Routledge Revivals

Private Justice

This book, first published in 1983, looks at discipline in industry and shows how private justice is integrally bound up with formal law. It is a timely examination of the forms of social control that exist ostensibly outside the formal legal system but on which it crucially depends. *Private Justice: Towards Integrated Theorising in the Sociology of Law* will be of interest to students of law, sociology, and criminology.

Dr. Stuart Henry is currently Professor and Director of the School of Public Affairs at San Diego State University where he has been since 2006. Since leaving Trent Polytechnic (now Nottingham Trent University) in 1983 he has held positions in the United States at Eastern Michigan University, Wayne State University, and the University of Texas at Arlington. He is the author or editor of 30 books and over 100 articles on crime, deviance and social control.

Private Justice
Towards Integrated Theorising in the Sociology of Law

Stuart Henry

First published in 1983
by Routledge & Kegan Paul

This edition first published in 2015 by Routledge
2 Park Square, Milton Park, Abingdon, Oxon, OX14 4RN
and by Routledge
711 Third Avenue, New York, NY 10017

Routledge is an imprint of the Taylor & Francis Group, an informa business

© 1983 Stuart Henry

The right of Stuart Henry to be identified as author of this work has been asserted by him in accordance with sections 77 and 78 of the Copyright, Designs and Patents Act 1988.

All rights reserved. No part of this book may be reprinted or reproduced or utilised in any form or by any electronic, mechanical, or other means, now known or hereafter invented, including photocopying and recording, or in any information storage or retrieval system, without permission in writing from the publishers.

Publisher's Note
The publisher has gone to great lengths to ensure the quality of this reprint but points out that some imperfections in the original copies may be apparent.

Disclaimer
The publisher has made every effort to trace copyright holders and welcomes correspondence from those they have been unable to contact.

A Library of Congress record exists under LC control number: 83010926

ISBN 13: 978-1-138-91170-3 (hbk)
ISBN 13: 978-1-315-69247-0 (ebk)
ISBN 13: 978-1-138-91171-0 (pbk)

PRIVATE JUSTICE

TOWARDS INTEGRATED THEORISING IN THE SOCIOLOGY OF LAW

STUART HENRY

Routledge & Kegan Paul
London, Boston, Melbourne and Henley

For Sally Miller whose private justice was very rough

*First published in 1983
by Routledge & Kegan Paul plc
39 Store Street, London WC1E 7DD, England
9 Park Street, Boston, Mass. 02108, USA
464 St Kilda Road, Melbourne,
Victoria 3004, Australia
Broadway House, Newtown Road,
Henley-on-Thames, Oxon RG9 1EN, England
Set in IBM Century, 10 on 12 pt
by Hope Services, Abingdon
and printed in Great Britain by
The Thetford Press, Norfolk
© Stuart Henry 1983
No part of this book may be reproduced in
any form without permission from the publisher,
except for the quotation of brief
passages in criticism*

Library of Congress Cataloging in Publication Data

Henry, Stuart.

Private justice.
Bibliography: p.
Includes index.
1. Law — Philosophy.   2. Justice, Administration of.
3. Sociological jurisprudence.   4. Social control.
I. Title.
K240.H46   1983   340'.11   83-10926

ISBN 0-7100-9703-4

Contents

	Preface	vii
	Acknowledgments	ix
1	Deceptions of order in law: social structures and law forms	1
2	Impressions of diversity: from informalism to integrated theorising about law	32
3	Images of legal reality: the ideology of constructing forms of factory law and their institutions of private justice	70
4	Beneath the public face of private discipline: the authoritative law of managerial justice	98
5	The negotiated law of participatory justice; accommodation, protection, legitimation and co-option	132
6	Celebration, co-operation and contamination: the collective law of community justice	179
	Conclusion	220
	Appendix	223
	Bibliography	229
	Index	237

Acknowledgments

I owe sincere thanks to: James Cornford, director of the Nuffield Foundation, for his early enthusiasm for the project; Gerald Mars, the supportive and encouraging director of the Centre for Occupational and Community Research where the research for this book was carried out; the Social Science Research Council who funded the study; Ann Lea whose secretarial and administrative wizardry together with total loyalty to the project, sustained us through bureaucratic obstacles and enabled her to type a sheer mountain of words; Rue Bendall of Warwick University's Department of Law, without whom the theoretical underpinning of this book would have been much less developed — chapters 1 and 2 draw on her dissertations, '"Legal" pluralism: a critique of holistic conceptions of law' and 'Towards an integrative approach to the study of law' both mimeo, University of Kent, 1981 and 1982 respectively; Ruth Shelley who not only managed to squeeze editing and typing the manuscript into an already overcomplicated life and did so more for love than money, but who also provided the inspiration necessary for the book's completion; and to Philippa Brewster of Routledge for her tolerance in accommodating to delays, excuses, problems and disasters.

A special thanks is due to all those people* who so generously allowed me to use their time, thoughts and words. Such is the parasitic nature of authorship that without the preparedness of ordinary people to 'be researched', books would be of considerably less value and certainly of less interest.

*To safeguard the confidentiality of individuals and organisations, all names appearing in chapters 4 to 6 and the appendix are fictitious.

Preface

This book is about the law and justice that goes on outside of the formal legal system. It is about the private systems of social control that operate in institutions, organisations and groups. But it is also about formal law, since my central argument is that formal law and private justice are integrally related. Each is mutually interdependent upon the other such that some of the relations of one are the relations of the other and vice versa. The position is taken that in order to understand law in society it is necessary to understand the nature of this interdependence between the public and private, the formal and informal, the part and the whole. Theorising which seeks to clarify and separate law as distinct from other forms of social control, or that which analyses informal or private justice in isolation from the formality, is guilty of contributing to the ideological process whereby law is constructed as a reality. This book sets out to expose such a process.

I did not begin the research on which *Private Justice* is based with this approach in mind. Rather, drawing on an interest and understanding of hidden and informal institutions which seem to proliferate in any society, I began with the view that private justice existed as a separate, alternative form of justice and one which might promise us a glimpse of future forms of law suitable to post-capitalist or even socialist legality. In the course of the research it became apparent that this view was simply wrong. Not only was it found that state law relies upon private justice to exercise some of its control functions, but private justice itself relies on state law to exercise *its* discipline. The one form is not separate from the other but each are necessary parts of the other. At the same time, however, each part has its own limited autonomy. They exist together as mutually dependent but semi-autonomous parts of a totality of social control. Theorising which subsumes private justice as a function of state law, absorbs and denies the autonomy of informal institutions, but that which acknowledges and elaborates such autonomy has so far failed to show how it is limited by the structure of the totality. This book, then, seeks to integrate these approaches and to transcend the dichotomy between structure and agency, part and whole, state law and private justice. It aims to demonstrate that whatever private justice is, it is not wholly private.

1 Deceptions of order in law:
social structures and law forms

Introduction

Arguably the most important contribution made by sociologists and anthropologists to theorising about law is to identify the structural conditions that appear to give rise to particular kinds of law and to their related systems of criminal justice. Thus the works of Maine, Durkheim, Weber and the Marxist sociology of law, found a tradition of theorising which transcends the universalism of those natural and positive law philosophers (Aristotle, Hobbes, Austin, Kelsen, Hart) and question the universalism of functionalists (Llewellyn, Hoebel, Parsons, Bredemeier), all of whom assume that there are essential and irreducible components of legal systems common to all societies.

The sociological contribution is to relieve the natural law theorist of his embarrassing inability to explain how the 'natural' is to be articulated by locating precisely who it is that decides what constitutes 'natural', 'essential' or 'moral', values. The debunking of the slippery notion that law is a spontaneous and uncontrived product of the continuous flow of life, made accessible to man through reason, is as refreshing as the exposure of the processes under which law is legitimated by reference to the gods, the popular sense of right, or the general will. What sociologists and anthropologists clearly and often uncomfortably demonstrate is that law is formulated in a socio-political context; that it serves some interests rather than others; that different social structures or forms of societal organisation display different forms of law and legal systems, and that a combination of coercive and ideological processes are at work to ensure the continuation of existing systems of law and through these the perpetuation of existing social structures.

Not only is the 'naturalness' of natural law an obvious target for such critical scything but so too is the mystification stemming from the dubious distinction made by positive law philosophers between law and other rules, such as morals and customs. That Austin (1832) saw law as an independent, isolated, logical and self-consistent system, separate from other kinds of rules and their enforcement and comprising only those rules commanded on a subject by a sovereign, does not mean that is what law is, as Ehrlich (1913) with his notion of 'living law' was one of the first to point out. Nor does it make sense to say that the commands of a sovereign add up to a closed system, since, as Pound (1959) explained, individual actions are necessary for the system's day-to-day operation and 'the law in action is not the law in books'. Kelsen's attempt to refine the positivist conception of 'pure law', whereby law is that created in a manner prescribed by, consistent with and validated through the 'basic norm' (*Grundnorm*) of the state takes us back to the question of how one establishes the basic values of a society. He may well be correct in observing that: 'A norm becomes a legal norm only because it has been constituted in a particular fashion, born of a definite procedure and a definite rule' (Kelsen, 1934, pp. 517–18), and that, 'Law is valid only as a positive, that is, state law.' Indeed he argues that, 'only by referring the human behaviour to law as a system of valid norms . . . is it possible to distinguish sociologically between . . . legal and illegal behaviour' (Kelsen, 1945, p. 177). But if the distinction between law and other social norms is arbitrary then so too is what counts as legal or illegal. Worse, if the distinction is the product of a process whereby some groups of people enact their views and interests in the name of God, the state, or the people, then the law is as sinister as Proudhon feared when he proclaimed 'Whoever puts his hand on me to govern me is a usurper and a tyrant. I declare him my enemy.'

Some universalists like the functionalist theorists try to side-step these issues and justify positive law in terms of its functional needs to society. Parsons's notion, for example, that law has an 'integrating function' as a 'generalised mechanism of social control and that it serves to mitigate potential elements of conflict and to oil the machinery of social intercourse' (Parsons, 1962, p. 57) is as compelling as Hoebel's view (1954, pp. 275-6) that the primary job of law, 'is the ordering of the fundamentals of living together'. These functions are even more convincing when they are elaborated into universals which provide: legitimate rules for living; rules for judging when these rules are broken; rules authorising the application of sanctions to rule breakers; and rules for changing rules (Hart, 1961). But the functionalist argument withers under the structuralist critique. This forcefully asserts that in assuming a consensus of value, the functionalist, like the natural law theorist, glosses over fundamental differences of power and interest between social groups and thereby fails to account for how legal rules actually emerge, are administered and are enforced. As Hunt (1978, pp. 52-3) says in criticising Llewellyn's (1960) *The Common Law Tradition*, notions of societal values and essential functions are now held to be the height of reductionist thinking and normative imposition:

> To adopt the functional analogy often detracts from the central methodological problem of the social sciences, namely to grasp and to be able to give expression to the complexity of the interaction and interrelationship between the constituents of the social reality.
> This tendency to simplistic reduction is compounded by . . . the utilisation of an equilibrium model . . . the dubious assumption that there is detectable some optimum functioning of the social system or a part thereof, which is essential to the preservation of that equilibrium. Any departure from that optimum balance is regarded as producing negative consequences for the stability or preservation of the system as a whole . . .
> The further and more unacceptable consequences of the functionalist position is that it renders analysis static . . . every facet of the present is seen as necessary and inevitable and social change is consequently perceived as potentially destructive.

4 Deceptions of order in law

Unfortunately, positivist assumptions about law have carried over into sociological theorising and not simply that of the functionalist tradition. As Schur (1968, p. 9) says,

> Social theorists attempt to develop analytical models of the legal system in order to determine the hallmark of the distinctively legal and to delineate clearly the lines of demarcation between the legal system and other subsystems of the social order ...

The consequence of this has been that when such theorists have sought to advance theorising about law by identifying the social structures which shape it, they have neglected to consider the whole of the law-society relationship. By omitting to consider the body of informal behavioural imperatives, norms and obligations, they contribute to, rather than analyse, the very ideological processes that render formal law the dominating social control institution. In order to unmask this kind of mystification it is necessary to re-establish the relationship between positive law and its informal counterpart. As part of that endeavour this book is concerned to re-emphasise the important place of private and informal mechanisms of social control in the context of total social control. Fundamentally, it seeks to integrate theorising about the structural conditions which shape a society's system of law and its system of justice, with those approaches which explore the less formalised, though nonetheless coercive and ideologically significant forms of private justice. Only by considering these approaches together can we hope to comprehend what constitutes the totality of social control. Such analysis must begin with an examination of basic structural conditions, together with their corresponding forms of law and associated systems of criminal justice. In this chapter I draw out the characteristic features of these structures and law forms as they have been identified in the literature, and go on to show how these are products of the ideological distinction between law and non-law which in turn give the deception of order and the appearance of reality to the face of law. Examination of the literature shows remarkable agreement among commentators that at least three types of social structure can be classified each having a characteristic form of law and associated system of criminal justice. I shall examine each in turn.

Community structures and their law form

As both Tönnies (1912), in his distinction between Gemeinschaft and Gesellschaft, and Durkheim (1893), in contrasting mechanical and organic solidarity point out, small-scale social units tend to have a minimal division of labour, such that each member shares in the whole range of tasks necessary for maintaining that unit and that any member can replace any other. Individual members relate to one another spontaneously, through their social status within the group and do so for the purpose of the relationship itself The members are held together as a community by this spirit of similarity, which Durkheim called, 'collective sentiment', and by the ties of tradition, friendship, understanding and the common acceptance of a belief system. Classic examples of these structures are to be found in the small-scale feudal agrarian village community, and in some non-industrial societies.

Under the community structure what counts as an offence is any action which shocks the 'collective sentiment' or 'common conscience'. Clearly, since individuals are represented through statuses and are in multiple relationships with others, any dispute between two people is likely to affect many others' relationships. But those actions especially shocking to the collective morality are those threatening the essentially conservative values of the community. They are offences precisely because they threaten the sense of tradition, the status hierarchy, the community values, its kinship network, authority structure and religious orders. As Young (1981, p. 275) says in his characterisation of conservative thinking about crime, 'for social cohesion to be maintained, self-interest must be subordinated to the general good' and 'order must take precedence over justice.' He says that, 'for the conservative, the causes of crime lie in the pursuit of individual gratification (usually incommensurate with effort) and the undermining of traditional loyalties and the consequent unwillingness of the individual to accept discipline' (ibid., p. 277).

Durkheim was the first to elaborate the kind of justice that would accompany the community structure. He said that societies held together by the undifferentiated principle of integration would have repressive laws whose sanctions imply blame or moral condemnation in the form of punishment, deprivation or public reproach. The punishment, though crude, retributive, unreflective and instinctive, is essentially defensive and conservative, 'a passionate reaction of graduated intensity' (Durkheim, 1893, p. 96), whose intensity is greater the more closely the societies approach the undifferentiated form. 'It cannot ... regulate itself but responds somewhat haphazardly to blind causes which urge it on and without anything moderating these activities' (Durkheim, 1969, p. 21).

For Young (1981, p. 278) the central goal of justice corresponding to the conservative community structure is to maintain order. 'To achieve this aim, coercion is necessary ... a central part of social control which is undermined if any laxity in the exertion of authority occurs.' Young (1981, p. 279) summarises the conservative perspective:

> Conservatism would stress the actor him/herself. The person's relative position or reputation in the social order becomes of considerable importance. For here we are dealing with a school of thought which makes much of the symbolic and public nature of punishment. The conservative preference for the simple moral lesson, deriving from unchallengeable authority, is reflected in the residual (and obsessive) belief in the efficacy of physical punishment. Punishment should be expressed as publicly as possible ... The moral lesson of punishment for the individual must extend its salutary effort to the population as a whole for it is here that the greatest social good can be achieved.

As a conservative expression of the community sentiment, then, the justice favoured by community structures is substantive and has a wide concept of relevance, with little emphasis on abstract formal criteria. As Kamenka and Tay (1975, p. 136) say,

The person at the bar of judgement is there, in principle, as a whole man, bringing with him his status, his occupation and his environment, all of his history and his social relations ... Justice is thus substantive, directed to a particular social context and not to the establishing of a rule or precedent ... The formalism of procedures in this type of justice can be considerable, but they are linked with magical taboo notions, they are emotive in content and concrete in formulation; they are not based on abstract rationalistic conceptions of justice and procedure ... For the Gemeinschaft is above all, as Tönnies notes, a religious society held together by a common religious ideology that cannot tolerate the breaker of its taboos; its symbols are the seal and the pillory.

Importantly, for Durkheim, the repressive law of community structures is administered collectively, not by any special judicial machinery. 'It does not function through the means of a special magistracy, but the whole society participates ... it is the assembly of people which renders justice' (1969, p. 19). He says, 'since it is the common conscience which is attacked, it must be that which resists, and accordingly the resistance must be collective' (1893, p. 103). It is in this sense that Durkheim argues that 'Crime brings together upright consciences and concentrates them' (1893, p. 102). Indeed, as Unger says, the issue of what in fact happens can never be kept clearly separate from what should be done. 'There is a point at which deviations from the rule remake the rule itself. Thus every act leads a double life: it constitutes conformity or disobedience to custom at the same time that it becomes part of the social process whereby custom is defined' (Unger, 1976, p. 49).

However, Durkheim also argues that under the community structure's repressive law, responses do not have to be collectively administered, but need only reflect community sentiment. If one man or office captures that sentiment then the same expression can occur. Thus Durkheim observed that community responses can be organised through certain intermediaries as when power is vested in the hands of a tribal chief. But, 'simply because collective sentiments are enforced only through certain intermediaries, it does not follow that they have ceased to be collective while localising themselves in a restricted number of consciences' (1969, p. 20). It might not follow but it might soon follow, since it becomes very difficult to maintain a man or office wholly responsive to collective sentiment without becoming at the same time normative, and then the whole force of the community's collective response rests on how effective is the process of legitimating the system of judicial administration. It may begin as in Weber's (1922) charismatic form of leadership, where justice is administered in a specifically personal way with decisions relying on 'devotion to the specific and exceptional sanctity, heroism, or exemplary character of an individual and the normative patterns of order revealed or ordained by him'. But unless there is sufficient power in the community to redisperse the localised and restricted embodiment of sentiment from the few to the many, the extent to which it will remain a community response is questionable.

Perhaps the clearest illustrations of the form of justice expressing community sentiment can be found in the anthropological studies of non-industrial societies and particularly acephalous societies — those without any central government. Malinowski (1926), in his ethnography of Trobriand Islanders, showed how the rules were backed up by sanctions ranging from peer group pressure to withdrawal of economic co-operation from the essential reciprocal obligations. These sanctions could be so severe that the recalcitrant would be forced back into line or made to live elsewhere, outside the community. Moreover, the psychological threat that this *might* happen make 'it impossible for the native to shirk his responsibility without suffering in the future' (Malinowski, 1979, p. 96).

But it is not necessary to rely on relatively obscure non-industrial societies to illustrate shaming, ridicule or ostracism as examples of the way community structures shape the system of justice into a particular form. Indeed, as we shall see later, to do so may be misleading. Even where apparently formal legal structures exist, these may be overriden by community sentiment. A good illustration of this is to be found in the criminal justice system of early colonial America. There the family, community and church maintained a firm grip on the society's members. The few newcomers who were not members of established groups, were required to join within a reasonable period or leave the community altogether. As Ferdinand (1977, p. 2) says, in his excellent review of early American criminal justice, 'There was no room, especially in New England, for independent individuals, and those who would not submit to close community control over their lives were not welcome.' He describes how many New England communities instituted town meetings where local matters could be considered, solutions proposed and a policy established by a voice vote of those attending. Few individuals felt strong enough to defy the consensus of the town meeting and those that did were often obliged to depart as a result of public pressure. In the New England community then, the law was little more than an extension of the community and its mores. Community sentiment was more powerful in determining who was to be arrested than the written law. Ferdinand (1977, p. 3) says:

> Thus the court and its officers were tied to the local community in a hundred ways and followed closely the initiatives and guidelines established by community leaders. The principal bulwarks against deviancy and crime, therefore, were the community and the church, with the formal law and the courts simply reinforcing their authority in nearly all matters.

As will become apparent, a fundamental argument of this book is that the existence of one structural influence does not necessarily mean the exclusion of all others. In particular, the dominance of particular structural forms in a given society does not deny the influence of existing or 'subordinate' forms, even though it may appear to do so. As in Brinton's (1953), *Anatomy of Revolutions*, what appears to be the 'old' order is never completely expunged by the radicalism of the 'new'. The emergence of 'new' structural influences and their associated law forms has not prevented the influence of the community structure and its judicial form. Thus recent analysis of western adjudicatory justice, which is the characteristic law form of Gesellschaft-like society (see below), has revealed both the repressive crime control and the status degradation elements, characteristic of the community structure. Packer (1969, p. 158), for example, has pointed out that alongside the more apparent due process form, 'the repression of criminal conduct is by far the most important function to be performed by the criminal process'. King (1981) shows how this overall concern with the punitive effect of justice is manifest through an implicit presumption of guilt in which police are seen as filtering out the innocent, allowing only the guilty through to the next stage. From this perspective, defence lawyers are seen as an expensive luxury and eloquent pleas of mitigation detract from the certainty of severe punishment for those caught and convicted and undermine the necessary 'feeling of speed and finality' (Packer, 1969, p. 159). As King (1981, p. 19) points out, this perspective can shape the atmosphere of the proceedings and the attitude of the officials toward the defendant:

> If it is believed that almost all defendants who appear before the court are 'guilty of something' and if they are acquitted, that they are 'lucky to get off', then it is also permissible to regard the courtroom experience itself as an exercise in deterrence, and to attempt to make it as unpleasant as possible for defendants.

Thus the defendant's isolation in the court as an object of ridicule, the public exposure of his shameful behaviour and the stern reprimand of the judge or magistrate, are, says King (1981, p. 102), 'direct deterrents designed to shock and humiliate him and discourage him from further involvement in crime'.

As well as acting as deterrents these elements, which have no place in a strictly western adjudicatory system of justice, reflect another influence of the community structure, that of 'status passage'. Drawing on the work of Garfinkel (1956) and Glazer and Strauss (1971), King says that a central aim of criminal justice is the imposition of a new social status on the defendant, who is seen as a symbol in a ritualistic process. The new status is invariably of a lower social position in the hierarchy of society. The various stages of the court proceedings are designed to separate the individual's moral career from that of the rest of the society, to condemn and degrade it through a series of rituals and then to culminate in the shaming and stigmatising of the defendant as guilty. As Garfinkel (1956) showed, this degradation ceremony has two aspects. One is to shame the individual such that he wants to hide himself from the community. The other is the effect on the community which is brought together in moral condemnation of the offence at the same time clarifying and reasserting the rules that are shared by the members and thereby reaffirming the existing social order.

In summary, from this kind of analysis it appears that community structures shape a form of justice that is concerned to repress individual deviation and to elevate social harmony; to express the conservative sentiment of the community's sense of traditional values as of overriding importance; to strip a man of individual pretensions and to judge him as an integrated status bound up with other relationships, expressive of the totality and indeed essence of the community; but also to deny him a place outside of his status.

Individualistic structures and their law form

Individualistic structures are seen to be characteristic of large-scale societies where people perform different specialised functions and where social relations between them are instrumentally employed as rational and efficient means to achieve the overall societal goals. The idea is captured in Durkheim's (1893) notion of 'organic solidarity' which he contrasted to the 'mechanical solidarity' of community structures. Organic solidarity is the principle of integration between members of societies with a high degree of division of labour. Members are indispensable to one another, integrated because of their dependence on each other's specialised functions. Their relationships are, therefore, instrumental.

Tönnies (1912) called such structures Gesellschaft-like and in contrast to the Gemeinschaft-like structures, he saw these as being underpinned by a rational will in which ends alone determine the means most suitable to achieve them. The rational achievement of societal goals is seen to be best attained where people are free agents capable of defining their own self interests and of contracting with other individuals for their own individual benefit. As Kamenka and Tay (1975, p. 137) say, this individualistic Gesellschaft-like structure is,

> linked with social and geographic mobility, with cities, commerce and the rise of the bourgeoisie. It assumes a society made up of atomic individuals and private interests, each in principle equivalent to the other, capable of agreeing on common means while maintaining their diverse ends . . . everything in principle becomes saleable, alienable, exchangeable. The economic is divorced from the social, the political, the religious, and treated in its own abstract terms . . . the Gesellschaft, legally and ideologically, is above all a simplifying phenomenon, an attempt to reduce all things to the same level and the same currency, the single medium of exchange.

Under such a structure, crime is also viewed as the outcome of a rational decision to break rules, especially the rules protecting the individual's freedom to contract and to accumulate private property. But no external causes are seen to drive or motivate rule-breakers, nor is it shocking that rules are broken. If rules are broken then this is because it is in the individual's rational interest to break them. The aim of criminal justice policy is seen, therefore, to make crime less attractive to those people. The response to crime is not a collective community attempt to repress that which undermines the spirit of integration since, in contrast to the community structure, there is not, as Durkheim pointed out, a collective conscience, but rather, the development of different moralities around differential occupational categories. Instead, the form of justice that is adopted is itself both rational and restitutive. It is designed to protect the differentiation and specialisation of functions and to guarantee the division of labour. It is not concerned with an expression of emotion or loss of honour. Rather it involves sanctions designed to 'return things as they were . . . to their normal state' (Durkheim, 1893, p. 69).

To achieve this rationality in justice it is necessary to have a system which separates and dissociates an individual from any other status that he might have and one which renders him formally equivalent to others. For Kamenka and Tay (1975, p. 137) the due process system satisfies these requirements:

> It emphasises formal procedure, impartiality, adjudicative justice, precise legal provisions and definitions and the rationality and predictability of legal administration. It is oriented to a precise definition of the rights and duties of the individual through a sharpening of the points at issue ... it reduces the public interest to another ... private interest. It distinguishes sharply between law and administration, between the public and the private, the legal and the moral, between the civil obligation and the criminal offence. Its model for law is the contract and the quid pro quo associated with commercial exchange, which also demands rationality and predictability.

Under the due process model of law, then, the rules are discrete in being clearly distinguishable from other kinds of rules such as etiquette and morality and are seen as being of superior authority. The same characteristic of separateness runs throughout the entire criminal justice system and is especially evident in the courts of western adjudicatory justice. These courts are, as Roberts (1979, p. 19) says, 'remote places we only visit in the event of a dispute, presided over by specialists who conduct their business against a background of unfamiliar ritual'. Their sole function is to administer the law in the context of disputes which are brought before them. The courts are not used for any other purpose and the specialisation and separation from the rest of the society is reinforced by the unique ceremonial procedures associated with dispute settlement, the highly specialised legal language and the dress of courtroom personnel.

Central to the due process model is the presumption of innocence and the principle of legal rules governing the admissibility of evidence and ultimately the decision. The issue is clear: rule determines outcome. There is little compromise between disputants and little opportunity for them to influence the outcome of the hearing since this is determined by legal rules and a narrow concept of relevance which 'requires that a precise issue in dispute is separated from any larger complex of relations between the two disputants and dealt with in isolation from other aspects of the relationship' (Roberts, 1979, p. 21). Equally important are the procedural protections of adversarial confrontation between two parties as formal equals, the testing of witnesses in cross examination and the establishment of proof beyond a reasonable doubt. Young's (1981, p. 262) characterisation of classicist thinking about crime and criminal justice serves as a useful summary of the law form appropriate to the individualistic structure:

> According to the principles of legal equity, crimes should be judged by a jury of one's peers — that is by other rational and equal individuals. Judges should be guided by a clear and systematic legal code. And sentencing should be limited to applying a prior, agreed and fixed set of penalties — a tariff system — equally across the board, allowing only adjustments and discretions for 'mitigating circumstances' . . . Punishment should be strictly applied, irrespective of the status or the background of the accused, but also applied efficiently and effectively . . . punishment should be seen to be 'just' — but it should also be strict, regular and disciplined. Justice should be doled out without delay and to the maximum of offenders the police can apprehend. The law is an instrument not only of control, but also of education. And 'educating the public' into the calculus of law requires that irregularities, due to either lack of detection or evasion of penalties or irrational prison regimes, should be eliminated. Any deviation from strict disciplinary uniformity simply encourages crime.

Bureaucratic structures and their law form

Drawing on the work of Weber, Renner and Pashukanis, Kamenka and Tay (1975) identify a third structure which they describe as bureaucratic administrative regulation.

A similar structure is also outlined by Unger (1976) as 'bureaucratic regulation'. Bureaucratic administration occurs at both state and organisational level. At state level it occurs in order to achieve rationality, regularity, predictability, efficiency and cost effectiveness where the national economy or public interest is at issue. A crucial feature of its operation is that scientific experts replace lay individuals in informing its decision-making. Similarly, where organisations centralise capital in order to maximise the profitability of large-scale production, monopoly and multi-national corporations appear with their own internal administrative regulation. Kamenka and Tay (1975) say that the ideal situation for the development of bureaucratic administrative regulation is where: state law begins to control finance and credit; the large corporation displaces the individual entrepreneur; property is subject to internal organisation, direction and control; and administration is elevated above ownership. Under these conditions, whether at state or organisational level the individuals are subordinated to the abstract category, whether this be 'consumer', 'employee', 'one-parent family', or whatever.

The relegation of individuals to a subordinate role is especially significant to the view of crime held under bureaucratic administration. This is a positivistic one in which rule-breakers are not individually responsible for their actions but are the product of some external cause. They do not choose to break the law but are deterministically driven to do so by some force. This may be physiological, genetic or psychological; it may be the result of an error in the individual's socialisation process within the family or even as a result of incoherent or inconsistent values in the social or cultural milieu. Whatever the source, as Young (1981, p. 270) says in his characterisation of positivist thinking about crime,

> The causes of crime are thus rooted in defects in the past of the actor, in his or her determinant antecedents ... The criminal or deviant would be a rule-breaker in any culture. It is not necessary for the positivist to explain the context of the norms that are violated, merely the propensity of the individual to violate them.

Thus response to crime under this structure has two central concerns. One is to diagnose and treat the causes of crime; the other is to administer this form of justice in the most bureaucratically efficient way, irrespective of individual rights or the notion of due process. The first of these goals follows on from the view of crime as caused, and the assumption that causes can be identified. As Young (1981, p. 271) says, for the positivist,

> If the criminal is determined and not responsible . . . we must replace punishment by *treatment*. We must substitute for the jury system of lay people, a panel of experts who diagnose the conditions of the individual and prescribe the appropriate treatment.

The preferred judicial system, then, is one characterised by a reliance on scientific representation in decision-making, with no participation or representation. The role of the court is to identify those who are blighted by their past; to diagnose through the use of scientifically trained experts such as probation officers and social workers. These experts are relied upon to compile information about the offender's social background, medical history, family situation, work record, previous offences and the sanctions received for them. From these social inquiry reports specifying the cause or multiplicity of causes, the courts put together the most appropriate individualised sentence to reflect the specific therapeutic needs of the defendant. This is applied with the hope of correcting, restoring, or rehabilitating the offender to a position where the pressures and demands of the society will no longer lead him to behave criminally; where his state of mental and social health will enable him to cope with these demands without further intervention being necessary.

In this process there is no regard for the effects that intervention may have on his individual rights which will be blatantly disregarded. As King (1981) says, the objects of rule-following under this form of justice are not to protect the individual against the arbitrary power of the state, nor to adjudicate disputes between individuals, but to process defendants through the system in the shortest possible time, at the least possible cost and with the maximum degree of efficiency. Indeed, these goals are best achieved by minimising the conflict between different interested parties; by maintaining records in order that any required information is readily available on file; and by socialising the different specialists into informal, friendly, co-operative relations. It is not surprising then, that Blumberg (1967, p. xx) has described the criminal justice that operates in this way as a 'people processing machine' in which police, lawyers and judges live and work in a 'symbiotic relationship of convenience and necessity'. It is he says, 'characterised by the superficial niceties of traditional due process, but not its substance' (Blumberg, 1967, pp. 4-5) and that,

> The rational instrumental goals of the court organisation, in its urgent demand for guilty pleas, have produced a bargain-counter, assembly-line system of criminal justice which is incompatible with traditional due process.

Similarly, Bottomley (1979, p. 103-4) describes this bureaucratic process as one of routinised justice,

> concerned above all with getting through each day's crowded court lists as efficiently as possible . . . an established set of institutional arrangements involving several groups of more or less permanent actors dealing with an essentially transient group of 'consumers' or 'clients' . . . involved in the business of purveying bargain justice and committed to the production ethic.

Deceptions of order and the social construction of law

At first sight it appears that the identification of the range of structures and their corresponding law forms is an advance over earlier positivist theorising. This, despite its universalistic pretensions, restricted its concerns to what can now clearly be seen as the adjudicatory due process model of law, characteristic of an idealised individualistic social structure. That structural theorists recognise other law forms as 'law' is helpful, but unfortunately this is not all they do. It would not be unfair to suggest that the separation of types of law according to social structure and then arranging these in some evolutionist sequence is, in some cases, deliberately designed to promote a particular configuration of the social order and in other cases to serve an ideological function to the same end. This can be a seductive journey as in Maine's (1861) discussion of the 'movement' from the 'primitive law' of community structures under which laws are based on one's social status in the family, to the liberation of law in those few 'progressive societies' where 'law is brought into harmony with society' (Maine, 1979, p. 19); where the individual becomes the relevant legal unit; and where rights and duties are determined by 'free agreement' and voluntary consent in the form of the contract. Indeed with Maine we are deceived into pondering upon what it might have been like to live under informal law as if this was in the past and into celebrating that we no longer have to. We might more profitably have examined the reality and relationship of informal law to its positive counterpart and explored the day-to-day constructionist processes whereby the reality of law is carved out of the continuum of social control.

The ideological process clarifying and nurturing a single conception of the social order is just as forceful in Durkheim's genetic evolutionism. Like Maine, Durkheim was keen to eschew the crudity of unilinear evolutionism between his two types of social structures and their corresponding law, qualifying his analysis by suggesting that the historical development is not as simple as it appears, but a fragmented course which can never be combined into a continuous line. But, as Gurvitch (1947) points out, Durkheim was ultimately unable to escape his 'hierarchy of phases of development' because his classification of the forms of social integration was too simplistic. As with Maine, the Durkheimian dichotomy assumes that the existence of formal written law is indicative of the substantial structural differences between different social orders. But this, as Gurvitch (1947, p. 93) maintains, is a deception which

> excludes from the reality of law one of its most important sectors ... the spontaneous, dynamic law, which is constantly being modified, the life giving source of organised law, with which it is constantly coming into conflict.

As Gurvitch points out, Durkheim is blind to the reality of 'jural pluralism'. By concentrating on the total structure of society rather than on its component parts, Durkheim glosses over the complex way community structures and their law forms can occur in groups while individualistic structures and their law forms can occur in other groups or even in the same group. As a result his analysis tends to perpetuate the myth of positive law that holds some forms of social control to be more important and admirable than others.

Perhaps surprisingly, even when it has been at its most critical, the structural analysis of society and its law forms has often failed to transcend the ideology to which it addresses its appraisal. One example of this is to be found in the Pashukanis version of Marxist sociology of law. Although Marx wrote little on law, his general theory has been developed by some to imply that as the economic relations of production of a society proceed through a number of epochs, from feudalism to capitalism to communism, each particular mode of production has a characteristic form of law. Indeed, the view expressed by Marx in *The German Ideology* and by Marx and Engels in *The Communist Manifesto*, is that when the antagonistic classes of capitalism disappear, when there is no longer a ruling class, the state and the law would necessarily wither away to be replaced by a moral consciousness, the general will of the community and by communist self-administration. As Engels argued, the seizure of state power and the subsequent dictatorship of the proletariat would replace the government of persons by both the administration of things and the direction of the process of production. Thus, as Pashukanis (1929) interprets it, law is not independent of the relations of production but changes its form in accordance with the historically specific mode of production.

However, as Renner (1904) has forcefully pointed out, there need not be a change in the form of law in line with changing social structure, only a change in its function. He argues that whether it is a feudal, capitalist or socialist society, there need be no change in the law form since these are meaningless frameworks, and it is the content, meaning or function of law that changes with changing structural conditions. He shows how, that although the structure of property has changed and become socially and economically powerful over the masses of wage labourers subjected to it, juridically, the law of property has remained purely individualistic. However, as Gurvitch (1947, p. 152) argues, even this view is concerned with formal written law

> without observing that there are deeper levels of law, varying in direct and immediate functional relation with the totality of social life, the transformation of the structure of jural institutions being in action independently, and even in opposition to, abstract propositions of law.

Another example of a critical appraisal of structures and law forms which seeks to subvert the positive law-centred approach but which serves to reinforce it, is that of the separatist anthropologists. Some of these, notably Roberts (1979), occasionally give the impression that non-industrial societies are the only ones having a range of social control institutions. In his efforts to castigate law-centred approaches, Roberts sometimes presents an over unified and skewed picture of law in western industrial society. Thus he (Roberts, 1979, p. 17) says,

> Despite the prominence of our legal institutions we must recognise from the beginning that they represent a special feature of one society which will not necessarily be duplicated within any of those we are concerned with here.

Indeed, rather than following through the Malinowskian inspired observation that 'a large burden of social control must be born in *all* societies by extra legal mechanisms' (Roberts, 1979, p. 12), he slithers into the structuralist trap he is criticising by making a somewhat tenuous distinction between societies with centralised governments and acephalous societies. The former he depicts as having adjudicatory, third-party, dispute settlement procedures, while the latter have a wider concept of relevance and a range of social control mechanisms (Roberts, 1979, pp. 26-7):

> Even where judicial institutions are found, they do not always enjoy the unchallenged pre-eminence in the business of dispute settlement, which our courts claim and manage

to exercise. Fighting and other forms of self-help, resort to supernatural agencies, the use of shaming and ridicule, or the unilateral withdrawal of essential forms of co-operation may all constitute equally approved and effective means of handling conflict.

While this analysis is a long overdue unleashing of non-industrial societies' social control from the constraints of western legal ethnocentricism, it is considerably less liberating for industrial society whose formalised dispute settlement machinery conceals beneath it an equally significant range of non-legal mechanisms of social control. It is tempting to turn his own criticism of law-centred anthropologists toward this view of western industrial societies and to agree that 'mechanisms of control, however specialised, do not operate in isolation, and that to segregate them for the purposes of study can only lead to distortion ... damaging attempts to fit indigenous data into alien categories' (Roberts, 1979, p. 203). One could go further and suggest that the answers to his key questions of why some modes of dispute settlement are 'dominant in one society and not in another' and why 'talking was a mode of dispute settlement better established in some societies than others' (ibid., p. 201), are to be found less in the structural conditions, economic relations, or political forces, than in the ideological processes which lead us to construct such distinctions.

Undoubtedly, though, the most recent contributions to the debate over social structures and their law forms are the most disturbing since their proto-pluralist stance perpetuates old myths in a new, less detectable guise. These theorists pretend a kind of analytical neutrality in which different law forms are not so much the products of different epochs, civilisations or societies, but are competing ideal-types, models or paradigms existing within any one particular society. Each proto-pluralistic analysis, however, purveys a definite preference for one particular law form or for one particular mix of forms. In either case, questions about the relationships between the forms, takes precedence over those about the ideological implications of the distinctions on which they are founded.

Full honours for refining the pluralist trick must, however, go to Weber (1922). His insistence on the theoretical and heuristic nature of the 'ideal-type' as a neutral construct drawn from reality by accentuating selected features, at the very least allows him to smuggle through the cues for developmentalism. At most it exports the assumptions about distinctions between law forms to the debate about developmentalism and thereby provides the ideological scaffold on which to hang any genuine pluralistic concern. Freund (1965) and Eldridge (1970), suggest that Weber was more concerned to stress that legal development was a product of the dynamic interaction of various facets of legal systems, in particular between formal and substantive rationality. In contrast, Parsons (1937) believes, along with Walton (1976) and Grace and Wilkinson (1978), that Weber is positing no less than a 'law of advancing rationalisation'. Hunt (1978, p. 101) appears to resolve the conflict:

> It may fairly be insisted that Weber does quite frequently slip from the limitations which he places upon the ideal-type method; he does slip into the habit of treating them as evolutionary descriptive models. This is particularly marked with respect to his typology of legal systems.

But although Weber (ibid., 1978, p. 106)

> may be consistently understood by recognising that his philosophical and methodological position does lead him to advance a 'law of advancing rationalisation' . . . at the same time he has sufficient insight to realise the ambiguities and tensions involved in this process . . . he sees the rationalisation of formal law inhibited by the demand for substantive justice.

But the debate is false. The issue is not whether rationalisation is rampant or fettered, nor whether legal forms are sequential or interactive. Rather it is whether the analysis itself serves to reconstruct the existing positive law form or whether it critically transcends it. Since Weber does not even address this issue it must be concluded that his 'insight' is ideologically myopic. Again Gurvitch (1947, p. 30) highlights much of this problem in Weber's work:

Above all, we must ask whether his legal sociology has not suffered overmuch from his way of accepting the elaboration of coherent systems of legal norms which are, so to speak, suspended in the air and which lack any connection with the living reality of law, of which they are but more or less rigid symbols ... Weber does not notice that under these rigid rules there are flexible and ad hoc principles, that beneath these there are living collective beliefs which give law its real effectiveness and which reveal themselves in 'normative facts', spontaneous sources of the positivity of law, of its validity, 'sources of sources' and basis of a perpetual dynamism constituting the real life of law ... The problem of functional relationship between concrete forms of social structures and meanings which inspire them and in the constitution of which they participate, this central problem of the sociology of the noetic mind is not solved even by Weber.

Nor do the most recent contributors to structural ideal-type pluralism offer a more enlightened vision of its ideological limitations. Unger (1976), for example, identifies three ideal-type law forms which he calls 'customary law', 'bureaucratic or regulatory law' and 'legal order'. (These correspond to the law forms identified from the literature at the beginning of this chapter.) He then asks the right critical questions; whether the alleged autonomy of the 'legal order' is an illusory mystification which 'confuses a dominant theory and the mentality which that theory represents, with an accurate description of the actual place of law in society' (Unger, 1976, p. 56). He points out that the symbols and traditions which make this law-form appear radically autonomous should not be taken at face value. But then he traps himself on to a narrow path by observing that the generality and autonomy of the legal order should not be dismissed as a mere ideological pretence since 'people often act on the belief that the legal system does possess a relative generality and autonomy' (ibid., p. 56). And he says that to treat people's understandings and values as mere shams 'is to assume that social relations can be described and explained without regard to the men who participate in those relations attributed to them' (ibid., p. 57). Shams they are not. But the crucial issue is not to seek an explanation which takes for granted the objective reality of the products of action and belief, but to delve beneath this paraphernalia of doings to expose the process of its construction and reconstruction. This Unger does not do. Instead he restricts himself to exploring how 'the rule of law ideal is rooted in a particular form of social life'. Following up his analytical distinctions between law forms with an historical account of their emergence, he omits any reference to the understandings and meanings of the participants and thereby contributes to the reconstruction of the positiveness of the existing conception of the legal order.

Kamenka and Tay's (1975; 1978; 1980) identification of the three types of law, which as we saw earlier, they termed Gemeinschaft law, Gesellschaft law, and bureaucratic administrative regulation, is equally concerned to deflect a critique of developmentalism before succumbing to its irresistible lure. They (Kamenka and Tay, 1975, pp. 141-2) point out that the three ideal types are not so much characteristic of different historical eras or societies in different stages of development, but feature together in any society:

> The typology suggested here does not imply a simple straightforward evolutionary scheme, in which each stage is replaced by its successor and then thrown into the dustbin of history. It recognises on the contrary that Gemeinschaft, Gesellschaft and Bureaucratic Administrative strains will co-exist in all, or at least in most, societies, standing in comparatively complex relation with each other . . .
>
> Social relations, even in allegedly 'primitive' societies, are complex and they will display at least incipient Gemeinschaft, Gesellschaft and Bureaucratic Administrative characteristics at all stages of social development. *But certain historical periods and certain countries do provide us with classical epochs in which a particular strain comes out with special clarity, comes to self-consciousness, as it were, serves as a paradigm that illuminates in a new way our understanding of the present, past and of the*

foreseeable future... in the western world there is no doubt that the immediate trend is toward the immeasurable strengthening and extension of bureaucratic-administrative strains at the expense of Gesellschaft and Gemeinschaft strains. (My emphasis)

However, it is not the obvious contradictions that should concern us here, nor even the way developmentalism seeps into the argument. Rather it is that the ideal-type analysis is drawn on as a resource through which to celebrate the particular merits of the western Gesellschaft-like due process law form. The message is that there is a 'contemporary crisis in law and legal ideology' because the balance in which one particular form appears to dominate is being threatened. The 'movement' toward bureaucratic administration is depicted as a blind alley placing East and West on a convergence path to totalitarianism in law, if not in politics. But, worse than this in their view, is the recent re-emergence of the Gemeinschaft strain with its emphasis on not treating men as objects. This they dismiss as a romantic, utopian quest to return to the dark ages; no more than a 'humanising cosmetic' for bureaucratic practices and one which contains the same 'great dangers to liberty and human dignity' that it has always done (Kamenka and Tay, 1975, p. 142). Having established their ideal-types, the force of their preference for one type rather than another goes unqualified. They (Kamenka and Tay, 1978, p. 52) ridicule the growing disenchantment with the rational legal form and its concomitant retreat from values of objectivity, technical rationality and goal seeking:

> Objectivity has now become... a dirty word, a synonym for the unfeeling and inhuman. The emphasis is on personalisation... the belief that only the sufferer can provide the remedy, that only the worm can know the heel, or ... that all knowledge is shot through with subjectivity and that only the irrational, inexplicable action is truly free action... Much of the revulsion... presents itself as a conscious demand for a return to the face-to-face society, the organic community of living social bonds and commonly shared ideologies and interests... as an

elevation of the non-commercial, pre-industrial organic community, the Gemeinschaft.

And they (ibid., pp. 54-5) chastise those who embrace such a position, those who,

> are much happier talking about 'community' than about the state, about participation than administration and planning, about 'self-expression' than about emulation. There is a remarkable longing for the personalisation of law and legal proceedings, for the restoration of man to a place in the organic community that recognises him as a total person, and that makes justice, at least in principle, the work of the whole community and not a specialised branch of learning and experience. There is a parallel enthusiasm for a 'situational ethic' to replace general impersonal principles of conduct ... people's courts and people's judges seem more human than the bewigged and begowned representatives of a complex and learned art, which still believes that men must be judged by universal principles grounded in and shaped by long-mulled-over and carefully recorded experience and that hard cases make bad law. The sentimentality and superficiality of the new picture is reflected in its comparatively fleeting impact; it is always being undermined by concrete, *real* developments.

Now it seems that Kamenka and Tay want it both ways. Either their Gemeinschaft strain or ideal type co-exists and contributes to the reality of law or it does not. If it does, then there is no way its contribution can be undermined by 'real' developments since it is a part of these: if it does not contribute then Kamenka and Tay are back with no less a developmentalist perspective than the one they themselves criticise. The central and unasked question is how far is the 'coming out' of particular strains or ideal types and the clarity of their self-consciousness, a product of the ideological manipulation designed to underpin a favoured form? How far is *this* process the 'concrete reality' through which any appreciation of the totality of law is suppressed? Perhaps, even more fundamentally, whose models of law are these and what is their purpose?

The limits to structural pluralism can be best exposed by

examining the multi-paradigmist interpretations of law forms. This appears to overcome the latent developmentalism of the ideal-type pluralist, since it fully accepts that different models or paradigms co-exist within a society. Although this promises comprehensiveness the promise is an illusion since the multi-paradigm approach is equally unclear about whose paradigms we are dealing with and indeed, from where these are derived. Are they normative impositions organising the subject matter from outside and thereby reflecting a consensus among the scientific community as in Kuhn (1970) or Ritzer (1975)? If so, they are mere social constructions designed to have a high degree of internal consistency that is not present in reality. Alternatively, are the paradigms supposed to be distillations of reality? The two are not the same, however much theorists would like them to be. Thus duality of origin for the paradigms, whether these be social structures, law forms, or criminal justice systems, is a major and significant weakness of the multi-paradigmists' position. It can be illustrated through the work of King.

King (1981) following Rich (1979) provides us with a number of competing models of the criminal justice system. He identifies six which he calls 'due process', 'crime control', 'medical', 'bureaucratic', 'status passage' and 'power'. (Some of these were drawn on at the beginning of this chapter to elaborate the forms of law associated with different social structures.) He argues that the models, 'do not claim to represent the attitudes of individual actors. They are each distillations of a perspective, an approach to criminal justice which one would expect to prevail among particular groups of participants' (King, 1981, p. 29). But only three of the models, the due process model, the crime control and the medical model are given the honour of being, 'participant approaches in that to a greater or lesser degree they reflect the values and perspectives of one or more of the groups of regular participants' (ibid., 28-9). Thus King suggests that defenders of the law such as the Bar and the Law Society and organisations like Justice and the National Council for Civil Liberties and some lawyers specialising in defence work, would favour the due process model. Similarly, victims of crime, magistrates and police might favour the crime control model, while social workers and probation officers would prefer the medical model. The other three models are 'analytical and theoretical; they are derived from the work of social theorists' (ibid., pp. 29-30). King argues that all these six models may be in existence at any one time and that 'some participants . . . may apply them selectively depending upon their perception of the type of case or the type of defendant they are dealing with' (ibid., p. 29). He justifies the advantages of using such a multi-paradigm perspective on the grounds that the picture offered by each individual model is only a partial one and that 'the full picture . . . will emerge only after applying several different models, viewing the system from several different perspectives' (ibid., p. 30). The framework is useful, he says, in that it 'may raise questions which tend to be ignored and provide new and stimulating interpretations of the routine and the familiar' (ibid., p. 31).

From this problems are apparent over the ambiguity of whether we are dealing with models of 'reality', that is participant models, or whether such models are the theoretical creations of commentators. In one sense the two are not mutually exclusive since some commentators hold the participants' views and many participants hold the theorists' views; court administrators are obvious candidates for the bureaucratic model whereas court reporters and even victims and community representatives are likely to hold the status degradation view. The point is, as the ethnomethodological leveller about commonsense knowledge and the natural attitude reminds us, that the distinction is purely arbitrary. So too is the number of models chosen; it is rather simplistic to identify occupational groups as having certain interests and therefore carrying certain models which supposedly reflect those interests. How many different groups are there? Should there not be a different model for each group? But even the answers to these questions would not be adequate since it is individuals who make up a group and they may each have a range of changing interests and pressures and thereby carry a range of models in their heads. To address that issue, and then to probe into how and why people select the models, or more accurately the fragments of models to suit particular current or future goals, might begin to get nearer to the kind of analysis that is needed.

Similar problems can be identified in the theorists' own paradigms, since each theorist may use different criteria for constructing his view on the range of paradigms that exist. Indeed, this is precisely what has happened. Some sociologists distinguish different paradigms according to the methods employed. What one takes to be a paradigm and even what one calls a paradigm is often not the same thing. The resultant paradigm chaos has reached a stage where some multi-paradigmists, such as Rich (1979), are having to talk of 'The paradigms of Ritzer', 'The paradigms of Reasons', 'The paradigms of Chambliss' and 'The paradigms of Quinney' (Rich, 1979, pp. 71-81) and to lament that (ibid., pp. 74-5):

> It is possible that if Reasons knew the work of Ritzer before creating his paradigms he would have utilized the concise system devised by the latter rather than the vague descriptions he uses that in actuality overlap with two of Ritzer's paradigms or are part of the same paradigm.

So what started out as a recognition that there are competing models in a framework of criminal justice, ends up in a battle for who has the best collection of paradigms. We now no longer bob from theory to theory in our failure to transcend one-sided interpretations of social reality (see Young, 1981, pp. 306-7), but scamper from one multi-paradigm set to another.

The tragedy is that the multi-paradigm approach does not mean a more comprehensive understanding of law forms or a full picture of the system of justice. Not only does the approach leave gaps between paradigms, through which vital nuggets of the total reality of law slip, but by presenting a range of models as the full range, it also tricks us into believing that all of law is covered. But this is not so. The potential number of models is as diverse and extensive as the numbers held by the participants and because the structuralist methodology, even in its pluralist form, does not actually ask the participants, but imposes models on them, then it can never alone capture the quality of the diversity that constitutes law. However, the problem with the multi-paradigm form of structural analysis is that we are so deluded by its appearance of diversity that we lose sight of what is missing and may even be mislead into thinking that because 'all' the positions are covered then the theorist is politically neutral. This sense of neutrality is dangerous not only for legitimating that which is left out, but because it also legitimates that which is presented. Each one of the paradigms within the limited range somehow acquires a false equality with its neighbours. This levelling has the disarming effect of allowing dominant models, and more crucially, the processes whereby their dominance is created and sustained, to go unchallenged. As a result the multi-paradigm approach itself becomes a part of the process of ideological mystification, restraining any genuine understanding of the totality of law.

How then, are we to transcend the deceptions of order created by structuralist theorising and achieve the kind of comprehensiveness in our understanding of law promised but not delivered by the more pluralist of its approaches? How are we to lay bare the ideological processes whereby some forms of law are rendered dominant while others are suppressed? To achieve these ends it is necessary to adopt an approach that from the outset recognises a genuine pluralism. This requires that we first break down the positivist separation of law from other forms of social control and to picture this broad concept of law as a continuum rather than a discrete series of ideal types, models or paradigms. Further, it requires us to recognise that a continuum of 'law' is in existence in societies at any particular point in time, though this is not to deny that some aspects of the continuum may appear to be more dominant at some times than others and more dominant in some places than in others. Crucially, it demands that we adopt a more micro-analytical, interpretive perspective which takes *seriously* the meaning and conceptions of 'law' for the participants; and not just the participants in the formal legal system but also those in the whole range of control institutions. Only then can we, as observers, point to models of 'law' that might exist as social constructions. But these will be the commonsense typifications of the participants themselves, as they are used by actors in constructing their legal reality. Nor is it likely that the models so identified will be logically complete, nor necessarily separated, nor even restricted one to a man. Rather it is likely that they will comprise a rag-bag of ingredients which are drawn on as a resource, as and when a situation demands. Finally, only when we have sketched out this position will we be able to examine the way some constructions of law attain their autonomous and dominant appearance in the face of the range of competition and thereby might we liberate ourselves from the ideological shackles of structuralist theorising.

Paradoxically, those approaches which go farthest in this direction have proved the most susceptible to ideological manipulation because they fail to even acknowledge the appearance of order which the structuralists take for real. It is this naked naivety that leaves them defenceless against the charge of failing to address the totality. I shall examine these approaches and their limitations in the next chapter.

2 Impressions of diversity:
from informalism to integrated theorising about law

Introduction

In the previous chapter we saw how the structural analysis of law, in its attempt to undermine the universalism of natural and positive law theorising, actually served to reinforce the social construction of its positiveness. In seeking to account for the structural causes of differences between law forms, it failed to examine how that which is formalised and accepted as law, is only one aspect of the totality of social control. In either relegating informalism to past history or future dreams, or else by mistakenly assuming that it was competing with, rather than a part of the reality of law, structural theorising lost sight of the crucial importance of informal and private non-legal social control. But without acknowledging that informalism is integrally bound up with the process whereby law is constructed and maintained, it is impossible to explain that process.

For some time now, it has become increasingly clear, that there has been a significant shift in thinking about law, from macro-analytical theorising, to a micro-empirical approach, which has been especially sensitive to the importance of the informal as a part of law. Kamenka and Tay (1980, p. 3) for example, have observed that:

> there has been a growing trend in Western societies toward so-called legal realism, toward discounting the internal coherence and historical integrity of law, its claim to mould society and to represent specifically legal traditions

Impressions of diversity 33

and ideals . . . The trend has been to de-intellectualise law, to pit life against what is written in the law books, to demolish the fences that an earlier generation had put up to distinguish law from custom and from the legally irrelevant. We now insist, above all, that law stands neither above nor outside society, but within it, and that it does not make its own history.

It does not follow, however, that the recognition of informalism in law results in a more ideologically liberated body of theorising. Indeed, the reverse is true. Within the trend towards micro-theorising two major themes can be identified, both of which contribute more to the ideological construction of positive law as a reality, than to any comprehensive understanding of the process whereby that reality is produced. One theme, founded on legal realism and sociological jurisprudence, recognises that positive law is comprised of *informalities*, such as discretion, negotiation and bargaining resulting from human involvement. It sees these informalities as discrepancies from an ideal, the achievement of which might be accomplished by making them explicit. The other theme, asserts that law has become too bureaucratic and formal, and suggests that it should be *informalised* and decentralised in order to make it more humanistic. But in seeking this 'purer' alternative form, no attention is paid to the ideological processes whereby characterisations of law as 'purifiable', purvey a false sense of its realness, as a concrete, achievable entity.

In contrast to these themes two further micro-analytical perspectives on informalism, legal pluralism and the ethnography of dispute processing, have recently developed to offer a promising way forward from the ideological impasse. Both start out from the recognition that formal positive law is only one of a range of social control mechanisms most of which operate privately and informally in groups and organisations. They go on to show that rather than being separate, or alternative forms of social control, these informal aspects are integrally bound up with the total system of control, of which the formal positive 'form' is merely a surface appearance. Unfortunately, in so far as these theorists are embedded in the micro-analytical approach, and ignore structural considerations of macro-analytical theorising, they are unable to explain how formalised law attains its crust-like appearance of autonomy and object-like reality. Furthermore, while they describe how formalised law is constantly being made, unmade and made again on the surface of a dynamically changing flow of social control, they are unable to explain why it is that some informal control becomes formalised as law, while other such control remains informal and ostensibly insignificant. In order to comprehend this part of the process without forfeiting the contribution of the micro-analysis, it is necessary to adopt a perspective which integrates both macro and micro. It is toward such an approach that this chapter leads.

Legal realists, sociological jurisprudence and the informalities of law

Legal realists, Llewellyn, Frank and Arnold and the sociological jurisprudence of Pound, although being critically opposed on a number of crucial issues such as the place of value judgements in law, bring two insights to theorising about law which they share in common. They recognise that positive law is comprised of many informal practices necessary for its day-to-day operation and they shift attention from the macro-theoretical concerns which impose order on legal phenomenon, towards micro-analytical, empirically based examinations of actual legal processes. Llewellyn (1930), for example, stresses the need to determine 'how far the paper rule is real, how far merely paper', and calls for studies of the actual behaviour of the courts since 'what the officials do about disputes is, to my mind, the law itself' (1960, p. 3). Pound (1903), the founder of sociological jurisprudence, engaged in a polemic against the credibility of analytical jurisprudence and legal positivism and though critical of realism, like Llewellyn, called for the study of law as it actually is — 'law in action' as opposed to 'law in the books'. This in turn raised the question of the relationship between law and prevailing behaviour patterns and that between what courts say and what they do.

However, although these critics recognised that the reality of law might be different to its theory, they did not see this as inevitable and indicative of the underlying process whereby positive law is generated and sustained. Thus, because of his view that law was a tool to achieve social wants by eliminating friction and waste, Pound, for example, was side-tracked into the issue of how to improve the tool. An accurate assessment of the actual legal process was essential if law was to be effectively used for social engineering. Moreover, although, like Ross and Ehrlich (see below), Pound acknowledged that law was but one of a number of mechanisms of social control, he was nevertheless wedded to the overriding importance of positive law for society. Drawing on Ross's (1901) notion of social control, Pound defined law as 'a highly specialised form of social control carried on in accordance with a body of authoritative precepts, applied in a juridical manner and administrative process' (Pound, 1942, p. 42). But as Hunt (1978, pp. 20-1) says,

> His concern became to elaborate the distinctive features and modes of operation of law. He ceases to pay any more than a cursory attention to the interrelationship and interaction between law and other forms of social control . . . His work is concerned primarily with the effects of law *upon* society, with the results of law, to a much greater extent than he is with the social determination of law.

Ironically then, because of his political desire to improve law, Pound's critique turns into another elaboration of the ideology preserving a positive form of law as *the* law. Indeed, although these theorists did shift attention towards the micro-empirical approach, the political use of their work has seldom been absent. The mass of empirical research that has emerged on every aspect of law, from how it is created and administered in the courts to how it is enforced in prisons and on the streets, has been desperate in its concern to highlight informalities and discretion, and to pin-point these as abuses in order to either reform, reject or protect the perceived existing dominant law form. Far less has it stressed the importance of informalities for positive law theorising. The problem is that the ideological analysis does not extend to include a discussion on how concentration on the discrepancies between ideal law and law in practice lose sight of their centrality to the process whereby the reality of law is constructed. A good illustration of this can be found in the empirical study of plea-bargaining, the way in which justice is negotiated informally within the context of formal legal processing.

Plea bargaining epitomises the neo-realist shortcomings. According to legal theory, courts should be governed by the rule of law and the principles of due process, which include an adversarial trial, protection of individual rights and a sentence determined by the rules as interpreted by the judge, after the jury has weighed the evidence and given its verdict. In practice this process has been found to be not infrequently pre-empted by informal negotiations between prosecutors, defence council, defendant and judge, which results in a guilty plea *before* the jury has considered the case and this is done in return for either a reduced sentence or dropped charges. (Blumberg, 1967; Newman, 1966; Dell, 1971; McCabe and Purves, 1972; Bottoms and McClean, 1976; Baldwin and McConville, 1977). The most recent surveys have found that among those who change their intention to plead at the last minute, from 'not guilty' to 'guilty', almost three-quarters were involved in some kind of negotiated justice. Eighteen per cent were involved in a genuine plea bargain and the rest understood something had gone on 'behind the scenes' as a 'nod and a wink' bargain (Baldwin and McConville, 1977).

However, having established the existence of plea bargaining, commentators do not go on to examine what it means for theorising about law and about the role informal practices play in maintaining the reality of formal law. Instead they use the evidence as a resource in a political battle over what should be happening to real law. Thus one group (Baldwin and McConville, 1977; Bottomley, 1979) see the evidence of plea bargaining as strengthening the need for 'open justice' and for discretion somehow to be made accountable. Bottomley (1979, p. 121), for example, says,

Areas of discretion must be defined and the exercise of
that discretion structured; overall policies must be clearly
stated and criteria for decision making articulated in ways
which allow for public debate in advance of their implementation. Effective means of accountability should be
established at every possible stage so that the community
knows and approves of what is being done in its name.
The defendant must be kept fully informed of what is
happening to him and given meaningful opportunities
to participate in the process.

The problem with these approaches is that they obscure the way in which positive law is inevitably dependent on informal practices and in proposing that a purer form of law can be achieved, perpetuate the myth that provides the ideological underpinning for positive law. How this operates can be seen most clearly from the legal establishment's reaction to the evidence of plea bargaining. As the Court of Appeal judge said in the case of Atkinson 1978:

Plea bargaining has no place in the English Criminal Law
... our law having no room for any bargain about
sentence between court and defendant; if events arise
which give the appearance of such a bargain, then one
must be very careful to see that the appearance is
corrected.

The crucial point here is not simply that the legal establishment is trying to preserve and protect a particular ideal of
law, but that we are able to glimpse into the ideological
process whereby positive law is constructed, as an appearance
of reality, and no less so by those with alternative views of
what that 'reality' should look like.

From the plea bargaining example, then, we can see that
although the emphasis on informalities advances thinking
about law in that it recognises formal positive law's reliance
on informal practices, it does not go nearly far enough.
It ultimately fails to recognise the inevitability of the
dependency and in striving to achieve a purer concept of
law reinforces rather than transcends the positive law
perspective.

The politicisation of informalism

The second theme addressing informalism but also failing to appreciate its significance to the production of positive law, is that of community justice reformers. These commentators accept the ideology that law has become formal and bureaucratic, and see a more desirable legal ideal in an informalised, decentralised, popular or community form of justice. Thus they argue that law has become separated from ordinary people, unaccountable, discretionary and riddled with expensive delays and ineffective controls. Versele (1969, p. 9) for example, argues:

> In the course of its development, the administration of criminal justice has become divorced from the people and entered an abstract realm . . . It is complacently isolated in an ivory tower, clothing a moralising approach in logical garb. It prides itself on a haughty independence which causes it to turn its back on society. The people have consequently lost interest in official justice and resigned themselves to the distortions which create a gap between their aspirations and legal concepts and criteria.

It is argued that this separation is reinforced as a result of legal functionaries adopting the 'iceberg approach': 'lawyers have been concerned with the exceptional rather than the typical, the few rather than the many. While the law may have applied to the whole population, only a few exercise their rights under it' (Whelan, 1981, p. 166).

Now the extent to which this kind of criticism rings true is a reflection of how far we are bound by the ideological processes which create one particular legal form as the reality of law. The separation that is pointed to between law and people is a conceptual one not a real one, since law is a product of men's minds. To conceive of law and then to act towards that conception as though it is autonomous and independent from the very thoughts that create it, is the height of reification. But to emphasise the separation in order to bring men back in, actually compounds the reification and can only deepen our sense of the reality of law and the objective facticity of its institutions. This is because such emphasis first denies the existence of human creativity, through its particular characterisation of the existing law form, and then falsely equates the physical presence of people-in-law with a change in its conception through which law itself is somehow seen as their product. Thus, instead of asking why the existing law is seen as separate from people, why it is that the rights of the few are not conceptualised by the many as having to do with them, and why it is that law is seen to be handling only the tip of an iceberg, the response has been to campaign for, and devise ways whereby, more bodies can be involved in legal processes. As Versele (1969, p. 10, p. 17) puts it,

> Criminal justice and community must be brought closer together, since those who judge and those who are judged are both part of the same society . . . the administration of criminal justice is in no sense the exclusive business of lawyers or of a social elite. It is the business of people as a whole . . . A direct and reliable means of accomplishing this is by public participation in the administration of justice.

As Whelan points out, this trend towards greater involvement in law has resulted in a variety of 'reform movements . . . the "access to justice" movement, the "justice with a human face" group, and the studies of dispute processing, particularly alternatives to the traditional judicial process' (1981, pp. 166-7). It has also resulted in the proliferation of the language of involvement, with terms like 'participation', 'decentralisation', 'informalisation', 'popularisation' and in the more humanistic sounding procedures of arbitration, conciliation and mediation, becoming vogue (Cappelletti and Garth, 1978; Eckhoff, 1966; Danzig, 1973; Fisher, 1975; Statsky, 1974; Longmire, 1981).

The general form of the machinery for such a decentralised justice is conceptualised as the 'community court'. For Fisher (1975, p. 1253) this is defined as 'a lay body dealing with a population that has objective features in common, with a jurisdiction over offences otherwise criminal and with the power to impose meaningful sanctions'. For Christie (1976, p. 20), 'The ideal is clear. There ought to be a court of equals representing themselves; when they are able to find a solution between themselves, no judges are needed. When they are not, the judges ought also to be their equals'. Under Eckhoff's (1966) version, because the task of the judge would be no longer to reach a decision about which of the disputants was right, information could be extracted from *both* sides, increasing the possibility of settlement and reconciliation through compromise and negotiation. Underlying disputes could be dealt with as well, ending any further grudge. Similarly, Fisher (1975, pp. 1286-7) says the model community court 'in many ways . . . resembles more primitive judicial systems' and that 'to be effective, a community court would have to have the ability to both conciliate the parties to a dispute and to impose sanctions sufficient to gain respect and support of the community should conciliation prove impossible'.

Of crucial importance is the way the community justice reformers see their informalised ideal relating to what they take to be the existing dominant formal system. For some, like Danzig (1973, p. 7), the relationship should be 'complementary': 'If decentralisation is to be successful, it will involve the construction of a complementary system, supplementing and in some areas substituting for, but nowhere destroying or totally displacing, the existing apparatus'. He justifies this on the grounds that it is not only more likely that such a formula would be more acceptable to the existing bureaucracy but, 'whatever the faults of the present system, it does some things well' and that, 'there is no virtue and much danger in decentralising what is done well centrally' (ibid.). Others propose their community courts as 'alternatives'. Fisher, for example, criticises limited versions, such as arbitration and domestic diversion programmes, which have been set up experimentally in the United States, for only sometimes being used as alternatives and which depend upon referrals from the formal system. He similarly criticises the use of disciplinary boards in universities and colleges, which leave open the possibility of additional criminal sanctioning and thereby duplication of legal processing under the formal system. And he rejects prison tribunals as models for they do not have exclusive jurisdiction and 'rarely allow for prisoner participation, thereby raising doubts as to whether the "judges" are really "community members"' (Fisher, 1975, p. 1271). Finally he dismisses the socialist experiments with community courts on the grounds that 'they are unfortunately subject to political controls by local party officials' and they 'must carry out the policies set by their respective political organisations' (ibid., p. 1278). For these reasons Fisher (ibid., p. 1287, p. 1278, p. 1282) is categorical about the relationship between formal and informal legal forms:

> A true community court should be more than an adjunct to the existing system, it should be an alternative to the formal system ... A true community court must remain independent of any political organisation and influence if it is to operate effectively as an instrument of justice ... its procedures should be overseen by the formal courts only to the extent necessary to ensure that the constitutional freedoms and protections are not infringed.

Perhaps the most extreme version of this perspective is that of Longmire, who adopts an anarchistic position in which a decentralised popular justice system is proposed as a 'radical alternative' to completely replace the existing formal legal system (Longmire, 1981, p. 22):

> At best, a formal system of control might be maintained in a much less significant form than the present system and with much less power and authority than it now exercises over citizens' lives. In its ideal form the proposed system will negate the need for coercive social control agencies and will therefore suffice as a complete replacement for, rather than complement to, the existing law enforcement system.

As with the legal realists, then, community justice reform movements, though recognising the importance of the informal in law, see this as the object of future legal development, rather than as the subject of existing law creation. But such a position misunderstands the nature of informalism. It cannot be achieved for it is already there. It is an inseparable part of formalism. To suppose otherwise, and to act towards formal law as though the informal could replace it, is to perpetuate the ideology which is responsible for the mythical distinction whereby formal positive law is conceptualised as an object-like entity having an existence apart from the process of its creation. This is not to say, however, that procedures could not be adopted that would involve more people in the law. Rather it is to assert that such a change, in itself, is not enough to bring about a change in the way law is conceived as a separate object-like entity, separate from those whose 'involvement' is a part of its creation. That this is the case can clearly be seen from experiments with decentralisation and community justice in both socialist and western industrial societies.

A form of community justice has been used under different names in a variety of socialist societies. These courts have been called comrades' courts in the Soviet Union, people's courts in the Republic of China, popular tribunals in Cuba, social courts in Hungary, disputes commissions in the German Democratic Republic and workers' courts in Poland. Although the origin of the socialist use of the community court concept is put at around 1919, with Lenin's philosophy that the workers should participate in the management of all state and communal affairs including the administration of justice (Ramundo, 1965), in most socialist countries the courts did not flourish until their reintroduction between 1959 and 1962. An illustration of how these serve to further entrench rather than liberate law from the dominant ideology whereby law is created as external to those who participate in its production, can be seen by an examination of Soviet comrades' courts.

The comrades' courts are based on two principles: first, that offences are not simply the fault of the individual, but of the whole collective, who must take responsibility for them through participation in their management or resolution; second, that only those people who are an offender's immediate community fellows can know his specific situation, conditions of life, relationships and similar facts which are seen to have a significant bearing on the correct resolution of the dispute. Thus, rather than being separate from the other activities of the community, comrades' courts are set up at enterprises, institutions and organisations, schools, collective farms, apartments and rural settlements, where their members are elected by special ballot for two years by general meetings of the collective. Thus, they operate with a wide concept of relevance, are very personal and are encouraged to consider the full circumstances in the background of the offender, as well as the total context of the case (Berman and Spindler, 1963; Ramundo, 1965; Lapenna, 1968).

However, far from being the autonomous law forms of an idealised community justice, the comrades' courts are an integral part of the total apparatus of social control. Although they are supposed to be independent of the more formal state people's courts, their elected members are encouraged to attend regional Councils of Comrades' Courts at which are present the best qualified members of comrades' courts as well as lawyers and workers from judicial bodies (Ramundo, 1965, p. 710). Moreover, Rogovin (1961, p. 305) talks of the two-fold aim of the comrades' courts in the context of the overall system of social control: to educate the public into the rules of the socialist society, by arousing public interest in social order through mass participation; and to act as a vehicle through which the individual is re-educated and returned to society as a useful member. As Ramundo (1965, p. 699) says, the socialist vision is that as a result of comradely censure and criticism, a new social morality will develop, become instinctive and cause crime to decline or disappear. But Rogovin shows how local party officials or union control can actually result in the fabrication of issues of dispute for the purpose of 'educating the public' (1961, p. 306). She argues that the function of the court is to give the state greater penetrative power via the collective, to encroach on the sphere of the individual and inhibit any deviation that may be thought of as 'dangerously individualistic'.

In short then, the socialist experiments with community courts highlight how participation by wider numbers of people can actually serve the dominant ideology which maintains the legitimacy of formal law, rather than disclosing to the participants their part in this process. The same co-option process can be shown to be true of experiments with community justice in western industrial societies.

Brady, for example, in his critique of Longmire's proposals

for popular justice says that 'informal sanctions of the community and the mobilisation of public consensus can be a powerful and yet relatively non-coercive form of social control' (1981, p. 36). He asks why it is that popular justice, community participation and neighbourhood justice are being actively promoted and indeed funded by the very government agencies and state representatives of which they were originally critical. He argues that this occurs because the new resurgence in citizens' participation and popular justice is not a challenge or an alternative to the existing legal order but 'can and do serve only to extend the legitimacy and power of the state in a time of fiscal and political crisis' (ibid., p. 31). Brady suggests that we need to distinguish between calls for popular justice that emerge outside the state as social movements for equality and which promise to remain independent from it because they are involved in the business of social change through consciousness raising, challenging social and economic inequalities and criticising the state and its justice system, and those which are 'sterile or even reactionary and racist' (ibid., p. 32). Brady says that the latter group mistake mere form for change. He points out that the experiments in community participation and action programmes show that as soon as these become a challenge to powerful interests they are abandoned by government. They are geared more to legitimacy than liberating a utopia of popular control over justice (Brady, 1981, p. 35):

> The programs which they have funded very clearly limit citizen participation to low priority roles, to enable justice professionals to concentrate their energies elsewhere.
> There is no intention to create an alternative justice sytem ... their role is strictly limited to low priority cases and their training and orientation is solidly dominated by the regular court professionals.

A similar critique is made by Abel (1981, 1982) who distinguishes between 'conservative conflict', which he sees as perpetuating the status quo, and 'radical' or 'liberating conflict', which 'transforms parties, disaggregating those that were corporate and organising previously atomistic individuals'

(Abel, 1981, p. 255). He sees the move towards informalism in law as part of conservative conflict arguing that 'the ideology of informalism exaggerates the differences between formal courts and informal alternatives and hides their similarities' (ibid., p. 250). He says that both informal and formal legal structures tend to render conflict conservative, rather than liberating; they shape conflict so as to preserve rather than challenge the structure of domination and exploitation. They incorporate political struggles into areas where they will be least disruptive to the state and do this under the questionable guise of a more just, more humane cheaper system giving greater access. But, says, Abel, informal institutions are partial in their implementation, occurring more often in trivial and peripheral areas such as neighbourhood disputes over noise, pets and fences than in 'conflicts between worker and capitalist, subordinate and superordinate, citizen and state, human being and polluter' (ibid., p. 261). Not only are the areas of conflict limited, but, says Abel, so too is the status of the disputants. These are restricted to atomised individuals, which has the effect of dispersing conflict and of distracting from inter-class conflict. And whilst informal justice is supposed to be separate from the state and be run by community members for community members, it is typically run by the government, and by conciliators, arbitrators and mediators, who increasingly become an institutionalised class; an 'aristocracy of good citizens'. Abel concludes by pointing out that informal institutions have their own inbuilt limitations (1981, p. 263):

> From the viewpoint of the capitalist state, their drawback is that they cannot effectively manage conflict and remain informal. If they take the latter course they will atrophy ... if they choose the former they will have to remain more openly coercive; but this will generate opposition and compel the liberal state to respond by adopting formal procedures ... Members of oppressed groups ... want to resist exploitation and domination, not reach an accommodation with it. They want a public hearing and moral vindication; if informal institutions do not provide this, grievants will find other arenas.

But this does not mean that informalism is sterile as regards advancing liberation, for, as Abel recognises, 'they must express some of the aspirations of the disputants or the latter would shun them altogether' (ibid.). This point is perhaps best made by Santos (1980, pp. 390-3) when he talks of the shred of content necessary for manipulation to be possible:

> It would be a gross mistake to analyse current reforms as sheer manipulation and state conspiracy . . . the main contradiction is that the reform movement carries with it a strong symbolic feature, the idea of participation, self-government and real community. This is a utopian transcendental element . . . Community justice cannot be ideological without at the same time being implicitly utopian as well.

However, liberation cannot come simply from participation. It requires an awareness that the informal is an integral part of the totality of law and not an alternative to it. If participation in the administration of law simply leads to the separation of those who administer from those who receive, then there will have been no transformation in conception, merely a change of personnel. For genuine liberation it is necessary for those who participate to understand the place of the informal in relation to the total structure of social control. The informal cannot be siphoned off for separate consideration, participation and analysis. It has no meaning outside of its relationship to the formal, just as the formal is meaningless without reference to the informal. The two are parts of the same whole. Their conceptual separation comprises the ideological process that constitutes one of them as the reality. Attempts to make the other part the reality do not advance our thinking about how that reality is constituted and fail to be aware of their own contribution to that process. Without such awareness there can be no liberation. Fortunately, however, two other perspectives on informalism, legal pluralism and the ethnography of dispute processing have developed out of an initial awareness of the importance of the informal to law, to a consideration of its dialectical relationship with the total system of social control.

Legal pluralism and informal law

Although some ideal-type structural theorists and some multi-paradigmists, discussed in chapter 1, appear to adopt a pluralistic stance, we saw how this was deceptive (pp. 21, 31). In each case the concept of positive law is actually reinforced, the former by relegating competing law-forms to the 'past' or the 'primitive'; the latter by restricting the range of paradigms to within the taken for granted limits of formal law. Legal pluralism proper, starts out from the observation that instead of there being only one kind of law, the positive law of the state, there are numerous other kinds of law that are generated quite independently of the state, and that these operate at various levels of formality. Legal pluralism can be usefully conceptualised as operating along two dimensions. The horizontal dimension distinguishes between kinds of law according to their different sources of generation in different groups or institutions. The vertical dimension, in contrast, recognises that law operates at different levels, from a superficial formality down to a spontaneous, unorganised informality. The most articulate version of legal pluralism, that of Gurvitch, integrates these two dimensions such that the horizontal and the vertical criss-cross. Here the horizontal dimension is not differentiated by group but by the form of integration to a group, there being many of these in any one group. Therefore there exist as many different kinds of law as there are ways of being bound to a group and for each kind there are a number of different levels, layers or depths of operation. Although the origins of these ideas are disparate, we can thank Gurvitch who, in constructing his pluralistic typology, found it necessary to draw together, for critical review, many of the key theorists who have contributed to this perspective.

Of particular importance to thinking on the horizontal dimension have been those writers who saw law as separate from the state. Those like Grotius, Krause, Proudhon and Gierke, argue that law is generated not by the state but autonomously by each group and they identify as many types of law as there are groups. Krause, for example, sees the state as no more than one sector of the total life of a society and one which is not dominant to other associations. In contrast, Gierke saw the state having pre-eminence over other groups but this did not inhibit him from recognising that all organised groups are subject to their own autonomous order of law. As Gurvitch (1947, p. 72) says of Gierke:

> Gierke characterised all organised groups as the subject of their own autonomous order of law (which regulates their internal life) as a complex collective person... He proclaimed law's independence of the state and went on to develop a methodical classification of the types of these collective persons and their frameworks of law.

A major difficulty with these early 'horizontal pluralists' is that they are dealing with a narrow concept of law. Although it was not state law, and although they distinguished between kinds of law, they none the less saw law as the written codified laws relating to the groups identified in their analysis. This conception was considerably broadened by Ross's (1901) notion of social control and by his listing of thirty-three different ways in which people were controlled in society. The more effective of these were informal controls such as tradition, spontaneous group pressure and public opinion, not least because people trust them, dread them and are obsessed by them. Unfortunately, Ross could not escape the evolutionism of his day and argued that the legal controls of advanced industrial society would displace informal controls more typical of 'primitive society'. He saw these artificial measures of control as unnecessary and actually weakening social instincts and 'primal moral feelings'. In this he failed to see that the two kinds of controls were interdependent, such that one cannot replace the other.

Gurvitch points out that Ross also confused kinds of control with the methods used to bring them about and with the agencies or groups for which such controls were exercised. This meant that he was unable to see how each agency, social group or organisation could use a range of kinds of social controls and that each kind of control could be accomplished by a variety of different methods. This, says Gurvitch, stemmed from a basic flaw in Ross's thinking in which he ignored the plurality of social groups in a society and assumed a monolithic social order (Gurvitch, 1947, p. 20):

> The problem of the relation between social control and the different types of groupings within an inclusive society entirely escaped Ross . . . He connected the various kinds of social control only with the inclusive society. He considered order created by social control as a unique order; as though order were an absolute and not a relative principle, and as though there were not in every society an inextricable pluralism of orders and agencies of social control for achieving them!

From this we can see that Ross's horizontal pluralism does not extend to a recognition of the different sources of law, only to a recognition of its different forms and therefore loses sight of the valuable contributions of the earlier pluralists.

In contrast to the horizontal pluralists like Ross and Gierke, there is the contribution of those, like Ehrlich and Hauriou, who developed thinking about vertical pluralism. Ehrlich (1913), for example, saw formal positive law as merely the surface crust of a series of layers which reach down to the source of law: 'living law: the law which dominates life itself even though it has not been posited in legal propositions' (1979, p. 125). Ehrlich criticised the positive law philosophers for focusing too narrowly on law and as a result, neglecting the broader form of which law was merely one manifestation. Although individuals were governed by state laws they were also embedded in many associations (Ehrlich, 1979, p. 122):

> Here in the social association, is the source of coercive power, the sanction of all social norms of law no more than morality, ethical custom, religious honour, decorum, etiquette, fashion . . . Man therefore conducts himself according to law chiefly because this is made imperative by his social relations. In this respect the legal norm does not differ from the other norms. The state is not the only association that exercises coercion; there is an untold number of associations in society that exercise it more forcefully than the state.

Beneath the abstract legal propositions that make up formal

positive law and which are elaborated by the state, are concrete rules for the resolution of conflict. Underneath these there is the spontaneous inner order of society itself, the centre of gravity of law and legal development; the association then is the source of law. Moreover, Ehrlich sees state law as being of less importance than 'living law', not least because of the latter's effectiveness in binding individuals together, and because of those same individuals' ignorance of state law and by contrast their profound awareness of the spontaneous, silent action of social groups. He also suggests that the generation of 'living law' goes on quite independently of the formal law and of the state, whose influence lags behind.

As Gurvitch points out, Ehrlich's pluralism is incomplete in that it reduces (horizontally) all law to being of the same kind, that generated by the association, and for ultimately restricting each to the same (vertical) level (Gurvitch, 1947, pp. 121-2):

> the law of societies is artificially impoverished by being confined to the spontaneous, as though it did not have its own abstract propositions in autonomous statutes of groups, and its own rules of decision elaborated in the functioning of boards of arbitration and similar bodies.

He indicts Ehrlich for seeking a universal source of law instead of distinguishing different sources in different kinds of association, and instead of describing the differing layers of depth of each kind of law.

Ehrlich might also be criticised for failing to appreciate that state law has a significant influence on the shaping of living law; that associations are not completely free to generate spontaneous living law which then becomes ossified as formal legal propositions. Even less free are the individual members of these associations, though they are completely subordinated neither to the state, nor to the association, but exercise a degree of freedom.

Like Ehrlich, Hauriou saw the association, in his case 'the institution', as the source of law and that this was differentiated into several different levels of depth. But he went beyond Ehrlich in attempting to integrate a horizontal

Impressions of diversity 51

pluralism, though this remained less well developed than his vertical pluralism. Vertically, the most superficial layer is that of the rigid rules that are 'fixed in advance'. The next layer is the more flexible dynamic rules 'established ad hoc' for particular cases. The final, deepest layer, is the institution itself as a spontaneous primary source of law, 'the real life of law'. As well as layers of law within and reaching down to the essence of the institution, Hauriou identified a horizontal pluralism by distinguishing between different kinds of law-producing institutions.

Gurvitch, however, not only criticises Hauriou for producing a sociology of law, 'whose merit lies rather in his analysis in depth of the reality of law revealing its "vertical pluralism" far more accurately than its "horizontal pluralism"' (Gurvitch, 1947, p. 115), but, more fundamentally, criticises him for failing to use the correct criteria for distinguishing between kinds of law in the horizontal dimension. For Gurvitch, the source of different kinds of law is not the group but what he describes as the microsociological elements within groups: forms of sociality or ways of being bound to the group. Since Gurvitch's analysis is the most highly developed attempt to integrate horizontal and vertical pluralism, it is worth looking at this more closely.

Gurvitch founds his 'systematic sociology of law' on what he takes to be the simplest and irreducible microscopic elements or 'social electrons'; 'such microsociological elements are not at all individuals *but the ways of being bound to the whole and by the whole, the forms of sociality*' (ibid., p. 156). He says that 'there is no observable society which does not include a multiplicity of groups ... a complete web of real collective unities' (ibid., p. 182). It is the way individuals are bound to these groups, rather than the groups themselves, that generate law. Each group has a range of ways by which members are bound to it. In other words there are a number of different forms of sociality. Since 'every form of sociality is capable of being ... the birthplace of law' (ibid., p. 158), 'there are as many kinds of law as there are forms of active sociality' (ibid., p. 166).

Gurvitch, a prima donna of distinctions, distinguishes between two basic kinds of sociality: direct, spontaneous sociality and organised, reflected sociality. The spontaneous kind of sociality provides the horizontal dimension to his integrated schema of differentiated kinds of law. Here, different intensities of fusion to the whole provide the criteria for distinguishing a range of different kinds of spontaneous sociality. He identifies twenty-seven different kinds of spontaneous sociality, each having its own corresponding kind of law.

In contrast, the organised reflected form of sociality provides the basis for his vertical dimension of differentiation. Each and every kind of law identified in the horizontal dimension can exist at a number of different levels of formality as 'a series of superimposed strata, moving from a more or less rigid schematisation and external symbolism to an increasing dynamism and immediacy (in descending direction), and inversely from spontaneity and flexibility to reinforced crystallisation and conceptualisation (in an ascending direction)' (ibid., p. 174). He identifies six different depth levels in the vertical classification: organised law fixed in advance, flexible organised law, organised intuitive law, unorganised law fixed in advance, flexible unorganised law and unorganised intuitive law.

The synthesis of the different kinds of law in the horizontal plane, each corresponding to a different form of sociality characteristic of a particular group, and each operating at a different depth of formality corresponding to different levels of sociality in the vertical plane, constitutes a framework of law. These different kinds and levels of law are dynamically interacting within the framework of law, like their source, the different kinds and levels of sociality, such that, 'the congealed schemes of the organised superstructures always lag and have again and again to be broken by the explosions and eruptions of spontaneous sociality' (ibid., p. 160). Further, the different frameworks of law combine and compete to constitute the system of law characteristic of the all-inclusive society. However, whilst these systems, frameworks and kinds of law are ranked hierarchically by Gurvitch, his location of the source of law in the form of sociality allows him to see law as autonomously generated, free from the influence of the all-inclusive society (Gurvitch, 1947, p. 158):

Having designated as a 'normative fact' each manifestation of social reality capable of engendering law, i.e., to be its primary or material source, we can conclude: the normative facts of the all-inclusive societies possess, in the jural life, primacy over the normative facts of forms of sociality. But this does not at all hinder each form of sociality from giving birth to its own peculiar kind of law; the forms of sociality play, beside and inside groups and all-inclusive societies, in which they are integrated, the role of primary sources of law and this role is a very important and decisive one . . .

It can be seen from Figure 1 that I have restricted representation of Gurvitch's twenty-seven different kinds of sociality and their corresponding kinds of law in order to clarify the overall picture. As he says (Gurvitch, 1947, p. 181),

the six layers of law distinguished by the vertical microsociology criss-cross with the multiple kinds of law differentiated by horizontal microsociology. Schematically speaking this would give not less than 162 (27 × 6) kinds of law which clash and balance with varying degrees of intensity and actuality inside every framework of law corresponding to each group, to each real collective unit. Obviously, we give this number only to help conjure up a picture of the true 'jural microcosm' which, in principle or at least virtually, is to be found in every active group, even small. It is this microcosm which forbids hasty generalisations and oversimplifications about the jural character of various groupings . . . and about the regularities which guide the transformation of systems of law corresponding to the types of inclusive societies.

Indeed, Gurvitch then goes on in systematic fashion to classify social groups and their corresponding frameworks of law and then all-inclusive societies and their corresponding legal systems.

Gurvitch's contribution to thinking about law is formidable. It renounces 'the evolutionist prejudice which believes that the "germ" of an uninterrupted unilinear development of jural institutions may be found in primitive society and

54 *Impressions of diversity*

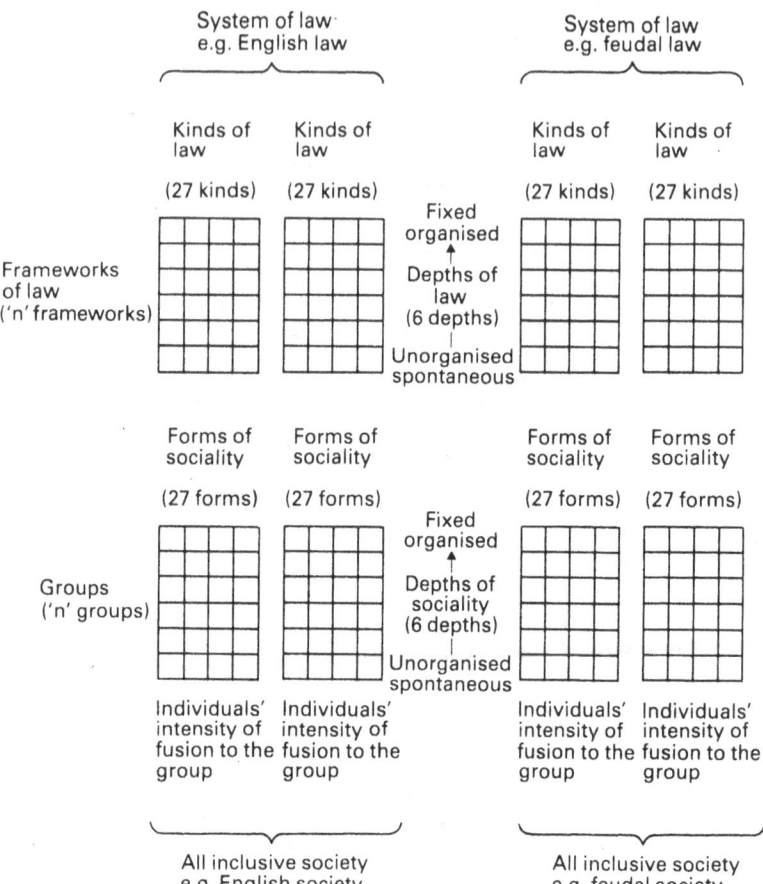

Figure 1 A simplified representation of Gurvitch's 'systematic sociology of law'

which confuses the problems of the legal typology of society with that of their origin' (Gurvitch, 1947, p. 227). It shows that law is generated spontaneously, and autonomously rather than being imposed by the state. It demonstrates that law is pluralistic in both range and in its depth of formality. Importantly, it goes farther than others in its attempt to incorporate the diversity and dynamism of law whilst trying not to lose sight of its relationship to the totality. In particular, and in the classic sociological tradition, it aims to look at both the organised and rigid structures and at the less obvious spontaneous, dynamic and volatile aspects which are concealed beneath the surface. Having said this, however, there are a number of fundamental weaknesses with the whole approach.

Firstly, Gurvitch's analysis suffers from an over-reliance on formalism, imposing categories on reality. He has a propensity for taxonomies and typologies and for 'criss-crossing' these together such that the whole schema becomes extremely complicated, tremendously involved, and cumbersome to the point of being unmanageable which ultimately obscures more than it clarifies. Nor is this helped by his conciseness. As an authority on his work observes (Bosserman, 1968, p. 288):

> Gurvitch waits for no one. He knows what he believes and he moves immediately into an explanation of this conviction . . . If he would have undertaken to do a more careful and elementary presentation of a number of key concepts in his theory, his readers would be aided in grasping more easily the core of his thought.

Secondly, the basis for his classification in terms of depth levels is questionable. Bosserman asks, 'Does an in-depth study necessitate arranging social phenomenon in depth levels, much as in geology? What reasons are there for arranging the formality of law hierarchically with the organised and rigid at the top and the spontaneous and intuitive at the bottom? Does this not imply one is superior to the other, as indeed Gurvitch suggests?' (ibid., p. 275). Bosserman (ibid.) continues:

> Why do total social phenomenon need to be hierarchised? The key notion is the relationship between the various phenomena . . . Gurvitch is not clear what constitutes significant distinctions among the various levels. Though he places these phenomena in a hierarchy, they have no structure without the horizontal plane . . . They are so intertwined there is little theoretical distinctiveness. What we need are the dialectical processes of reciprocity of perspectives and mutual implication to bring these two aspects together.

Thirdly, Gurvitch's notion that forms of sociality are the birthplace of law is highly contentious. No empirical evidence is offered that demonstrates how this generative process takes place. Indeed, it follows simply from Gurvitch's Durkheimian and Maussian inspired belief in the primacy of the collective mind or 'total social phenomena', which is held to be ontologically prior to the other aspects of social reality. Phenomena are studied for themselves but from the perspective that in reality they are an organic whole. But suppose this is not the case. Suppose, rather, that law is a product of the interaction between individuals or between individuals and the totality or even between the interactive products of that interaction. Then the root of law may be a feature less of forms of sociality than of the way in which individuals reproduce the appearance of real phenomena and then act towards that appearance of reality in a way which reconstructs and reconfirms its objective appearance. Moreover, Gurvitch may be accused of a degree of reductionism not dissimilar to that with which he charges Ehrlich. In Gurvitch's case, the reduction is to forms of sociality as a universal law producer, rather than the association as in Ehrlich's case. It may be, instead, that the source of law lies in a diversity of relationships that individuals have with apparent totalities and that any unity is a product of the process of interpretation and organisation of what is otherwise dissimilar behaviour.

This suggests a fourth criticism, that the obsession with the 'realness' of groups as total social phenomena and the identification of the form of sociality, as the source of law, subordinates the intentionality and freedom of individuals to engage in creative action with others and with the social structures that are themselves products of that creativity.

A fifth problem is that the appearance created in Gurvitch's writing of simultaneous attention to both diversity and totality is misleading. As Toulemont critically observes: 'The fact that Gurvitch never establishes real abstractions, but always stops somewhere between the abstract and the concrete has led to definitions which are hazy, elastic and elusive' (1955, p. 246). It has also led to the mistaken belief that he is addressing the dialectical relationship between structure and action. Unfortunately, the diversity of Gurvitch's pluralism does not spread to include individuals' action, and his concern with totality limits structural considerations to those of the group and even reduces the state to the status of just another group. In short, his dialectical posturing fails to transcend the limits set by the Durkheimian tradition of accepting social reality as fact, rather than seeing its very facticity as the subject for inquiry.

Studies of dispute processing

A third influence that has emphasised the role of informalism in law, and which has recently reached a similar level of plurality in its attempt to address both total and partial levels of theorising is the ethnographic study of dispute settlement in non-industrial societies but this too ultimately fails to achieve a dialectical analysis.

Studies of dispute processing grew up in a critical response to the 'law-centred' approach taken by many anthropologists and ethnographers who, 'consistently assert that legal rules can be distinguished from other kinds of norms . . . and that "law" must be regarded as no less than an irreducible phenomenal category' (Comaroff and Roberts, 1981. p. 8). The law-centred approach saw the study of law in non-industrial societies as an adjunct to the analysis of western legal systems. For these commentators (Radcliffe-Brown, 1952; Evans Pritchard, 1940; Fallers, 1969), societies without 'western-type' legal institutions of rules and of courts and constables, were often assumed to have no law at all. Those who did not take such a dismissive and ethnocentric view (Shapera, 1938; Gluckman, 1955), nonetheless attempted to force the social control mechanisms of such societies into the western legal mould and thereby sought universals of legal systems. As Roberts has said of such studies, 'all rules are treated as legal rules and all peace-makers are identified as judges' (Roberts, 1979, p. 194).

In sharp contrast to the law-centred perspective, an approach has emerged which builds on the foundation laid by Malinowski's (1926) study of the Trobriand Islanders and which takes a pluralistic view as to what is to count as law. As Comaroff and Roberts say, this perspective looks at all those processes concerned with maintaining social order, not just those taken to be 'legal': 'It is . . . in social processes, not in institutions, that the analysis of order is ultimately to be grounded' and this perspective marks 'a significant shift of focus from institution to interaction' (Comaroff and Roberts, 1981, pp. 12-13). Thus the work of ethnographers such as Colson (1953), Turner (1957), Bohannon (1957), Bailey (1960), Berndt (1962), Gulliver (1963), Young (1971) and Koch (1974) is important in that each shows how a variety of non-industrial societies uses a range of social control mechanisms in the resolution of disputes; from fighting and contest, through to resort to supernatural agencies, shaming, ridicule, ostracism, the withdrawal of co-operation, as well as settlement-directed talking, third-party intervention, arbitration and mediation. As Comaroff and Roberts say, even where special judicial institutions exist, they 'do not always enjoy the exclusive pre-eminence in dispute settlement that English courts ostensibly enjoy' (Comaroff and Roberts, 1981, p. 10).

The merits of the dispute processing perspective over earlier law-centred approaches are that it takes a broader social control perspective and recognises a wide concept of relevance (Comaroff and Roberts, 1981, pp. 13-14):

> An adequate account of a dispute requires a description of its total social context — its genesis, successive efforts to manage it, and the subsequent history of the relationship between the parties . . . Once disputes are no longer seen as discrete bounded pathological events, they may not be neatly excised from the ongoing flow of community life, even for heuristic purposes.

Thus the approach requires a shift away from focusing on judges and judgements, to the contextual background of the parties to the dispute (ibid., p. 14):

> since rivalry and dispute represent merely one phase in the intersecting biographies of the parties concerned, it is their respective circumstances, goals, strategies and actions that determine the nature of the interaction between them.

Impressions of diversity 59

The decision whether, or in what manner, to precipitate a public confrontation is often predicated on these factors. If the form and content of dispute settlement processes are to be explained, attention must therefore be given to the disputants' ostensible motives in pursuing a quarrel, how they recruit support, their strategic efforts to influence the procedural course of events and so on.

Finally, the perspective reveals that rules need not be laws directly determining the outcome of disputes, but may themselves be the objects of negotiation, such that the whole dispute settlement process is a 'conceptual and organisational framework for competitive bargaining, transaction and compromise' (ibid., pp. 14-15). What is required, then, according to Comaroff and Roberts, is 'the elaboration of an approach that can account for both the *total* logic of dispute processes and for their systematic contextualisation' (ibid., p. 247). They argue that 'norm and reality exist in a necessary dialectical relationship' that gives form to the manner of dispute settlement experience. Thus rather than reduce the dispute process to an institutional adjunct of social structure, Comaroff and Roberts try to show that the constitution of the socio-cultural system shapes an order of manifest linkages and values. These in turn configure the relations and interests that are negotiated in the context of disputes and therefore affect the form and content of the processes of confrontation. They (Comaroff and Roberts, 1981, pp. 248-9) conclude:

> There is something of an analytical mutuality — perhaps even a circularity — in all this. On the one hand, the logic of disputes is ultimately situated in the encompassing system and can be comprehended only as such. But, on the other, it is in the context of confrontation — when persons negotiate their social universe and enter discourse about it — that the character of that system is revealed.

A similar level of analysis is reached in Moore's (1978) *Law as Process*. Moore argues that there is a certain contradiction between the idea of an intentionally directed society and one which is causally driven. She (Moore, 1978, p. 3) rejects one or other of these saying that

60 *Impressions of diversity*

any analysis which focuses entirely on the orderly and the rule bound is limited indeed, and does not place the normative in the context of the whole context of action, which certainly includes much more than conformity to or deviance from normative rules.

She says that instead, 'one is dealing with *partial* order and *partial* control' and a central concern must be to identify those social processes which operate outside the rules, or which cause people to use the rules or 'abandon them, bend them, reinterpret them, side-step them, or replace them' (ibid., p. 4). Of course, established rules exist, but for Moore these operate in the context of changing moments of time, shifting persons, altering situations, improvised actions, indeterminacy, ambiguity, uncertainty and manipulability (ibid., p. 39):

> Order never fully takes over, nor could it. The cultural, contractual and technical imperatives always leave gaps, require adjustments and interpenetrations to be applicable to particular situations, and are themselves full of ambiguities, inconsistencies and often contradictions.

From this perspective, then, law is an active process, 'not something which once achieved, is fixed'. Rather, 'existing orders are endlessly vulnerable to being unmade, remade, and transformed, and that even maintaining and reproducing themselves, staying as they are, should be seen as a process' (ibid., p. 6). In order to analyse 'law as process', Moore proposed the concept of the semi-autonomous field. She argues that such a field can 'generate rules and customs and symbols internally', it has 'rule making capacities and the means to induce or coerce compliance' (ibid., pp. 55-6). At the same time, however, the semi-autonomous field is 'vulnerable to rules and decisions and other forces emanating from the larger world by which it is surrounded'. She argues that it is 'set in a larger social matrix which can and does invade it' (ibid.).

In an attempt to develop a radical theory of legal pluralism, Fitzpatrick (1981) draws on Moore's notion of law as process and argues that semi-autonomous fields have their own discrete legal order which is not ultimately subordinate to the overarching state legal order. Rather, law 'is seen as constituted, in significant part, by the interaction of legal orders and their social fields' (Fitzpatrick, 1981, p. 1). He illustrates this with the example of the family and its legal order which, while affected by the state legal order, is also set in its own social field. He (ibid.) says,

> The state legal order itself is profoundly affected by the family and its legal order. There is a constituent interaction of legal orders and of their framing social fields. One side of the interaction cannot be reduced to the other. Nor can both sides be reduced to a third element such as the capitalist mode of production.

Elsewhere Fitzpatrick (1982, p. 12) argues:

> It is not so much that the family relations function in support of relations of reproduction within the totality; family relations *are* some of those relations of reproduction . . . the family cannot be reduced to this totality or seen as only subordinate to it. There is an interaction between the two in which the family has both a structured and an historically based autonomy.

With Comaroff and Roberts, Moore and Fitzpatrick, then, we reach a level of theorising about law which promises to move away from the limitations of micro-analytical pluralism, whereby the only escape from what Hamnett (1975, p. 107) calls 'the theoretical desert of social control' is back to a form of law-centred universalism. By recognising the dialectical relationship between structure and social action and how these are interdependent and mutually implying, we begin to see the possibility of transcending the view that law is either the product of structure, or the outcome of interaction. We begin to glimpse how informalism is not so much an alternative form of law but a necessary part of the ideological process whereby the crystallised, formalised, objective-like qualities of law are created and sustained in an on-going manner. It is necessary to reveal the ways in which in acting at the informal spontaneous level of interaction, total social structures are conceptualised and implied as though they were objective realities having real consequences.

Thus, rather in the manner of Moore and Fitzpatrick, it is necessary to explore the processes of interpenetration of the micro-structures with the macro and vice versa. It is towards just such an approach that much of Giddens's work has been directed.

Towards an integrated theory of law

In his extensive writing in sociological theory, Giddens has repeatedly stressed the importance of both social structure and action. He argues that social order is the conscious product of human agency, but that men are not totally free to produce order in the way that they choose. Action is constituted structurally and yet structures are also constituted by action.

Giddens (1979) starts with a general critique of previous theorising, irrespective of its political persuasion, as presenting either/or alternatives but failing to bridge the gap. Both radical and conservative approaches present action theories (or micro studies) as antimonies of structural theories (or macro studies). Thus liberal consensus theory presents the antimony between the symbolic interactionism of Mead and Blumer, which deals with small-scale interpersonal relations, and the functionalism of Parsons and Merton which handles the relations making up the totality. Similarly, radical theories present the antimony between phenomenological Marxism as in Paci and Lukács against the structural Marxism of Althusser. Giddens says that writers operating at the micro level of action theory 'have paid little attention to or have found no way of coping with, conceptions of structural explanation or social causation' (Giddens, 1979, p. 49). On the other hand those writers preoccupied with structure accord a priority to structure over action, such that structure exerts a dominant influence over conduct. Thus 'each reaches a position in which subject is controlled by object: Parsons's actors are cultural dopes, but Althusser's agents are structural dopes of even more stunning mediocrity' (ibid., p. 52). Giddens argues that this separation between agency and structure is an incomplete analysis since examination of agency without referring back to structure, or structure without referring back to agency, loses the essence of the matter: that action and structure presuppose one another in a dialectical relationship. To overcome this limitation in theorising Giddens (1979, pp. 69-72) says it is necessary to address the,

> duality of structure which relates to the fundamentally recursive character of social life, and expresses the mutual dependence of structure and agency . . . the structural properties of social systems are both the medium and the outcome of the practices that constitute those systems . . . structure is both enabling and constraining and it is one of the specific tasks of social theory to study the conditions in the organisation of social systems that govern the interconnections between the two . . . every process of action is a production of something new, a fresh act; but at the same time all action exists in a continuity with the past, which supplies the means of its initiation. Structure thus is not to be conceptualised as a barrier to action, but as essentially involved in its production . . . According to the notion of duality of structure, rules and resources are drawn on by actors in the production of interaction, but are thereby also reconstituted through action. Structure is thus the mode in which the relations between moment and totality expresses itself in social reproduction . . . institutions do not just work 'behind the backs' of the social actors who produce and reproduce them. Every competent member of every society knows a great deal about the institutions of that society. Such knowledge is not incidental to the operation of society but is necessarily involved in it . . . all social actors, no matter how lowly, have some degree of penetration of the social forms which oppress them.

Now it might be argued that attempts at addressing both macro and micro concerns are not new. As Archer (1982, p. 455) says, 'The fundamental problem of linking human agency and social structure stalks through the history of sociological theory'. However, in recent years while most theorists 'have tilted *either* towards structure or towards action, a slippage which has gathered in momentum over time' (ibid.), those addressing macro and micro perspectives simultaneously go no further than stating the importance of both. What is new about the recent integrative approach of commentators such as Giddens (1979), Collins (1981a), Knorr-Cetina and Cicourel (1981) and Archer (1982), is that they explicitly seek to unite macro and micro perspectives in a single theoretical framework which above all else recognises that action and structure presuppose one another and as such cannot be addressed separately. However, it is also apparent that such integration does not imply a consensus or unity of approach. As in the case of the multi-paradigm approaches (see above pp. 27-30) we have different kinds of integrated theorising competing for precision of conception, depth of insight, and for the promise of liberating us from past inadequacies and omissions. But these differing approaches also display their own preferences and harbour the semi-autonomous histories of their own creation. Thus one of the first reviews of approaches to integrated theorising by Knorr-Cetina (1981, p. 29) points out that in spite of their common concern to integrate systematically notions of macro and micro, authors 'hold different views of micro-level phenomena and their relation to macro-level questions'. On this basis she identifies three kinds of integrated theorising. The first is the position of Collins (1981a; 1981b) who sees macro phenomena as made up of aggregations and repetitions of many micro episodes. He argues that the repetitive actions that make up social structure are explained by the micro mechanism of 'interaction ritual chains'. Thus he (Collins, 1981a) argues that, 'Such chains of micro-encounters generate the central features of social organisation — authority, property, and group membership — by creating and recreating "mythical" cultural symbols and emotional energies'. Indeed, he suggests that all macro phenomena should be translated into combinations of micro events: 'Microtranslation thus gives us a picture of the complex levels of abstraction involved in causal explanations' (ibid.).

A second position identified by Knorr-Cetina is that of those authors who conceive of macro phenomena in terms of properties which emerge as intended and unintended consequences of micro events such as Giddens (1979; 1981) Harré (1981) and some authors leaning towards a macroscopic view of social order in their integrated theorising such as the neo-systems approach of Lidz (1981), Luhmann (1981) and Archer (1982). But even within this category there are substantial differences of position. For example, while Archer (1982, p. 456) points out that both Giddens' structuration approach, which as we saw above depends on the notion of duality of structure, and her own morphogenetic neo-systems approach, recognise that action is 'shaped by the unacknowledged conditions of action and generates unintended consequences which form the context of subsequent interaction', she vigorously maintains that the two approaches differ. In particular they differ in their respective accounts of how 'they theorise about the structuring (and restructuring) of social systems'. Archer argues that Giddens' theory remains incomplete in its explanation of the mechanisms of stable replication versus the genesis of new social forms precisely because in its attempt to integrate via the notion of duality of social structure it abandons the notion of 'analytical dualism' which underpins general systems theory. In contrast Archer seeks to establish the greater theoretical utility of the morphogenetic perspective since she sees this as preoccupied with specifying the mechanisms of feedback that contain both negative stabilising and rigidifying elements as well as positive structure-elaborating or disorganising features.

A third perspective on integrated theorising is identified in the work of Cicourel (1981) and taken by Knorr-Cetina (1981) which she describes as the representation hypothesis. Under this, says Knorr-Cetina (1981, p. 34):

The macro emerges . . . not as the sum of unintended consequences of micro-episodes nor as their aggregate or network of interrelations, but rather as a summary representation actively constructed and pursued within micro-situations. In other words, the macro appears no longer as a *particular layer* of social reality *on top* of micro-episodes composed of their interrelation (macro-sociologies), their aggregation (aggregation hypothesis) or their unforeseen effects (hypothesis of unintended consequences). Rather it is seen to reside *within* these micro-episodes where it results from the *structuring practices* of agents. The outcome of these practices are representations which thrive upon an alleged correspondence to that which they represent, but which at the same time can be seen as highly situated constructions which involve several levels of interpretation and selection.

Clearly none of these perspectives on integrated theorising is exhaustive. Nor does Knorr-Cetina's selection and classification represent a comprehensive account of the possible range of approaches. Like theorists before them, those adopting an integrated approach to theorising are shaped by their own academic heritage, by their individual histories and personal biographies of micro interaction, by the unintended consequences of their own academic involvement and by the macro representations routinely accomplished in the micro-social action of their own everyday academic and practical lives. What has occurred, however, with integrated theorising is no less than a Kuhnian style paradigm revolution whereby theorising whose analysis proceeds in any one dimension alone will be ignored rather than debated, discredited rather than discussed. For a time the central debates in sociological theory will be between different varieties of integrated theorising, between those addressing in their different ways the interrelationship and mutual dependency of structure and action.

Hunt (1981) has recently taken an integrated stance to theorising in law. While praising the contemporary thinking of those like Unger and Kamenka and Tay, for returning to theory after years in the wilderness of micro-analytical empiricism, he observes that much of the existing theorising, whether consensus liberal or radical Marxist, is dichotomous. Like Giddens he (Hunt, 1981, p. 47) argues that,

> there exists a fundamental unity between the concerns of contemporary Marxist and non-Marxist theories of law, which manifests itself in the extent to which both traditions are impaled upon a dichotomy which inhibits further advance. This is the dichotomy between coercion and consent.

Hunt argues that this parallelism between different approaches in which 'alternative or divergent theories grapple with a common set of problems' (ibid.) and in which 'each theorisation is reduced unavoidably to emphasising "either" the element of consent "or" the element of coercion' (ibid., p. 52), undermines any integrated approach that might combine both macro and micro components. Hunt, like Giddens, suggests that a position is required that goes beyond the choice between opposites into a 'meaningful and fruitful dialogue' between the previously exclusive positions.

In our discussions in chapter 1 we saw how macro theorising stressed the structural determinants of law but failed to explain the process whereby law was created as a positive, object-like reality. It failed because law forms were mechanistically related to social structures without any acknowledgement of the human agency whereby those forms and structures were conceptually hewn from the continuum of social control. Seductive though the Gemeinschaft, Gesellschaft and bureaucratic regulative typology of Kamenka and Tay and Unger is, because of the way it feigns at a comprehensive explanation, it loses sight of the essence of legal reality by assuming the existence of law forms as being deterministically related to structure, rather than seeking to explain their constitution and reconstitution as the outcome of human action. Lost too is all sensitivity to the way such theorising itself contributes to the ongoing process whereby these phenomena are constituted as the legal reality. By suppressing, and defining away as 'primitive' or 'utopian' those aspects of law relating to human agency, such as the informal, spontaneous and intuitive, or by subordinating these to a lesser status, structural theorising itself became part of the ideological process reaffirming positive law as *the* law.

In this chapter we have witnessed almost the mirror image of this approach, as micro-analytical theorising has tried to bring human agency back into law through its emphasis on informalism. However, in seeing this as an alternative, purer form of law to be achieved, the crucial feature of the informal as an integral part of the totality of law, is denied. An advance over these theorists were the micro approaches of legal pluralism and dispute processing, for they placed emphasis on the informal as coexisting with the formal in the context of the totality and made some attempt to relate the two. But as these approaches ignored social structure they were unable to explain why it is that some informal law becomes formalised as *the* law while other such law does not. Only in the approaches of the most recent contributors such as Comaroff and Roberts, Moore and Fitzpatrick, and to a lesser extent Gurvitch, is there any attempt to reach the integrated dialectical analysis between structure and action of the kind that Giddens outlines. An adequate theory of law, then, must be sufficiently sensitive to capture both the totality of social structure and the particular of human action, the macro and the micro, without absorbing the one into the other. Neither is a product of the other, but each implies the other. Both have autonomy but neither is completely free from the influence of the other. From the integrated theoretical perspective then, law can only be adequately analysed through the processes whereby it is constituted. To do this we need to look into the ways people in their doings with each other construct and reconstruct the manifest appearances of law. This does not require us to start out from pre-existing conceptions of law, nor to examine law in those places where the dominant conception suggests it is typically done, such as legislature, courts and enforcement agencies. Rather, it requires an examination of typical settings of social interaction to see how some of that interaction is conferred with the appearance of legal reality; how that interaction is conceptually differentiated into the relevant and the non-relevant, the formal and the informal, offence and response, external and internal; how initial conceptions are underpinned by routine props and practices which reflect specific structural forms themselves subsequently drawn on as a resource, and thereby recreated in future interaction in a way which shapes and channels, guides and moulds, but never completely smothers fresh action; in short how the reality formed in such conception is both autonomously generated and simultaneously bound by the totality of wider social structure.

In order to carry out such an analysis of law, I have concentrated on the interactive setting of the workplace, though clearly any other could have been chosen, and I have focused on the processes whereby people construct the reality of 'private justice'. This amounts to the ways people discipline and control those of their work colleagues whose actions are deemed to be worthy of sanctions. Rather than take such 'factory law' and its institutions of private justice as a subordinate form of law to state law, or as illustrative of informal social control, I seek to show how it is both independent from and inter-related to state law and the wider system of social control. I show how private justice is a part of state law and how state law is a part of it. First, however, I examine the traditional approach to such 'factory law'.

3 Images of legal reality:
the ideology of constructing forms of factory law and their institutions of private justice

Introduction

> The factory is an establishment with its own code, with all the characteristics of a legal code. It contains norms of every description, not excluding criminal law, and it establishes special organs and jurisdiction. Labour regulations and the conventions valid within economic enterprises deserve just as well to be treated as legal institutions as the manorial law of the feudal epoch. This too was based upon private rule, upon the will of a Lord . . . The same applies to factory law, the general regulations of labour in economic enterprises. No exposition of our legal order can be complete without it. It regulates the relations of a large part of the population. (Renner, 1904, pp. 114-15)

Renner's suggestion that factory law is simultaneously an autonomous system of social control and a part of the totality of law might have founded the kind of integrative approach that would enable us to draw out the characteristic mutuality between non-state institutions of social control and formal state law. It did not. As was the case with theorising about law generally, theorising about factory law has taken either a macro-analytical perspective which, in both its liberal consensus and radical Marxist versions, subsumes the autonomy and independence of such law to reified structural processes; or conversely a micro-analytical perspective which reduces all structural constraints to resources in a game of

Images of legal reality 71

strategic interaction. Importantly, in the course of the debates between these perspectives, images of the forms taken by private justice have been constructed and these have ideological implications for the way such law is constituted as a reality. In this chapter I shall show how such dichotomous theorising results in the conception of a range of forms of private justice, each of which is seen as the product of a certain kind of organisational structure and each as operating at a different level of formality. I shall argue that such theorising not only misunderstands the nature of factory law, but is actually part of the process whereby it is constituted as a reality, separate from the actions of those who create it. As shall be seen in subsequent chapters, far from existing as separate and discrete forms, characteristic of a variety of organisational structures, or indicative of a range of levels of formality, the different 'forms' of factory law and private justice are each present in any particular social structure. The only difference between these forms is the way in which participants take some of their aspects rather than others to be the explicit legal reality of their factory law, and then act towards them in such a way as to confirm their concreteness. Moreover, the same is true of the relationship between the adopted form and the wider structure of social control; rather than private justice being separate from state law, it is a part of it as is state law a part of private justice.

Macro approaches to factory law: structural change and legal form

Macro approaches to the analysis of private justice at work take either a consensus or radical perspective. In either case the form of private justice adopted is seen as a function of wider structural change, in particular, the development of capitalist industrial production.

The consensus perspective sees factory law in terms of discipline and argues that this is necessary in order to bring about harmonious activity at the workplace. Its advocates argue that discipline first became necessary as a result of the change from domestic cottage industry to the form of manufacture based on large factory units. Until that point, they argue, workers had been free to work as and when they pleased but (Ashdown and Baker, 1973, p. 49),

> industrialisation has imposed a strict discipline on the daily lives of workers . . . Regular attendance; clocking in and clocking out; attending to the safety regulations; maintaining standards laid down for the job; obeying work orders; and generally conforming to the rules of the workplace — all impose restrictions on a worker's freedom.

The consensus theorists maintain that tradition made workers slow to accept change and slow to adjust to the speed of the new factory work. The new industrial proletariat was said to be much given to staying away from work, especially on Mondays and feast days, 'to poor timekeeping, to taking breaks during the day and, above all, to wandering from job to job' (Hudson, 1970, p. 10). As a result, say Ashdown and Baker (1973, p. 5), 'many industrialists reacted by introducing harsh and rigid forms of discipline, believing these to be the only way to establish control over workers'. Since, as Jones (1961, p. 9) points out, 'the right to use property as the owner saw fit was not only an economic right which found expression in the freedom of contract but it was also a divine right', non-owners were relatively powerless and were held to owe their owners zealous obedience. Any deviance from the rules brought harsh and irregular sanctions directed at the individual rule-breaker, the purpose of which was to exact retribution and to deter the offender and his fellow workers from committing future offences. The form of discipline adopted has been described as 'punishment centred', 'authoritarian' or 'coercive'. As Ashdown and Baker (1973, p. 5) say, the basic tenet of the authoritarian approach is that it is 'management's authority to make decisions, especially concerning such matters as discipline and that there should be no restrictions on this right, least of all from employees'.

Under the authoritarian form of discipline, as portrayed by the consensus theorists, rules were spontaneously established on an ad hoc basis and although they became formalised through precedent, they remained unwritten. They reflected the owners' standards and interests and their purpose was to facilitate the creation and maintenance of wealth and to preserve the existing structure of power and control. Any deviation from the rules was likely to be seen as deliberate and often as a personal challenge to authority, an act of wilfulness attributed to deliberate intent. The cause of deviance was less significant than the allocation of blame and the retributive punishment of the rule-breaker. Of little importance too, was the fairness or formality of administering disciplinary procedures which were often arbitrary and informal, with each case being treated on its merits in an ad hoc way. Any appeal relied upon the mercy of those imposing sanctions and was subject to varying degrees of tolerance, benevolence, inconsistency and whim, and this served to accentuate the fear, and enhance the overall deterrent effect (see Figure 2).

According to Ashdown and Baker (ibid.) there were a number of structural changes that caused this 'older' punitive model to be replaced. It was said to alienate workers, having an adverse effect on morale and efficiency. It was open to abuse as increased factory size resulted in the delegation of authority to unscrupulous foremen who were prone to arbitrariness and inconsistency. Skilled labour, particularly since World War 2, became scarce and expensive. Capital invested in training employees increased the value of human resources, making indiscriminate use of disciplinary action wasteful. Finally, organised labour grew and pressed for changes and reforms. The result, say the consensus theorists, was the abandonment of the authoritarian approach in favour of a more corrective/democratic disciplinary form.

The essence of the corrective approach 'is that punishment is no longer regarded as an end in itself, but as a means toward achieving a more constructive end; that of using the co-operation of employees and promoting self-discipline' (Ashdown and Baker, 1973, p. 6). Whereas consensus theorists describe the older punitive model of discipline in a way that divides the employer and employee, they present an image of the newer corrective disciplinary model as one in which the interests of these groups coincide. Factory rules are presented,

1 STRUCTURAL CONTEXT

1.1	Typicality	Common in small organisations, where unions weak and where legitimation based solely on ownership of property.
1.2	Image of Reality	World individually determined through contract relations, private ownership and accumulation of property.

2 RULES

2.1	Type	Unwritten.
2.2	Authorship	Property owner makes spontaneous, ad hoc precedent.
2.3	Membership Status of Rule Creators	Unequal and restricted to owners only.
2.4	Mode of Legitimation	Authoritarian, imposed, with no participation or challenge. Legitimation accrues to those owning property.
2.5	Interests Protected	Rules reflect interests and standards of behaviour of the dominant elite of owners.
2.6	Purpose	To facilitate creation and maintenance of private wealth and to preserve individual power and control.
2.7	Jurisdiction	All members except owners.

3 CRIME AND DEVIANCE

3.1	Nature	Individual and collective rule-breaking seen as a challenge to property owners' authority.
3.2	Types	Property, authority and competence offences: theft, damage, disobedience, negligence, manners and dress.
3.3	Attributed Cause	Individual. Product of wilfulness, ambition, greed, moral or physical weakness, lack of self-control.

Images of legal reality   75

4 PROCEDURES AND JUSTICE
  4.1 Type — Unwritten.
  4.2 Creation and Origin — Ad hoc, spontaneous.
  4.3 Membership Status of Participants. — Unequal: owner-manager v accused member.
  4.4 Jurisdiction — All members except owners.
  4.5 Mode of Administration — Authoritarian decision; hierarchical command.
  4.6 Machinery — Management investigation; owner-director: hearing and sanctioning. No participation, representation or appeal.
  4.7 Nature of Procedure — Arbitrary, subjective application of rules from owner's perspective.
  4.8 Notion of Justice — Treats like situations differently depending on the individual circumstances, where owner decides needs.
  4.9 Form of Justice — Substantive (by results).
  4.10 Form of Appeal — Arbitrary and informal. Relies on mercy and paternalistic sentiment of the owner.

5 SANCTIONS AND EFFECT
  5.1 Philosophy of Punishment — Imposition of harsh, punitive sanctions for retribution and individual and general deterrence of deviance.
  5.2 Type of Sanctions — Fines, dismissal, prosecution and public shaming.
  5.3 Effectiveness against Rule Breaking — Conformity from fear until low probability of being caught, then high risk of spontaneous hidden-economy crime, pilfering, fiddling, and collective conflict.

Figure 2 Punitive-authoritarian discipline

not as arbitrary and ad hoc but, as worked out in advance, in a planned and orderly fashion; based on contingent outcomes designed to reflect the company interests; and to coincide with what are held to be 'general' standards of behaviour. The coincidence between the rules and the employees' interests is emphasised in a number of ways. First, the formulation of rules is done in a representative manner, after a period of consultation and of 'sounding out' the opinions of employees. Employees are shown to have the right to modify and object to rules before they are written down as factory law in the company rule book. Second, stress is put on those rules that are in the employees' interests. Special reference is made to rules about health and safety at work which protect employees from accidents, injuries, mutilation and death and to those rules that are an extension of commonly held views about hygiene, such as no smoking where food is being prepared. Less mention is made of how health and safety rules might be in the company's interests in their competition with smaller companies who might be forced out of business if they cannot afford the concomitant overheads (Carson, 1974). And no emphasis is given to the fundamental rules of the company that are definitely in its interests but are not part of what is counted as rules for consultation, such as those concerning how production is organised, how profits are invested, how income is distributed; in short, rules having to do with how the company is run.

A third way in which consensus theorists present a coincidence of interests between the discipline of the corrective model and those of employees is through the conception of rule-breaking. A distinction is made between 'group indiscipline', which is said to result from the widespread rejection of a working arrangement or rule, and whose resolution is seen to be an issue subject to the renegotiation of working standards, and 'individual indiscipline'. The latter, is described as the action of a small minority, the majority of employees being seen as 'law-abiding citizens who want to conform to the established equitable standards of conduct and will do so when they know what is expected of them' (Jones, 1961, p. 11). Not only are the majority presented as in agreement

Images of legal reality 77

with the company rules, but they are also said to be in agreement with the need to sanction rule-breakers (Ashdown and Baker, 1973, p. 1):

> Most employees ... go about their work in a self-disciplined way; they usually adhere to company rules and to what is regarded as reasonable standards of behaviour, and accept that disciplinary action needs to be taken against offenders.

So while rule-breaking is presented as exceptional rather than typical, under the corrective model and the rule-breaker is portrayed as the product of circumstances, not as wilful, intentional, and responsible — his stereotype under the punitive authoritarian approach. The circumstances might be an adverse domestic situation, illness in the family, the influence of corrupt friends, carelessness, lack of motivation, incompetence, inexperience, poor supervision or failure to understand the rules. As Jones (1961, p. 4) says, 'the corrective approach calls for an analysis of causes, connecting the penalty with the purpose of the punishment and fitting the penalty to the individual's personality'.

Of fundamental importance under the consensus account is the image of the procedures whereby justice is administered to those subject to disciplinary action. A stark contrast is drawn between the arbitrariness, prejudice, and inconsistency of the old punitive approach and the fairness, objectivity and neutrality of corrective discipline. To achieve this appearance, the corrective model is imbued with the qualities of an idealised, formal system of justice, such that the worker subject to discipline is seen to be accorded the rights of natural justice, 'notably a right to a fair hearing, a right to be represented and a right of appeal' (Anderman, 1972, pp. 57-8). Thus worker representatives are invited to participate in proceedings as advocates for the accused, and are allowed to question witnesses, and examine records in the same way that management are accustomed to doing. While management still investigate the case, set the penalty and communicate this to the employee, this limited participation is nonetheless justified in terms of establishing consistency and fairness and in terms of lessening 'the risk of inconsistent or ill-considered decisions' (NJAC, 1967, p. 31).

78 Images of legal reality

1 STRUCTURAL CONTEXT

1.1	Typicality	Common in large unionised organisations, public companies and bureaucracies. Most typical of four types.
1.2	Image of Reality	World legally and scientifically determined via contract relations. Unitary perspective.

2 RULES

2.1	Type	Written, formal.
2.2	Authorship	Specialist elite (management) draw up contingent outcomes in advance to form policy.
2.3	Membership Status of Rule Creators	Unequal, restricted to management elite.
2.4	Mode of Legitimation	Representative; limited participation in the form of consultation with member representatives.
2.5	Interests Protected	Rules reflect company interests, appear to coincide with members' interests, reflect 'general' standard.
2.6	Purpose	A guide to harmonious working for creation of organisations' wealth to preserve demand for professional elite.
2.7	Jurisdiction	All members outside owners; management subject to separate set of rules from ordinary members.

3 CRIME AND DEVIANCE

3.1	Nature	Individual and collective rule-breaking seen as separate issues.
3.2	Types	Property, authority and competence offences: theft, damage, disobedience, incompetence.
3.3	Attributed Cause	Individual: temptation, influence, circumstances. Organisational: unclear rules, poor supervision.

Images of legal reality 79

4	**PROCEDURES AND JUSTICE**	
4.1	Type	Written, formal.
4.2	Creation and Origin	In advance, planned and systematic.
4.3	Membership Status of Participants	Unequal: management v accused member and his representative.
4.4	Jurisdiction	All members except owners and management; management are subject to separate procedure. Specialist decision; hierarchical command.
4.5	Mode of Administration	Warning, investigation, hearing, sanctioning, appeal.
4.6	Machinery	Member representative, participation in warning and appeal.
4.7	Nature of Procedure	Rational; neutral application of rules according to 'objectivity' of management.
4.8	Notion of Justice	Creating like situations as like, where rules and procedures define likeness.
4.9	Form of Justice	Formal procedural.
4.10	Form of Appeal	Formal to owner/managing director.
5	**SANCTIONS AND EFFECT**	
5.1	Philosophy of Punishment	Imposition of progressive sanctions to deter and educate, to correct through voluntary self-discipline.
5.2	Type of Sanctions	Warnings, fines, suspension, demotion, transfers, dismissal; rarely prosecute.
5.3	Effectiveness against Rule Breaking	Spending of sanctions. Risk of hidden economy crimes when education is demystified.

Figure 3 Corrective-representative discipline

Participation is also useful, say the consensus theorists, in its vital role in legitimating what had been decided in the course of the proceedings and 'to make the whole area less contentious to the benefit of workplace relations in general' (Ashdown and Baker, 1973, p. 26).

Another major area of distinction drawn by consensus theorists is that between the punitive and corrective approach to penalties. The punitive approach, in its alleged use of harsh penalties, is said to ignore the educational possibilities of disciplinary policy. In contrast, the corrective approach is described as being sensitive to the need to temper its response in order that the employee is given the opportunity to reform. Thus Jones (1961, pp. 3-4, 11) distinguishes between the two approaches in terms of the different purposes of their disciplinary action:

> Although the individual is still penalised for his improper behaviour, the action taken against him is not for the purpose of punishing him, but for changing his attitudes and behaviour so that in future he will meet expected standards of behaviour . . . there is no thought of 'paying him back' or 'getting even'; the purpose of the action is training. Management does not seek compliance with the rules through fear . . . when disciplinary action is requested it is for the purpose of changing the individual's behaviour so that in the future he will do what is expected of him.

It is argued that in order to achieve this individual reform, sanctions should be employed progressively, perhaps beginning with a verbal warning and increasing through written warnings, fines, wage deductions, suspension, transfer or demotion to dismissal. Dismissal, as the 'ultimate deterrent', is to be applied only where 'a major offence has been committed' or where the employee has 'shown himself unwilling to reform' (Ashdown and Baker, 1973, p. 6). Indeed, drawing on their research Ashdown and Baker (1973, p. 21) argue that dismissal, 'as the ultimate deterrent did have a part to play in every organisation's disciplinary policy; but when used too readily in an arbitrary fashion, its value as a corrective device tended to decline'. Similarly, Jones (1961, pp. 12-13) argues that although

Images of legal reality 81

deterrence remains an important aspect of disciplinary action, under the corrective approach . . . the penalty assessed . . . should be corrective in terms of the individual, it must also serve as a notice to others that conformance to standards is important; the penalty will thus deter others from deviance from proper conduct.

Jones (ibid., p. 166) concludes that the progressive sanctioning of the corrective model has advantages over the punitive approach because it is more likely to bring consensus on disciplinary issues:

Because discipline becomes impersonal and is meted out evenly when someone violates these standards, it is accepted as fair that such an individual should be disciplined. When the individual is given a series of penalties and still fails to behave properly the group accepts as just and without resentment, more severe action. Although employees believe the disciplined individual should have his day in court, this does not alter their belief that disciplinary action is justified.

Finally, it is pointed out that unlike the punitive approach to discipline, the corrective model incorporates the explicit right, via formally laid down appeals procedure, to challenge any disciplinary action that is thought to be unjustified, or too excessive (this form is summarised in Figure 3).

In short then, as was the case with theorising about law generally, consensus macro theorists make sense of factory law and its private institutions of justice by distinguishing between different forms and by placing these in some developmental relationship, driven by structural change. Thus they identify punitive/authoritarian discipline as separate from corrective/representative discipline, and see technical changes as causing a corresponding change in discipline from the punitive form which is rendered 'older', 'cruder' and 'less sensitive', to the corrective form which is seen as 'newer' and more sophisticated. Although taking a very different political position, radical macro theorising produces a very similar analysis.

Radical macro theorising about factory law and private justice at work proceeds along similar lines as that of its consensus counterpart with respect to the way in which forms of private justice are treated in an evolutionary way and related to reified societal structural changes. Kinsey's (1979) radical theory is illustrative. (See also Henry, 1982; Lea, 1979; South and Scraton, 1981). Kinsey (1979, pp. 46-9) argues that the question,

> what form does the despotic control of capital assume at different periods in the development of the capitalist production process? — seems relatively straightforward . . . As changes in the production process occur — in technology, in the composition of labour, in the extension of the division of labour — so the control of capital over labour assumes different characteristics . . . Too often, however, it seems that, while it is widely recognized that the material conditions of the labour process undergo quite fundamental and dramatic transformation, it is assumed — quite wrongly — that the form of the despotic control of capital remains constant and invariable . . . The principal object . . . is to argue that three periods in the development of capitalist production are broadly identifiable within which qualitative changes in the control and organisation of the labour process are visible. These are: the period of manufacture which is identified with simple co-operation, and the exploitation of skilled labour; the early period of modern industry or advanced capitalist production which is to be identified with the high organic composition of capital; and the intensification of scientific 'man' management. Within each period I shall seek to establish the 'peculiar form of despotism' as it is assumed within the material conditions of the labour process.

According to Kinsey then, during the first period of manufacturing of early capitalism, skilled artisans and craftsmen co-operated in the workshop. They had power based on their protected interdependence. Throughout this period, the workshop owner had constantly to wrestle with the insubordination of workers. This 'power-sharing' formed a short-lived period under which discipline was founded on coercive law and the right of capitalists to lock workers in the factory.

Images of legal reality 83

The second period came with the transition to factory production and the replacement of skills by machines, which rendered workers homogenous, interchangeable and thereby replaceable. In this phase the form of disciplinary control shifted to the 'lock out' and the threat of dismissal and unemployment. Kinsey argues that here, factory owners no longer needed to control workers directly by law, but simply had to preserve the 'freedom' of the individual under law to sell his labour power. Workers then had to 'choose' between the authority of the capitalist inside the factory or economic need outside the factory gates. In this period a new form of co-operation is established within the factory in the form of the 'factory code' or company rules. This is not, says Kinsey, the power to physically control labour, but the power to organise and co-ordinate production. All that is now required as the disciplinary function is the coercion of the 'free' market.

The final period in the radical view of disciplinary development is the establishment of capitalist discipline as automatic and self-regulating. This is achieved, says Kinsey, in the 'contract of employment' which is the most highly developed medium in that it presupposes 'voluntary' and willed obligations between employer and employee as formal equals. In advanced capitalist production the voluntary contract becomes the generalised form of control and organisation of the labour process. The compulsion of the worker to sell his labour voluntarily is apparently removed and the worker consents. 'It is with this coincidence of organisation and control that discipline, properly so called, obtains' (Kinsey, 1979, p. 60).

In Kinsey's radical macro analysis, then, private justice at work is not autonomous, but is seen as a function of the general sophistication of ideological domination accompanying capitalist development. Indeed, even the most recent changes in industrial discipline towards more formalised rules and procedures, increased participation and the adoption of corrective rather than punitive sanctions, are seen in the radical macro analysis as indicative of an underlying trend towards increased legitimation and ideological domination. Increased formalisation, for example, is seen as part of the development of capitalism towards a semi-autonomous form of subjugation. Radical theorists point out that participation is simply co-option in order to secure the objection-free application of disciplinary policy and to legitimate the existing power relationships. South and Scraton (1981, pp. 58-9) for example, argue:

> In the transition to the capitalist organisation of the market, traditional paternalistic authority was geared to the new industrialism. By claiming a vestige of traditional legitimacy, capitalist discipline became capable of presenting itself as 'just', 'right' and even religiously ordained authority. For the legitimation of traditional authority to go unchallenged there had to be the concession of granting *participation*. Of course this was not genuine participation, for the very form of traditional authority thereby legitimated was immutably based on a stable hierarchy. Social justice *inevitably* must flow, according to this ideology, from the participation and association of all. By such arrangements the illusion is conjured of the legitimacy — by *moral* as well as material right — the subordinacy of labour to the superordinacy of capital.

Similarly it is argued that the use of corrective rather than punitive sanctions merely reflects that capital no longer needs to resort to harsh measures in order to achieve control. As Pashukanis (1929) has said, crude repressive justice is only necessary when subtler forms of control would be ignored or when more sophisticated techniques break down.

In short then, both the radical and consensus macro theorising reduce discipline at work to a dependent aspect of developing capitalism. In the course of asserting such argument, these theorists throw up forms of discipline. Any anomalies to the forms, such as participation, are themselves taken to be evidence of the emergence of new forms and indicative of the general developmentalist argument. No attempt is made to examine whether the 'emerging' phenomena, such as participation or corrective sanctions, are autonomously generated. Nor is the possibility explored that the so called new developments in disciplinary form have always been generated, but only recognised at certain times, such that the forms are more a function of theorising than of the reality of private justice. Just such criticisms are made by the opposing theoretical position of the micro approach, but as we shall see, their arguments, rather than transcending the ideological production of images of legal reality in the shape of forms of private justice, actually inadvertently produce a third form and so perpetuate the ideological process of which they are so critical.

Micro approaches to factory law: informality and plurality in private justice

As in the case of theorising about law generally, micro approaches to private disciplinary justice at work criticise the structural analysis of the macro theorists for masking the plurality of social control that operates at different levels of formality. They argue that discipline is, and always has been, a battle between competing interest groups, fought out both formally and informally through collective bargaining and they see the debate about changes in disciplinary form as just part of that struggle. They reject the view that any real changes have taken place in disciplinary form as a result of changes in social structure. Mellish and Collis-Squires (1976, p. 167), for example, argue that the rules which characterise different models of discipline and the different ways these are enforced, 'cannot be explained in terms of older values being replaced by newer ones, but have to be analysed in terms of the functions such rules serve for different sections of management or employees and the type of response evoked'. Indeed, they reject the macro theorist's argument that change has taken place between the so-called punitive model and the corrective model, pointing out that the historical evidence of those like Thompson (1968) suggests that a range of approaches always coexisted, even under the authoritarianism of the nineteenth-century capitalist entrepreneur. They argue that although the new industrial entrepreneurs of the nineteenth century gained a reputation as severe disciplinarians ready to dismiss, fine or worse at a moment's notice for anything they saw as an offence or a challenge, 'these same entrepreneurs had also tried to win the co-operation of their new industrial workers by concessions like time off on traditional feast days. And they tried to inculcate the norms of the new industrial discipline by sponsoring religious and secular education' (Mellish and Collis-Squires, 1976, p. 165).

Mellish and Collis-Squires argue that not only is there historical evidence to refute the evolutionary developmental perspective of the macro consensus and radical theorists, but contemporary work such as that of Gouldner (1954) shows that a range of approaches to discipline can co-exist in any one organisation. Drawing on Gouldner's (1954) study of *Patterns of Industrial Bureaucracy* and on their own empirical inquiry into discipline in the British docks, Mellish and Collis-Squires argue that even in the modern plant, the social reality of discipline is constituted through negotiated relationships between conflicting interest groups which go on both formally and informally and may range from punitive to a corrective and, moreover, may be instigated by either management or employees. The negotiation of company rules is a good illustration of the micro theorists' approach.

Gouldner points out that participation in rule creation may go on at a formal level and need not require a correspondence of interests for acceptance. He gives the example of a company's safety programme in which both workers and management make modifications to the programme at periodic meetings at which 'they were, moreover, encouraged to make suggestions from the floor ... The safety meetings provided workers with frequent opportunities for the expression of complaints and with a chance to make and immediately see the response to, safety suggestions' (Gouldner, 1954, p. 192). He showed that while management legitimated the safety programme by tying it to production, workers legitimated it via their values of improved conditions of employment such as personal cleanliness and increased, if limited, control over the work process.

But Gouldner also showed how this participatory rule creation is not restricted to that which is formally accepted as jointly negotiable, but extends, informally, into all areas of workplace activity. Although formal rules might exist, informal rules might be operative. He describes how an informal agreement might grow up to disregard some rules such as the 'no smoking rule' insisted on by an insurance company. This 'concession' on the part of management serves the management's interests in building up a trusting relationship among employees. Thus the existence of the formal rule becomes little more than a resource in the internal strategic battle between conflicting interest groups. Dalton (1959) has similarly shown how employers use concessions such as allowing perks or fiddles, which are strictly against theft rules, in order to get co-operation in achieving production targets and so as to reward some employees for extra offort considered to be 'beyond the call of duty'. Mellish and Collis-Squires (1976, p. 169) argue that 'such individual concessions quickly become precedents and may then be established as informal custom and practice rules ... relationships of informal co-operation and interdependence between foreman and employees'. Thus it is argued that informal agreements between management and unions not to invoke some rules, and setting up informal rules which turn a blind eye to pilfering or fiddling in exchange for extra co-operation, are no less jointly agreed rules reflecting the interests of both groups, as are the formal rules of say a joint health and safety committee.

Nor, from the pluralistic micro-analytical perspective, is deviance from the rules as simple as breaking the formal rules in the company rule book. An awareness of the 'informal' means that following formal rules can itself be seen as deviance from an informal rule. For example, the tightening up on pilferage and the redefining of perks as theft, and the subsequent disciplinary action by management, may be treated by employees as deviance from the informally accepted practice. As such it might be met by employees taking their own punitive action against the management in the form of a walkout or some other form of collective action. As Mellish and Collis-Squires (1976, p. 172) argue,

> What is a disciplinary issue depends in part on what management care to treat as such ... on the interests they

have in controlling any particular aspect of employee behaviour and on their use, habitual or otherwise of disciplinary rules to control behaviour. But it will also depend on whether employees collectively allow an issue to be treated as an individual one. This in turn will depend in part on their bargaining interests, strength and history.

For these theorists then, the distinction made by the macro approaches between individual and collective deviance is one of conception rather than of form. Not only does it contain the mistaken assumption that management are free actively to institute changes in the face of passive union co-operation, but it also diverts attention from the real issue about the nature of the factory rules that discipline is designed to enforce, and as such is no more than an ideological device serving to 'individualise a collective issue' (Mellish and Collis-Squires, 1976, p. 167). This they argue only results in delaying the inevitable joint collective bargaining necessary to resolve the dispute, and repair the breached relations.

In contrast to macro theorising then, the micro analysis of factory law, displays with insightful realism, what discipline is about on the shop-floor level of workers' and managers' attitudes and meanings. Rather than seeing discipline as a determined product of reified social structure, the micro analysis shows that it is an autonomous and dynamic resource in the calculus between competing interest groups, where, as Mellish and Collis-Squires (1976, p. 168) argue:

> Procedures may be operated or ignored for motives other than the settlement of issues technically falling within their scope . . . [and] 'sticking to the rules' or 'applying the procedure' can be a tactic used by either management or employees during disputes.

There are, however, certain weaknesses in the micro-theoretical approach. Primarily, it fails to relate the meanings, interests and motives of individual workers and managers to the total structure of social control in which they operate. It ignores the constraints within which the autonomy of factory law is limited. It is not enough, for example, to explain away the recent apparent changes in disciplinary technology as part of an ongoing struggle between conflicting interest groups. The intervention of the state and the courts behind the particular form of discipline needs to be explained. Nor is it enough to assume that participation by employees in the disciplinary process will occur, whether formally granted or informally claimed, and as such mitigate the sanctions on individuals who without such representation would have suffered harsher treatment. Where informal sanctions have to be relied on the balance of power is inequitable. The tragedy is that the micro-analytical approach is so captured by its own insightful realism that it fails to perceive changes in the total power relationship. The irony is that these changes take place in the shadow of pluralistic protection which itself becomes part of the ideological mystification process strengthening the total structure of control.

Arguably, then, the most fundamental flaw in the microanalytical approach is that in pointing to the ideological implications of macro theorising, such as the false distinctions between 'older' punitive and 'newer' corrective forms, and between individual and collective rule-breaking, the micro approach loses sight of its own ideological contribution. In displaying the range of informal and formal ways in which employees participate in discipline, the micro theorists are responsible for creating yet another image of private justice as though it were the real form. As was the case with the micro analysis of formal law, the identification and elaboration of the informal has been seen by some as indicating the nature of a purer form, and there have been calls for the decentralisation of formal corrective discipline to a more participatory, accommodative form (see Henry, 1978; Henry and Mars, 1978). Under such proposals, the informal disciplinary practices and collective bargaining are instituted in a 'joint disciplinary procedure', in which management and trade unions take responsibility jointly for disciplinary action (see Figure 4). My own initial observations on private justice were guilty of precisely this ideological naivity. I proposed a system of private justice based on the 'spontaneously' evolved normative controls whereby groups of employees sanction those of their peers who are seen to deviate from the informally agreed norms. I called for,

1 STRUCTURAL CONTEXT

1.1	Typicality	Common in large-scale private paternalistic companies with unions and democratic tradition.
1.2	Image of Reality	World determined by negotiation and bargaining. Contracts reflect agreement. Pluralist view.

2 RULES

2.1	Type	Formal written and informal unwritten custom and practice.
2.2	Authorship	Joint specialist elite (management and unions) establish post hoc precedent by bargaining.
2.3	Membership Status of Rule Creators	Equal, restricted to interest group reps.
2.4	Mode of Legitimation	Democratic; implementation after participation by member reps., in joint negotiation.
2.5	Interests Protected	Rules reflect the plurality of dominant group interests and behaviour standards.
2.6	Purpose	To ensure justice when conflicting interest groups compete and to preserve bargaining position.
2.7	Jurisdiction	All members except owners and management who are subject to separate set of rules.

3 CRIME AND DEVIANCE

3.1	Nature	Individual rule-breaking seen as both an individual and a collective issue.
3.2	Types	Only more serious property and authority offences: theft, damage. Also rule imposition.
3.3	Attributed Cause	Individual: temptation, influence, circumstance. Structural: unequal rewards, ambitious interests.

Images of legal reality 91

4 PROCEDURES AND JUSTICE
- 4.1 Type — Written, formal.
- 4.2 Creation and Origin — In advance, planned and systematic.
- 4.3 Membership Status of Participants — Unequal: management and member reps., v accused and his 'friend'.
- 4.4 Jurisdiction — All members except management and owners; management and union subject to separate procedure.
- 4.5 Mode of Administration — Joint-specialist decision; hierarchical command.
- 4.6 Machinery — Warning, investigation, hearing, sanctioning, appeal. Member rep., participation at all stages.
- 4.7 Nature of Procedure — Substantive; negotiated application of rules according to conflicting views of situation.
- 4.8 Notion of Justice — Treating like situations as like, where likeness is socially defined by interest groups.
- 4.9 Form of Justice — Formal procedural, natural, social, substantive.
- 4.10 Form of Appeal — Formal to same or another joint-elite body.

5 SANCTIONS AND EFFECT
- 5.1 Philosophy of Punishment — Progressive sanctions to educate and rehabilitate. Also restitutive to repair breached sociation.
- 5.2 Type of Sanctions — Warnings, fines, suspensions, demotions, transfer, shaming, dismissals. Accommodates minor offences.
- 5.3 Effectiveness against Rule Breaking — High level minor rule-breaking; low level major. Increase where bargaining seen to fail.

Figure 4 Accommodative-participative discipline

'some form of court, situated in the workplace and composed of elected workers and management' (Henry, 1978, p. 160) and argued that it was crucial to involve employees in disciplinary decision making. As South and Scraton (1981, pp. 56-9) argue, not only does this 'uncritical idealism' forget and deny the significance of real divisions within the factory and society, but it also creates a distorted image of the nature of existing disciplinary justice as being of one particular form and thereby contributes to its construction as a reality.

Towards an integrative analysis of private justice

In short, then, neither the totalising macro theory nor the partial micro theory provides an adequate level of analysis. The macro theory denies the autonomy of private justice, explaining this in terms of its function to the totality. Conversely, the micro theory confers upon private justice a degree of autonomy that implies its complete independence from the total structure of power and control. But it is not the case that private justice functions solely to support the capitalist relations of production, neither does it generate assent to the totality of social control and thereby the social order. Yet nor is private justice independent of that totality of control. Rather, the relations of private justice exist actively and creatively as some of the relations comprising the totality. Private justice defies reduction or subordination to social structures. Instead, there is an interaction and mutuality between the two; between structure and the action that constitutes it. As a result, not only does the totality rely on the autonomy of private justice but it also intervenes to strengthen, refine and redefine it. At the same time, however, private justice acts on the totality in particular on the state law and penetrates into its construction and formulation. In the remaining chapters of this book I shall seek to elaborate this integrative approach through its application to a study of private justice at work. I shall hope to demonstrate the interpenetration and mutual dependence of private justice and the totality of social control by drawing on the actual conceptual distinctions used by participants to private justice.

Images of legal reality 93

At the same time I shall endeavour to show how such conceptualisation is part of the ongoing process whereby private justice and state law are reproduced as appearances of reality.

In adopting this integrative approach, I have foregone the temptation to distinguish between separate forms of private justice as though these were somehow separate from each other and the totality. I have similarly resisted the lure of relating such forms to organisational structures and of arranging forms and structures developmentally. Indeed, such an exercise would not have proved difficult. As we shall see below, the research on which this book is based was originally planned with a view to comparing and contrasting forms of private discipline that seemed to be characteristic of different social structures. A range of different companies and organisations were examined from the view point of their discipline and from an initial analysis it might have appeared that different forms were a product of these different structures. Thus the punitive authoritarian form of discipline was sought for and 'found' in private capitalist, free enterprise companies, where unionisation was weak or non-existent; the corrective representative form appeared to be typical of large-scale capitalist corporations and public companies, that evinced a high degree of unionisation; the accommodative participative form, though seeming to be less common, occurred where a paternalistic management structure prevailed, where unions were strong or where there had been a deliberate shift towards some form of decentralised industrial democracy.

Moreover, it was even possible to identify a fourth, as yet undocumented form of disciplinary private justice that seemed characteristic of socialistic and co-operatively organised collective enterprises. This fourth form appeared to locate the authority for its action in a notion of individual autonomy, rather than in that of hierarchy, as is implied in the other three forms, and seemed to be limited by and closely controlled from below. The rules and standards of this form reflected the sum of interests of the collectivity, but no individuals or specialists represented or made decisions on behalf of any others, since every individual seemed free to deliberate and make decisions himself and these were then

1 STRUCTURAL CONTEXT

1.1	Typicality	Common to small-scale non-unionised equal membership organisations, especially co-operatives.
1.2	Image of Reality	World seen as collectively determined through shared social relationships and communal ownership.

2 RULES

2.1	Type	Unwritten, spontaneous.
2.2	Authorship	Non-specialist members reach a collective consensus post hoc. Does not set precedent as rules can change.
2.3	Membership Status of Rule Creators	Formally equal and unrestricted, though in meetings views of founder and experienced members carry more weight as do those of the more articulate.
2.4	Mode of Legitimation	Collective participation in all aspects; product of actual consensus, but affected by who attends meeting.
2.5	Interests Protected	Rules reflect the interests and standards of the membership at any one time; sometimes skewed to factions.
2.6	Purpose	To ensure social justice in contributing to the creation of community wealth and collective autonomy.
2.7	Jurisdiction	All members; sometimes a problem with non-member employees.

3 CRIME AND DEVIANCE

3.1	Nature	Political and collective issue.
3.2	Types	Individualistic, political self-interest; establishing monopolies of control and information; unequal contribution and participation; unco-operativeness.
3.3	Attributed Cause	Natural diversity; external structural pressures; political ambition or immaturity; personal resentment.

Images of legal reality   95

4 PROCEDURES AND JUSTICE

4.1	Type	Unwritten.
4.2	Creation and Origin	Ad hoc, spontaneous, determined by circumstances, experience and members present.
4.3	Membership Status of Participants	Equal: all members v accused member, other members.
4.4	Jurisdiction	All members.
4.5	Mode of Administration	Collective decision and consensus.
4.6	Machinery	The single meeting, with all members participating who are present.
4.7	Nature of Procedure	Subjective application of rules from a collective perspective according to context and circumstances.
4.8	Notion of Justice	Treating each situation differently depending on its own special requirements.
4.9	Form of Justice	Natural; community; substantive.
4.10	Form of Appeal	Informal to the whole collective at another meeting whose composition may be different from first by chance.

5 SANCTIONS AND EFFECT

5.1	Philosophy of Punishment	To off-set outside influences and individualistic tendencies, to celebrate opportunity for development.
5.2	Type of Sanctions	Warnings, shaming, ostracism, withdrawal of co-operation, rejection from group; change of policy; division of group.
5.3	Effectiveness against Rule Breaking	High conformity; few problem cases which eventually lead to separation of group. Deviance then becomes norm of one of the new groups and is absent from other.

Figure 5 Celebrative-collective discipline

shared with the similarly arrived at decisions of others. Deviance from these shared and collectively agreed rules seemed to be met either by shaming, ostracism or rejection or else was celebrated for providing the grounds for further clarification and modification of the rules (see Figure 5).

However, closer examination of the evidence showed that these forms and structures were no more than surface appearances of reality. They were the conceptual products of the participants to different organisations. What became very clear from the research was that different kinds of organisational structure accommodate aspects of the whole range of theoretically identifiable forms of private justice. Thus, for example, companies with a hierarchical decision-making structure and which were firmly committed to the private ownership of property, not only exhibited aspects of the punitive and corrective forms of discipline, but also relied on collective peer group discipline — sanctions taken by workers on their fellows. Conversely, worker co-operatives, although explicitly adopting collective decision-making policies and conferring equal status on their members, also exhibited an executive form of elite decision making in discipline which might be thought to be exclusive to the harsh authoritarianism of the punitive disciplinary form. Perhaps most surprisingly these co-operatives also relied on state law, in spite of their professed independence and 'alternative' approach.

Now had the evidence been examined from conventional macro- or micro-theoretical perspectives, it would not have been difficult to explain away such evidence as 'anomalies'. Thus the forms of private justice might have been described as 'models', not found in their pure state. They may have been depicted as 'ideal types' simply aiding the understanding of the complexity of social reality. Alternatively, it might have been possible to explain away the 'anomalies' as by-products of change. In so far as structures might have appeared to have been changing in an evolutionary way, then discrepancies would become merely evidence of residual forms or vanguards of emerging forms. Had the micro approach been taken, the 'anomalies' would represent no more than the reality as opposed to the theory. But then this would leave unexplained why structures and law forms *appeared* to be different and why it was that some of these appearances were more profuse than others. As should now be clear, it is my view that all these approaches to private justice are inadequate. They either absorb the reality and autonomy of private justice or else they ignore the totality of social control. If, as the evidence suggests, there exist aspects of the range of theoretical 'forms' in any one organisation, an adequate analysis must explain how these forms are constituted as apparent realities, how they interact with one another and how they are part of and mutually dependent on the totality.

The research on which the analysis of private justice that follows is based, was a study of the internal private disciplinary rules and procedures used by a range of different organisations (see Appendix). From the analysis of this material, it will be seen that rather than forms of private justice, we are dealing here with semi-autonomous parts of the totality of social control. In the chapters that follow we shall see how members of different organisations, with ostensibly different disciplinary policies, and what might be thought to be different forms of private justice, actually rely on a similar range of semi-autonomous parts that comprise their discipline. These parts are neither determined by nor determining of that discipline. Rather, they are interdependent with it, such that discipline at work relies on and is comprised of its own autonomy together with the semi-autonomy of other semi-autonomous parts. Although, as we shall see, there are numerous semi-autonomous parts, the principal ones referred to by those taking part in the study will be considered in three groups: the state, economy and society; industry, organisation and management; and the union, co-workers and individual workers. Each group of semi-autonomous parts will be discussed in relationship to its mutuality and interdependence with different organisations' discipline. This interdependence will be demonstrated in the context of different stages of disciplinary process, from rules and procedure creation, concepts of crime and deviance, hearings and meetings, sanctioning and appeals. It will be displayed through the accounts of a range of different levels of participants, from managers and union officials, to employees and co-op workers.

4 Beneath the public face of private discipline:

the authoritative law of managerial justice

Introduction

In the previous chapter it was shown that one of the ideological implications of the debate within and between macro and micro theorising was the construction of the appearance of a number of forms of private justice. Nowhere did these forms exist in any pure or real sense. They were images thrown up by the selection of some aspects of discipline rather than others; the outcome of contrasts and distinctions conceptually created and reaffirmed in the debates between perspectives. In this and subsequent chapters I intend to deconstruct these images, taking each in turn and showing that what is taken to be the reality of private justice, that is the manifestation of its different forms, is merely one surface appearance of a wider range of social control. Moreover, I shall show that this range is not separate from the more formalised parts that become a disciplinary policy, nor is private justice separate from state law. This is not to say, as in Gurvitch or the other legal pluralists, that there exist different depths of formality or informality within each different kind of law. Nor is it to claim that the informal is somehow 'more real' than the formal, as micro theorists are wont to do. Rather, in applying the integrated analysis laid down in the previous chapter to the phenomenon of private justice, I aim to show how the explicit disciplinary policy of an organisation, irrespective of its apparent form, and regardless of the peculiarity of the organisation's structure, exists only as a semi-autonomous part of the whole. It is mutually dependent on other semi-autonomous parts of the totality of social control, but at the same time creatively contributes to that overall structure, not as an addition running alongside the apparently dominant control institutions, but as an integral part of the totality of control. Thus I shall explore how other semi-autonomous parts of the totality of social control are relied on in order to exercise private justice and in turn how private justice is relied on by these other parts in order to accomplish their control.

The parts may be distinguished according to the source of their autonomy. Thus some of these parts are structural wholes such as 'the state' and 'the economy' whose source of autonomy rests *outside* the organisation whose disciplinary policy they penetrate. This does not, however, mean, as macro theorists have assumed, that these holistic or structural parts are completely determining nor even fully penetrating of the discipline that they influence. Rather, because disciplinary policy and practice have their own historically specific autonomy, they exist in part outside these structures and indeed penetrate them. It is in this way, as we shall see, that some of the relations of state law are those of factory law while some of the relations of factory law are those of state law.

Other semi-autonomous parts such as 'industry', 'the corporate company' and 'the factory' have their source of autonomy *at* the organisational level and as such are much more obviously penetrated by and penetrate disciplinary policy and practice. Yet other semi-autonomous parts, such as 'management', 'trade unions' and 'the community of workers' have the source of their autonomy located *within* the organisation whose discipline they penetrate, but they are, likewise, mutually dependent upon the wider groups of managements, unions and workers, whose autonomy and history is extraneous to the particular organisation and exists more as a structural whole. Finally, there are those seemingly powerless semi-autonomous parts that are the very individuals whose action creates and recreates that which comprises the other semi-autonomous parts. But as Giddens has said, that some are more powerful than others should not be taken to deny autonomy for 'all social actors, no matter how lowly, have some degree of penetration of the social forms which oppress them' (Giddens, 1979, p. 72).

In this chapter I shall concentrate on what has been claimed to be the typical form of private justice at work: corrective representative discipline which might loosely be called managerial justice. I shall begin by showing how this 'form' has been established as typical, before going on to illustrate how it has been penetrated by, and penetrates, the range of other semi-autonomous parts which form the totality of social control. I shall examine in depth the mutual interdependence between these semi-autonomous parts and through this show not only how each relies upon and indeed constitutes a part of the other, but also how that which constitutes the formal disciplinary policy is merely one of the semi-autonomous parts.

The interpenetration of externally autonomous parts and managerial justice

An examination of the evidence on discipline in the typical hierarchically structured company of western capitalism suggests that the shift from a punitive-authoritarian 'form' to a corrective-representative 'form' indeed occurred (see chapter 3). This is not to say that these 'forms' actually exist. Nor even that discipline has actually changed. Rather, that in so far as discipline is a publicly discussed phenomenon, the typical company now adopts a *policy* that is more formalised, more representatively participative, and more corrective than the *policy* of say ten or twenty years ago. This can be seen by looking at survey data collected between 1965 and 1969 (NJAC, 1967; Dawson, 1969) and comparing it with similar data collected between 1978-1979 (Dickens *et al.*, 1979; IPM, 1979, Henry, 1981a). This shows that the proportion of companies having formalised procedures has increased from around 10 per cent in the earlier period, prior to government legislation and judicial intervention, to approximately 75 per cent in the second period, though large companies are more likely to have formalised procedures than small ones. Dawson, for example, found that only 2 per cent of firms with under 50 employees had formal procedures compared with 19 per cent of those with over 500 employees (Dawson, 1969, p. 63). By 1979, Dickens et al. were able to report that 51 per cent of those with under 10 employees had formal procedures, compared with 99 per cent of companies with over 500 employees (Dickens et al., 1979, p. 247).

A similar pattern was found for participation in the creation of procedures. Whereas in 1969 only 20 per cent of procedures were the outcome of consultation and negotiation with trade unions, by 1979 this figure was approximately 65 per cent. Further while in 1969, less than half of companies involved trade unions in disciplinary procedures, in 1979, only 3 per cent did not do so (IPM, 1979; Henry, 1982). Finally, if we examine the sanctioning policy of companies, we can see that the trend towards a corrective approach is repeated. There has been a shift from the use of harsh sanctions such as 'warnings' and dismissal, to progressive sanctions notably demotion, transfer and suspension. A survey in 1978 showed that 'the rates of dismissal had fallen over the eight-year period. And there had been a marked change in the number of establishments having high levels of dismissal' (Daniel and Stilgoe, 1978, p. 60). The authors conclude that 'The chief change was that there were substantially fewer plants having relatively high rates' (ibid.).

From the evidence available then, it would be difficult to deny that the explicit disciplinary policy of industrial companies has changed towards the adoption of more formalised rules and procedures, greater representative participation by trade unions in the various stages of the disciplinary process and greater use of corrective rather than punitive sanctions. But the significance of these changes depends crucially on the place of disciplinary policy in the total context of industrial social control. It also depends on the policy's relationship to the particular practices that are relied on to exercise that control, but which do not appear as part of that formal policy. Of major significance here is the relationship of managerial justice to state law.

'State law': the ACAS Code of Practice, industrial tribunals and law courts

Private justice at work is penetrated by state law in a variety of ways, the principal ones of these being, direct legislation on industrial relations, the government's arbitration and conciliation service, and the decisions of the legally constituted industrial tribunals. It is also less obviously penetrated by the decisions of formal courts of law as well as by the quasi-legal terminology of the due process model of justice.

Until the early 1960s, the disciplinary policy of British companies remained outside the state's direct concern, though not outside general legislative and structural influence. Discipline was considered a matter for management and employers to decide internally and privately. As Martin (1962) showed, even when employee deviance broke state theft laws as well as company rules, as in the case of 'employee theft', employers generally preferred to settle the matter privately and were allowed to do so. Martin found that in large firms the police were contacted in only 31 per cent of cases and in small firms this rate was a mere 21 per cent (Martin, 1962, p. 90). Moreover, even when the police were contacted, only 41 per cent of cases in large firms resulted in prosecution and only 24 per cent in small firms (ibid., p. 86).

By the mid-1960s, however, the state had explicitly entered into industrial relations legislation and one area of concern was that of discipline at work. This concern arose out of a desire to reduce what was seen to be a growing number of strikes, one of the causes of which was identified as the arbitrary use of disciplinary and dismissals procedures. The belief among government and industrialists seemed to be that if a formalised and standardised set of procedures could be adopted, this would reduce the number of grievances that arose from dismissal situations and thereby reduce the number of strikes. As we have seen above, surveys commissioned (Dawson, 1969; NJAC, 1967) confirmed the expectation that firms did not operate a formalised procedure. These also conveyed the kind of disciplinary policies that were considered to produce 'good personnel records' and, were particularly concerned to identify those companies having 'developed fairly formal disciplinary procedures and *prima facie* appeared to follow what could be considered "good" practice in discipline' (Ashdown and Baker, 1973, p. 2).

On the basis of these surveys the notorious Industrial Relations Act 1971 included provision for 'employee protection' if the internal handling of a case was deemed 'unfair'. Guidelines about what counted as fair were subsequently given in the *Code of Industrial Relations Practice* (1972), the Department of Employment's *In Working Order* (Ashdown and Baker, 1973), the various Employment Protection Acts and the decisions of the newly established industrial tribunals. The new formalised and corrective disciplinary policy was finally all brought together under the government's Advisory Conciliation and Arbitration Service's Code of Practice on *Disciplinary Practice and Procedures in Employment* (ACAS, 1977). According to the Code, disciplinary procedures should not be viewed primarily as a means of imposing sanctions and should,

(a) be in writing;
(b) specify to whom they apply;
(c) provide for matters to be dealt with quickly;
(d) indicate the disciplinary actions which may be taken;
(e) specify the levels of management which have the authority to take the various forms of disciplinary action, ensuring the immediate superiors do not normally have the power to dismiss without reference to senior management;
(f) provide for individuals to be informed of the complaints against them and to be given an opportunity to state their case before decisions are reached;
(g) give individuals the right to be accompanied by a trade union representative or by a fellow employee of their choice;
(h) ensure that, except for gross misconduct, no employees are dismissed for a first breach of discipline;
(i) ensure that disciplinary action is not taken until the case has been carefully investigated;
(j) ensure that individuals are given an explanation for any penalty imposed; and

(k) provide a right of appeal and specify the procedure to be followed.

The crucial issue here, however, is not simply that the state intervenes to pressurise companies to change their disciplinary policy. Rather, that its creation of a universal policy in the form of a Code, draws selectively from the existing range of practices and emphasises some rather than others. It is these practices, conceptually distinguished and considered to be good practice in discipline, that are distilled off from the range of social control, and made to constitute the state 'law', which is subsequently backed up by industrial tribunal decisions, that provide an additional dimension of control and a new resource that can be relied on. This mutual interdependence in the creation of state law and factory law is well illustrated by the manager of Paper Products Ltd:

> The form our discipline takes is that adopted in the Code of Practice . . . since going about these things in a different way might lead towards an industrial tribunal. It makes some sense to adopt the approach that the tribunals consider to be appropriate . . . The Code of Practice does, in fact, reflect the practice of industry. In drawing up the Code of Practice, ACAS, and the NJAC before them, did consult extensively with industry to find out what the practice was for discipline. They have to some extent brought all those agreements, practices and customs together and said this appears to be what industry does and finds acceptable and therefore this is what we will recommend in the Code of Practice . . . We had disciplinary procedures for some years which predated the Code, but the Code certainly raised questions which we had to consider, and we had to adopt similar provisions in our agreements. So yes, there has been a pressure on our agreements to mould things into the shape of the Code of Practice, but only minor things. The general philosophy is identical to the Code.

In other words, there is no directly determining role of state structure; but nor is the private company free to do as it pleases. Despite the autonomous generation of disciplinary rules and procedures, these become selectively embodied into the Code and state 'law', which then, in turn, acts back on the original disciplinary policy through the decisions of tribunals and the interpretation of the implications of these events by individual managers. The process is a dual one between human action and the creative product of that action, which appears as structure — in this case the state law.

For a company disciplinary policy to be penetrated by state law it is not necessary for that company to be directly involved in the decision of a tribunal. An awareness of the existence and significance of tribunal decisions, and their powers of enforcement, is sufficient for there to be penetration. The manager of Paper Products Ltd further explained that,

> It's not so much a case of changing our policy. It's a case of constant education to ensure that the principles under ACAS, the Code of Practice are adhered to. That means both education of managers and employees ... I think we have a set of criteria we have to observe in so far as the tribunals have said — when I say tribunals I mean Code of Practice which the tribunals use as a yardstick — that in order to be fair both legally and morally you should follow procedures and agreements where they exist, certain principles involving those procedures and also you must act reasonably ... Warnings have got to be adequate and opportunities given for improvement. Those warnings should be recorded. They should have the various elements in writing which if a tribunal, if it ever came to it, could say yes that qualifies as being a warning.

A similar point was made by the works manager of the Washing Machine Co., who denied that disciplinary policy had changed as a result of government pressure but acknowledged that it had been influenced:

> The ACAS Code and the industrial tribunals have not significantly affected the way we work our discipline. I mean, before all the industrial legislation of the past four or five years we had a 'code of practice' on this site, which dealt with disciplinary matters and so forth and it has been

modified as legislation required but in essence it hasn't been submitted that we ought to change it.

Perhaps surprisingly, then, the intervention by government into the disciplinary arena does not produce a dramatic transformation but adds to and reinforces existing procedure. As the manager of Paper Products Ltd, explains:

> I think we are better with the Code . . . It enables the manager to manage more effectively in the secure knowledge that he is behaving in a way which is regarded as reasonable. I constantly argue with managers who say 'Oh the tribunals mean we can't sack anybody' and I say on the contrary what the legislation has given us is the means by which we can dismiss someone fairly as a result of his own misconduct.

So, although industrial tribunals might appear to favour the employee, in practice they become an extension of the internal system and can be relied upon by it. This was illustrated by the works director of Paper Distribution Ltd, who described how an industrial tribunal can be used to provide an excuse to dismiss an employee who the company wish to sack because of his poor overall work performance. The existence of the tribunal allows him to be sacked in a way which reassures the management and relieves it of taking the ultimate responsibility:

> Whilst I won the tribunal case, in my own heart, I've got to say this looking back at it, to a certain extent the driver was right. I think he did have a case but he was a very slow, ponderous driver who took a long time and he didn't keep the vehicle clean and all these things came into it. And it transpired that, you know, we felt that we wanted to get shot of him in the warehouse and then he had his letters and then he went.

Indeed, the branch manager of Public Transport showed that although tribunals seem to place restrictions on management's 'right' to hire and fire, they actually do no more than build in delays by ensuring that dismissal decisions take on a uniform appearance:

Beneath the public face of private discipline

Dismissal is the ultimate power that we've got and even that is, of course, very very much restricted by the legislation in the recent years — the Employment Protection Act. Everything is now dealt with, with the view that it might go to one of these tribunals, so you've got to have hard, very very good cases. But to be fair, I understand that if this is dealt with properly through our own procedures, a tribunal will *not* throw it out.

Even where the employee appears to win a tribunal case, the company may still be relying on the tribunal as part of its disciplinary policy, though, as the manager of the Washing Machine Co., related, doing so need not deny the disciplinary policy its autonomy:

> If we take a decision and are subsequently taken through tribunal and we lose the case, that would not deter us from taking precisely the same kind of action in a repeat case. Because we do what we think is right and if we are unlucky and trip up at the tribunal or get caught on the technicalities, or they think otherwise, then we will foot the bill. Because otherwise you put yourself in blackmail situations and I think once you start asking 'what will happen if we did take it to a tribunal?' then you've lost your objectivity which it is essential to remain . . . If we have got a bad apple in the barrel and we discipline him and he chooses to take us to a tribunal and they find against us and order us to — not to reinstate obviously — but to pay compensation of £3,000 or £4,000, then the company is still better off to be rid of that individual. It's what, 6 or 9 months' wages to him but how many thousands of pounds of damage could he do to the company, carrying on as he did? So, overall we are better off and that's why I won't be deterred by what might or might not happen at an industrial tribunal.

However, the reliance on an industrial tribunal was not simply a case of economics since, as a partner in discipline at work, state law, in the form of industrial tribunals, could be drawn on in the company's battles with the trade unions. As the same manager explained:

Over the last three years we have been taken to a tribunal
four times and we've won four times. Now that has an
effect on the union people. They think 'Christ almighty!
Four times the company have been and four times they've
come up smiling.' So it can put pressure on them as well
as on the company. I mean, if we had been four times
and lost four times, the pressure would be on us.

In addition to its reliance on industrial tribunals, private
managerial justice can also rely on the state courts of law.
Although the proportion of cases taken outside the internal
disciplinary proceedings is relatively small, where that option
is available, as when employees break both state law and
factory law, it is sometimes exercised. Thus for certain theft
offences the National Catering Co., for example, operated a
policy of formal court prosecution rather than internal
discipline:

As soon as we have suspicion, as soon as he has been
charged, he will be suspended from duty without pay
pending the court trial. And if he's found guilty, then
there's an automatic dismissal from the service. It's not
often they get off.

But whether the option of prosecution in the formal
court is exercised or the internal system is relied upon,
depends on whether managers judge that the courts will
work in their favour. The same manager explained that,

The system is very biased in favour of the criminal . . .
it's now clearly established among people that go into
court, that anybody that pleads guilty is an idiot even
though you've caught him 'red-handed'. They will plead
not guilty at the Magistrates' Court and be remanded and
they'll go forward for Crown Court proceedings. They
will normally, nowadays, elect to go for trial by jury
which is their right and quite frankly the cost that you
are involving the legal system in for this £1.50 that's
allegedly at stake, is frightening. Then there are the
complications of explaining our control procedure to the
jury, the complications of presenting a case, making it
understandable. So there are a number of cases where we

say to ourselves, 'Well it's going to be highly difficult to make this one stick in court' and we would deal with that under formal disciplinary procedures within this company.

Whether public court action is taken or not, depends on the degree of rapport that can be anticipated or built up between the local courts and the company. The manager of the National Catering Company said that when they brought a court case they would do so only if they could ensure they would be heard in the same courts:

> Mayhem Magistrates' is almost a favourite. There is a knowledge built up there of our procedure. We've had the odd situation where we have had to take action in one or two isolated places where there has only been the one case ever gone into court and there is total misunderstanding of the explanation of our procedure.

Yet a third way in which there is a mutuality and penetration between state law and factory law is the reliance by company managers and trade unionists on notions, terminology and concepts, drawn from the formal legal system. A good illustration of this can be seen from the way the manager of the Public Transport Company describes his organisation's disciplinary hearings:

> They can conduct their own *defence* . . . They are not allowed to bring *witnesses* at the *appeals stage*. At the first stage they are entitled *to call witnesses*. They can call who they like to be *advocate* — a fellow employee. Some of the men have much more faith in a *barrack room lawyer type*, who is usually a trade union representative at a lower level . . . So the system *attempts to apply justice and justice is seen to be done*. We take a very serious view of discipline, that it should be applied with justice. My view is quite firm that . . . the punishment ought to be geared to what is necessary to correct a man for the error he's made, not merely to kick him in the teeth just to be tough with him. (My emphasis)

A manager of the National Catering Company reflected how penetration by law words can actually create the impression that the private system is the 'same' as the formal legal system:

Our disciplinary procedure in fact is almost comparable to the *court procedure*. The individual will be taken through the *alleged offence*. If the manager feels satisfied that there is a *serious misdemeanour* committed he will immediately issue formal *charges* as we call them. It is up to the fellow to advise the group manager whether he wishes to appear before him at a formal interview where he gives his *defence*. The formal interview then takes the appearance, as it were, of a *Magistrates' Court* in that the man will come before the manager on an appointed date to *answer the charges*. The group manager will act as the *prosecution* and the person has the facilities for bringing with him a trade union appointed spokesman or fellow employee. Usually the group manager will have a *note taker*, taking down the exchange of *evidence*. If the chappie turns up at the interview minus the representative and in the view of the group manager it was a comparatively serious case . . . the group manager will *caution* that he would much prefer not to proceed in the absence of an *advocate*. We've no wish to take any advantage over this and we've every wish that he should be given good *professional advice*. The group manager will have to *weigh up the evidence* on both sides, whether or not he'll find the individual *guilty or not guilty* and then decide on the *punishment*. The individual has got the right to lodge an *appeal*.
(My emphasis)

Clearly from the above examples, then, we can see how state law penetrates factory law and how the latter relies upon it. But the reverse is also true. It has already been mentioned that the bulk of offences against state law are handled privately and internally by companies and organisations. If all such cases were fed into the formal system of criminal justice, the courts could not cope without relying to an even greater extent on the discretionary autonomous decision-making of their own functionaries who would need to discount vast numbers of indictable offences. The reason this is not necessary is because the state legal system actually relies upon private disciplinary justice. But in this exchange of autonomy, the state must accept that it will be penetrated by the definitions and conceptions of private justice. Principally this penetration concerns a reinterpretation of what counts as crime and deviance, and what the appropriate severity of response should be. Perhaps not surprisingly, agencies of the state take the view that where there is a clash between formal courts and private justice, the state should take precedence. A senior metropolitan police officer clearly explained how he saw this relationship:

> You see, a factory, in my opinion, should only deal with offences against its own code of discipline, not with those against the criminal law ... The factory is only a part of the community as a whole. When I see in my mind courts of justice, those courts deal with the community as a whole rather than part of it. They may deal with a local part of it but they deal with anyone from anywhere else in the community that commits an offence in that area. It's a bit like the police service. The police are only competent to deal with offences against their own code of conduct, not criminal offences. They go outside. Where we have a factory it should only competently deal with offences against its own codes as opposed to criminal law. So, then, how do we get criminal law dealt with by the factory courts?

The answer to that question was given by another member of the police force who explained that there were very good reasons why formal law enforcement agencies do not get involved in all the criminal offences that occur in factories:

> The present situation, of course, in relation to theft is that the management have a legal obligation to draw this to the attention of the police. Very often they don't because to do so would create more industrial distress.

From the company's point of view, indeed, the retention of the right to discipline its own members is not simply to do with industrial relations, economics, publicity, or even that, as victim, it should decide what is to be done. Instead, internal dispute settlement is seen as providing a better context for understanding why an offence is committed irrespective of whether one is dealing with theft offences that break state laws or those that break only the factory code. A manager of the Public Transport Company explained:

> On technical offences, an outsider wouldn't really know what it was all about would he? If you take a signal passed at danger, for example, no outsider would be able to debate that with an advocate. How could an outsider form a judgement? He'd hear what the driver said. 'I know that signal was off, I saw it off. I can produce Joe Bloggs and somebody else who can say they also saw it off.' Then you've got the railway technical evidence ... If it came to whether a man was guilty of having fiddled his time sheet or not, I suppose an outsider could assess it, but I think the trade union would take the same view 'why bring an outsider in he doesn't know the conditions that this man works under? He doesn't know the stresses and strains and temptations that are there — the reasons why a man would resort to a fiddle.' I think the unions would support in all cases the company dealing with its own discipline.

As we shall see below, this penetration of state law by private discipline is compounded, since private discipline itself relies upon the autonomy of various internal groups and indeed, individuals, who all have some influence on the definition of what counts as crime. Before examining this, however, it is important to look at the other externally autonomous structural parts that are mutually interdependent with private managerial justice.

'The economy': unemployment, corporatism and industry

Although less obvious than the connection between state law and private managerial justice, there is a significant interpenetration of factory disciplinary policy by the wider economic structure. The industrial relations manager of the Rex Rubber Company explained how the political economy can set the scene for internal decisions:

> You can be overtaken by events. I don't think you can ever dissociate yourself from the broad picture. You can

have little things happening within a broad picture but in
the fullest sense there are so many things impinging upon
you that it's almost mathematical. An example of this is
that today the union movement are far more likely to
assist us in finding a joint answer to a situation than they
were say three or four years ago. Why? Because of the
economic situation. We are working a two day week which
is a result, not of the inefficiency so much of this plant
as a total UK, worldwide, situation. There's an old joke on
this — setting up the deckchairs at an angle of 45° on the
Titanic when it makes its last slope into the water. It is a
little bit academic. It is reflective of the political situation.
You can't ignore it. There are relative strengths at any one
time and people are imposed on by circumstances outside
and I feel that there was a time when union strength was
out of balance with company strength, and they were
imposing circumstances and in fact were often supporting
people who should not have been supported. I think this
was a kind of a reaction from the days when management
would have had you jumping through hoops. You know
you get the sort of swing thing happening. But there are
degrees of this. It's never really black and white. It never
really happens that way and sometimes, I mean in a period
of high employment where people can come and go, even
to dismiss a person is not what it would seem to be. You
simply move from here to there, you know. You suddenly
shovel the bad guy around. You don't really do anything
about it. You just remove your piece of the problem and
give it to somebody else and you wait for the next guy to
come along and then you remove him. Its like a merry go
round, an ever changing face all the time. People come
and leave and get older and die and so forth. It's a kind of
a system and you're in the middle spinning the plates just
trying to keep them all going . . . So here we are then, this
system is reflective of the political circumstances of that
moment in time and I do feel even so there is some kind
of rapport here — it isn't completely a negative thing. And
at the end of the day it isn't a light decision to put a fellow
up the road. I don't like to do this. I'm a working bloke.
I come from the same background and the same village as

these fellows and I see no victory in putting a young man up the road. On the other hand if there's an influence whose presence is to the general disadvantage of the group then I am afraid that he is the one that has to be sacrificed. You're throwing the baby to the wolves to keep the rest of it going.

The same effect can occur where the economic situation has strong overriding local influences. The works director of Paper Distribution, for example, explained how when labour was in short supply, disciplinary policy was penetrated to the degree that it became inevitably more lenient:

> We are in a very run-down part of London and we therefore find staff difficult to obtain. One is terribly careful when it comes to disciplinary procedures that you do the right thing because if you try to take action then you may have even greater difficulty in trying to get a replacement. So I think this totally conditions the thinking of management. I think if we fired a man and he then goes to another paper merchant, and says he has been fired by us you get a bad name in the trade.

Conversely, where there is a surplus of labour such as in times of high unemployment, or where an individual is in fear of losing his job, this has a dramatic effect on disciplinary policy. Some companies rely on such situations and even try to engineer them, such as the National Catering Company, who prefer to take on catering student casuals, because their employment situation exercises its own 'natural' discipline:

> We prefer to engage for the casual summer period students from catering colleges. We're helping out in two ways. We are solving our own casual problem and we're giving job experience to the students, which eliminates a lot of the problems because here you're engaging a casual group and their whole career depends upon what happens to them during that period. And obviously if they step out of line and they're caught doing any of the fiddles . . . that's them killed for life. So there is a natural control over them to begin with.

As well as the local economic situation, a company's

disciplinary policy can be influenced by the industry within which it trades and by the wider corporation to which it may belong. The works director of Paper Distribution Ltd, for example, was confident that he could overcome his disciplinary problems by introducing an incentive to prevent employees from fiddling the sick-pay scheme. He was frustrated in this attempt, however, by the fact that his company was part of a larger concern:

> The biggest problem is we are part of a large group with 6,000 employees in the UK and if I was to suddenly say, 'well look, because of this run-down area of London and because of the staff, I am going to pay an attendance allowance', they would say you can't do that because of the rest of the group. But the rest of the group are all in different areas of the country; they don't have our problem. You go back to the group situation with the contract of employment.

The general level and even the kind of activity that is considered to be 'crime' is related to what is understood to be typical for the particular industry. Thus an industry as a semi-autonomous part penetrates the state law via its influence over the internal company disciplinary policy. The manager of the National Catering Company described how the catering industry sets its own level for what counts as theft:

> We have exactly the same problems as the catering industry in general. I don't think that our degree of pilferage is any greater. It's a little bit more difficult to deal with in that it is usually cash that is going. There is some pilferage of property, i.e., food. There are accepted tolerances that over many, many years have been built in. Well we know, of course, from our experiences of the catering industry in general, that there is a deal of turning a blind eye to these things and you find reasons why they are accepted.

However, as we shall see in the next section, this penetration of state law by private justice owes more to individual managers and trade unionists in their interaction with each other and employees, than it does to penetration by industry.

A resource for strategic alliance, coercion and conflict: the interpenetration of internally autonomous parts and private justice

A company's disciplinary policy is not only dependent on semi-autonomous parts whose autonomy is externally generated, it also relies on those whose autonomy is located within the company or organisation concerned, such as management, unions and employees. As a manager of Public Security Ltd., said:

> Management to some extent is against the worker but at the same time it's got to be with them because that's what's earning its money. It can be to some extent against the union but on the other hand it's got to be with them because it's the union that's earning its money by keeping the workers happy. All three are intermingled.

'Management': consistency and diversity in disciplinary policy

That managers are individuals with their own autonomy means that although a formal policy on discipline might exist, a diversity of responses to rule-breaking may occur. Thus the manager of Paper Products Ltd said that, although his company has a formal corrective-representative policy, there was some difficulty in ensuring that managers followed the 'correct' procedure:

> We have a problem trying to achieve consistency, and one which requires constant education of both management and employees ... One manager may feel that an employee leaving his place of work is a dire sin and should entail being sacked; another may feel it's not at all that serious and perhaps a warning is sufficient. Then there'll be the manager who wants to short-circuit the procedural steps ... and another who will convince himself that he's given somebody a warning, when in fact he'd been so oblique in his reference to misconduct that the chap probably thought he'd earned some praise. It's no use turning round and saying 'I did tell you about that', when in fact you

didn't exactly tell them that, you told them about something else which they misunderstood.

Similarly, the industrial relations manager of the Rex Rubber Company said that diversity

> is almost inevitable. We are all human beings and if you say to me that every person who has been judged for an offence was judged by exactly the same criterion as everyone else — they are not,

and the same point was made by a manager of Public Transport Ltd:

> Disciplinary procedure is always subject to human application. However much you try and guide people on how they ought to apply punishments you always get the people who are perhaps basically a bit vindictive, and who want to hit a man.

So, although a company operates with a formal disciplinary policy, there are a range of tolerance levels and variations stemming from the different individual autonomies of managers. Since the policy relies on the manager's autonomy for its application, it would be surprising, not to say impossible, for consistency to be achieved. If managers were able to apply discipline consistently in accordance with the policy, they would not be capable of managing, since this requires the autonomy to act and interpret the action of others. The consistency of discipline, then, is more a property of the constant reference of diverse action to the policy; that is accounting for discipline in ways which make it appear consistent and by describing the need for attention to the policy, and reproducing that policy in various documentary forms and sending managers on special training courses. In this regard, a considerable impact is made by the numerous industrial relations training services and their literature (see *Industrial Relations Review and Report*, 1978; 1980).

Management and unions: power for co-option

Although the hierarchical decision-making structure of most

companies and organisations suggests that management are the sole agents for the application of disciplinary policy, a certain amount of reliance on trade unions occurs. This is accomplished by management drawing on the trade unions' representative role and incorporating this into some aspects of the disciplinary process in the form of a limited representative participation. I asked respondents to my survey whether they acknowledged this participation as a valuable component to disciplinary practice and if so why. Forty-seven per cent of the forty companies surveyed thought it was valuable and 40 per cent thought it was not, though this distribution did not correspond to those companies having some form of participation.

Those who did not think that participation was valuable often took the view that 'the onus/initiative on performance/attitude/behaviour rests firmly with management', that the matter was a 'management prerogative', and that the union role should only be to 'see that the rules are applied reasonably and equitably'. Others felt that 'workers did not want to participate in discipline' because 'it places them in an invidious position, which they do not like and will not accept' and besides 'this would not improve the situation because of the role expectation of employees'. Illustrative of this approach is the attitude of the personnel manager of Paper Products Ltd:

> My instant reaction is that participation is not a good idea. I suppose that's because it tends to lessen management control. Joint decisions as opposed to management decision . . . I don't like the word prerogative because that smacks of arbitrary decision making. It's more like the separation of functions, in a similar sort of way that management will plan production. But prerogative has a connotation of being the opposite of consulting about decisions . . . that's way I shy away from the word. Using it in the other sense, yes I would regard it as the prerogative of management to maintain discipline.

Those who thought participation was valuable did so either because it made the outcome of discipline less troublesome and easy to secure; it was more just and acceptable;

or it gave the workers greater responsibility. One employer, for example, felt that involving workers 'takes the acrimony out of a potential industrial relations problem and, if employees participate throughout the procedure, it assists in reducing the number of appeals against dismissal'. Another felt that participation was a 'safeguard against any residual element of autocratic management', while others said that where 'justice was seen to be done' and 'impartiality and fairness is seen to be applied' then there is a 'better acceptance of discipline' which is in turn 'strengthened by union participation' and which is necessary for rules and procedures to be enforceable and effective. Some pointed out that overall participation in this area gave a 'sense of involvement and responsibility' which one felt was useful 'provided that the commitment to worker participation succeeds in overcoming the individual urge to disobey reasonable rules of conduct'. For others the purpose of participation had the degree of subtlety expected of the corrective policy in that it provided an opportunity 'to communicate the company's attitude to offences and offenders'. Participation then, where it is seen as useful is only useful in so far as it is instrumental to the objection-free implementation of managerial control.

However, such reliance on and penetration of trade union activity by management for the purposes of administering discipline also works in reverse. Management are relied on by trade unions to maintain their own power position. This is not simply saying that unions discipline their own members, which as we shall see below, they do, but that management will be relied on by the unions to underpin this discipline and as such the relations of management over workers are some of the relations of the power of unions over their members. This can be seen in the account of the manager of Paper Products Ltd, who explained that,

> Well trade unionists are anxious to have rules the same as anybody else. Their representatives will often argue very strongly that unless I took some disciplinary action and sacked the person, I would lose all co-operation with the trade union movement. The unions have an interest in maintaining control and discipline because it reflects on

control of their own members. Maintenance of discipline and order is as important in the union hierarchy as it is in the management hierarchy. The idea of certainty about certain matters is important. If you are not certain of what the outcome of a particular action on this fellow is going to be then you are less able to control your own membership. You are saying 'Now look I'm the person that you deal with. I'm the one who says what can and what can't be done because that's important to me. I need that power in order to negotiate.' Anyone who breaches the norms set down by a union representative and gets away with it threatens that power. So the union representative will often expect management to take action and be very concerned if they don't.

Similarly, the manager of the Rex Rubber Company described how unions supported the dismissal of one employee:

They agreed to get rid of him. This is the union guys. You have to look at the politics see. He had nutted a shop steward. Now they obviously cannot allow that to go on anyway because otherwise you've got to have 7ft shop stewards around, you know karate experts. So the important thing is that when the guy went, that was it. There was no strikes, no walk-outs from sections. It is accepted as a good way to do business.

However, unions themselves, like management, are comprised of individuals who have their own autonomy, independent from the union, even though they are a part of it. Like individual managers, individual unionists can penetrate the collective union policy. As the industrial relations manager of Rex Rubber says,

The union convenor at the moment is C. P. Smith and in the early days he was referred to as 'Car Park Smith'. You know, out, out, out ... He's mellowed immensely. He's now on the executive of the union. He is a political animal ... His word carries a lot of weight ... He's got a certain amount of success under his belt. So there's this individual thing to the extent that they will say, 'What does Percy think?'

In short, then, both management and unions are interdependent in their reliance on each other to maintain control over employees, and each in turn also depends upon the autonomy of the individuals who make them up. These individuals are neither completely bound by the formal rules and procedures of the disciplinary policy, nor by their own group affiliations, but have a degree of autonomy which is relied on to make a settlement within the boundaries of the policy. Without this albeit limited autonomy, no settlement would be possible; with it, however, come the individual influences which make actual discipline sometimes different from the policy. In effect what happens is a kind of private justice version of plea bargaining, with the individual manager and unionist forming friendly relationships on which they come to a negotiated settlement. The manager of the National Catering Company explains how this interdependence between disciplinary policy, management, unions and the individuals that occupy these roles, operates:

> There is a rapport built up between the group manager and the union advocate. They get to know each other very well — just like solicitors. You begin to get to know how each others' mind ticks and that sort of thing. There will be the odd occasion where the advocate's been given access to the accused beforehand to discuss the case. He's been given access to the papers. Obviously from the evidence he will have a fairly good idea of whether the individual is guilty or not guilty himself and, on occasions, he will come in and have a word with you beforehand and say 'Well what are we going to do with this?' and feel the strength of feeling that you may have. It depends on the individual and the relationships between you. You've got to live with these chaps. You accept that. And they haven't got an easy job and there are one or two, obviously, that are hell-bent on getting their member off, whatever the circumstances. It builds up his credibility, he may be looking for election to another position this time next year. So you've got to try and sense it out. O.K., then I would review what had happened and then I'd say 'Well fine, I've made up my mind the chap is guilty, and what am I going to do with

him'. At that stage I would ask the advocate to come in and go over my decision with him and say to him 'Well in this case I think I'm going to give him 14 days' suspension, dismissal, whatever.' Usually an advocate will have a wee bit of an argument with you here and say 'Well couldn't you be more lenient, this that and the other.' So it's the old, old story. Usually ... you'll take it up a little bit to allow for him to come back a bit and make the fellow feel he's satisfied.

The manager of Public Transport Ltd gave a similar account, revealing how, in spite of a policy to the contrary, there are often pre-meeting, informal negotiations between individual unionist and management to sort out what the outcome is going to be:

I've already admitted to you that unofficially normally one discusses what one's got in mind with the advocate before the case is even heard. You often temper your case and go according to what he says. Sometimes I've known them even to say 'I reckon it should be harsher.' My sort of idea is to talk to the advocate before we have the bloke in because normally you'll find most of the chaps who represent people, if the facts aren't in dispute, are prepared to be reasonable.

Indeed, another senior manager with Public Transport Ltd explained how this reaching of an 'understanding' between the union representative and the management is used to get the employee being disciplined to accept a guilty plea and the 'sentence' reached by the hearing:

I would have thought it was in the interests of the man if one has an understanding with the advocates ... Very often they've told the man before he comes in that he hasn't any hope of winning the case. That he was wrong and that he'll have to take it, but he'll do his best for them.

The industrial relations manager of Rex Rubber Company explained that this informal negotiation of justice 'behind closed doors' was both necessary and inevitable; it was a product of the very nature of discipline and deviance — not the mechanical outcome of some driving force, but a reflection of the interdependence of these semi-autonomous parts on the range of others in the totality. While a policy might adequately respond to a cause, the reality of mutually interdependent parts requires this degree of informality and flexibility.

> This sounds very dishonest, but life is not 12345, black/white, black/white. So there is a certain amount of manipulation that has to be done all the way through. Read your bible it'll tell you all about it . . . We don't just go in cold. Christ! I mean if you look into any political organisation — the Labour Party, the Conservative Party, the interest groups — you'll see it's set up beforehand. Whilst it's not rigged there are pre-committees, if you like, on an ad hoc basis, maybe behind closed doors. If there's a bad situation I could talk to Smith and he might say 'Well look Bill, Christ, don't you understand what's going on.' Then, I can go to the plant manager and say 'Look the information is this . . . now this is the line that I would be going for and this is the logic.' (Again, I have to set this rapport up with my boss here.) 'He's given me reasoned support for this, not horse shit,' not wishing just to go blundering in. So, there's a little bit of toing and froing. It's the old political thing.

From this evidence it would appear that employees are somewhat dominated by the interdependent interests of management and unions who appear to form alliances and use the disciplinary policy as a resource against them. This, however, would be an oversimplification, since just as these semi-autonomous parts have their autonomy, so too does the community of fellow workers.

Fellow employees: the 'just' community

It has been well documented that employees exercise their own degree of informal discipline upon fellow workers whom they see as going beyond the taken for granted limits of pilferage (see especially: Horning, 1970; Mars, 1974 and Henry, 1978). Similar collective action can be taken by employees against those of their peers who deviate from certain company rules and working arrangements. In my survey it was pointed out that this was especially apparent where small teams or gangs are working for pooled bonuses. In such circumstances, said one employer, 'employees wish to be seen contributing to their working groups and are reluctant to disrupt the normal pattern' since, as another pointed out, 'equal effort is required by gang members'. Here there can be 'pressure from other workers on slackers' or 'sanctions on people whom the team don't feel are pulling their weight.' The position was summarised by the personnel manager of Motorcycles Ltd:

> They mete out their own justice really. Occasionally perhaps it has been thought that somebody has been swinging the lead, shall we say. Well if the others either side of him are hard working chaps they will jolly soon see that he comes into line in their own way. I don't know how they do it but we suddenly find that that chap is suddenly working quite well.

But this informal employee discipline is not solely restricted to some kind of separate sub-world of factory floor justice, as is often assumed. It also penetrates those disciplinary situations in which management had unions appear to be in full control. The manager of Paper Products Ltd explained:

> It is interesting from time to time when you have an issue, perhaps say a dismissal. Usually in practice someone will be suspended while the dismissal is being thought about and investigated. Now that sort of situation goes around the factory like wildfire — everybody is speculating as to what is going to happen. If we or the union are opposing dismissal then it's a straightforward confrontation, either the man goes or he doesn't go. There is usually very little common ground. But it is interesting when, for example, we see that the view of the factory is very much in favour of dismissal, irrespective of what the union representative might say. We know very well that the union representative has a part or a role to play regardless of the offence as a sort of advocate, but very often it is perceived that he is very happy to see the action taking effect.

Not only do the unions have their position penetrated by employee feeling, but so too do the management. Particularly illustrative here is the way management working in group settings may concede tolerance levels greater than those allowed by the company, at great personal risk and for no personal pecuniary gain. The manager of the National Catering Company explains how this operates within his company, via the employees co-opting the individual manager:

> The man in charge is the supervisor, the management agent. He's in total control of everything. He's responsible for the stocks, for the cash and for the behaviour of his own crew, which is fine in theory, but it does not necessarily work in practice because you get into the team thing. It's fair to say that the supervisor who falls by the wayside in a cash fiddle is not fiddling for his own personal benefit — the fiddle goes to the advantage of the crew entirely. It has to be admitted that the supervisor is under some considerable pressure. If he, himself, wishes to be an honest fellow, he has then got to face up to the problems that he will meet with the team. Everyone, apart from a few stalwart honest individuals, is perfectly happy to take part in any means of increasing their personal gain or wealth or whatever. So, there is this team thing that the staff to a large degree expect that part of their earnings are going to come from some degree of fiddling on the job. It's a very easy thing to do, of course, in a mobile unit where it's extremely difficult to supervise everything. As I say, a bit of pressure builds up on the supervisor to get involved and he's got to be a very strong fellow to stand up against his crew. Regrettably, most of them succumb. It is very unfair because when we take action it will normally only be the supervisor who gets the stick because we cannot really prove anything against the staff . . . And again there is the sort of unwritten law that none of them will 'shop their mates' and say well they were all involved. So the supervisor always takes the can. Obviously if he is not complying with the routine of things, then he is going to have difficulty in controlling his crew to get them to work as well as they might do and, again, no supervisor

wishes to be in a situation where the staff don't like him and wouldn't like to work with him. So its a way of buying the loyalty of his crew to work well with him.

Clearly, employees need not restrict their alliances to co-opting management in order to circumvent and, indeed, penetrate the company disciplinary policy. In service industries in particular they may form alliances with other semi-autonomous groups most noteably with the customer of the product against the company (see Ditton, 1977; Mars, 1973). But this leads us to a recognition that the individual employee himself can be relied on to have an autonomy of his own.

The power of the weak: the interpenetration of the individual employee and managerial justice

From the discussion so far, it might seem that the alliances and mutual dependence between the range of semi-autonomous parts which constitute the totality would completely overwhelm the individual employee and absorb any autonomy that he might possess into an adjunct of strategy or a resource in the conflict between competing interests. Not so. The integrative analysis, has been sensitive to the individual autonomy of those who occupy union and managerial roles as well as to the influence of the individual on the wider social structures that have their autonomy outside the confines of the factory. The same sensitivity shows that any disciplinary policy not only relied on the autonomy of the individual employee, but holds this as a most important element, without which discipline would be total coercion. In short, managerial justice is mutually dependent upon individual self-discipline. My survey of 40 industrial companies revealed that only 22 per cent believed there was no informal employee self-discipline, whereas 57 per cent said there was some and 3 per cent admitted to a lot. The form this took varied from self-discipline over behavioural standards such as, good attendance records without using clocks, 'awareness of time-keeping', 'dress', 'the importance of training', 'moral standards' to 'deciding on their own work priorities' and 'their own levels of acceptable behaviour'. Whilst some of this self-discipline might be a reflection of the individual's non-work background, some is definitely a product of the interdependence between formal company rules, backed up by state law such as the conditions of employment, and the freedom to contract, under which the individual makes an agreement to obey the company rules. In its most extreme version, this agreement takes the form of an oath, which not only relies on individual's commitment to their highest order of belief, but also lays the conditions for the acceptance of discipline should rules be broken. A manager of Public Security Ltd explained:

> We have a disciplinary code and we take an oath when we join the service. A disciplinary code backed up by an oath it's more specific. It's acceptable and accepted quite willingly . . . Indeed, it's part of the conditions of service. Out of that comes, if you like, a natural follow on of morality . . . This disciplinary code is imposed upon us with our full consent . . . One agrees in fact if I am in breach of it then I am entitled to be punished . . . It's like the armed services. One has imposed upon one military discipline which is a discipline of fear, because there is punishment if there is a digression. But out of the discipline of fear comes the self-discipline.

So strong can be the sense of self-discipline that the company may even rely upon the individual's autonomy, rather than invoking the disciplinary policy. The works director of Paper Distribution, for example, explained that it was sometimes unnecessary to bring a case before the internal disciplinary hearing since an individual could be prompted to exercise his own self-discipline and might actually dismiss himself:

> We had a case where a girl was off sick. She put in a doctor's certificate, but we knew she was 'phoning girls at the office having conversations and she had been seen about in the shopping centres by members of the staff. So to bring the thing to a head I said to my manager out there, 'Well look, why don't you write to her, say she's

been seen out etc. etc. The thing isn't working to her
benefit or to the company's and that she must come in
and have a conversation with you — just to clear the air.'
When she received the letter she put her notice in — which
is just what we wanted. Now had we have gone about it
in another way she could have said 'well you know you are
forcing me to go because I am sick, and that's not right.'

That individual employees have a certain autonomy in disciplinary issues is also reflected in the actual disciplinary decisions of managerial justice. Although 'standard' penalties for certain offences might exist, the individual employee may penetrate the formal policy such that account is taken of his personal circumstances and background. So much is this the case that some companies do not fix penalties in advance. The personnel manager of Metal Manufacturers said:

> The reason why we've not specified penalties is that in
> many cases things have to be looked at on an individual
> basis. If there's a guy, who has worked for the company
> for 25 years and something to do with his domestic
> situation means he is under pressure. He does something
> silly like taking a piece of metal which has got a fair value
> down the scrap yard, puts it in a shopping bag and gets
> caught going out the gate. Now he can say 'OK I know I
> shouldn't have done it. I know stealing material is gross
> misconduct, but I've worked for the company for 25 years
> and I've got all these domestic problems, I won't do it
> again. I know you've put on "final warning" but please in
> this case have some clemency.' We might well say 'Look
> the guy's worked here a long time, he's a good employee
> — yes we will exercise clemency.' On the other hand it
> could be a guy who's only been employed by us for
> about 18 months and we find 12 tins of paint in the back
> of his car. He's on his way. We deliberately don't write
> it down for that reason. You have to look at every
> individual case and use an element of common sense when
> it's being handled.

Similarly, a manager of Public Transport Ltd explained how an individual's background may so penetrate disciplinary policy as to render it wholly inappropriate:

> Sometimes, things come out that you didn't even know an inkling of. Somebody might have personal problems at home or there may even be medical reasons . . . and that can influence you. It's no good issuing a charge if you know the sort of problems he's got are not going to be resolved by it . . . He's not going to be helped at all.

Indeed, the manager of Paper Distributions Ltd pointed out that the acknowledgement of individual autonomy was not simply a concession by managers, but could be claimed and even relied on by individual employees to protect them, or even allow them to get away with certain action which would otherwise be sanctionable:

> Where you've men who have been here a number of years they get into the 'comfort zone'. There's no way we can really push them around because they can say 'Well you've put up with me for thirty years I can't be as bad as all that.'

In addition to penetrating formal disciplinary policy by relying on managerial discretion, individual employees can also penetrate the community justice of their fellow employees. It is not therefore only the case, as we saw in the previous section, that the community of employees penetrates the individual by imposing its own discipline upon him. Rather, there is a kind of duality in which individual employees may actually rely on management to bring sanctions to bear on fellow employees. A good illustration of this can be found in the case of the management of hidden economic rewards in the hotel and catering industry. The manager of the National Catering Company showed how this operated:

> There are two elements of earnings in the trade: The legitimate gratuities that the supervisor and staff pick up — that's the tips — that's at the discretion of the supervisor how he distributes it through his staff. We have nothing at all to do with that. The element of cash that is derived from whatever fiddle may be going on just goes in as part of the gratuity and becomes part of the spread. Legitimate and illicit, it all goes into one pile of money and then

that is distributed . . . If an individual isn't getting a
reasonable share compared to all the rest of them — which
he must know because he sees this going on — . . . , then
he'll start beefing about it 'supervisor so and so gives you
more tips.' If he doesn't get it sorted out we get a fair
inkling of what's going on. You get individuals that are
constantly asking for a change. Then there is a signal
flash that there is something wrong within that group.
It may eventually get to the situation where the individual
member of staff will come in and see his manager and tell
him the reason why he wants to change and the usual
reason is that, well he doesn't think he's getting a fair
share. At that stage of the game you begin to start asking
questions.

Finally, individuals may even rely upon state law and the public with whom they might form alliances to defeat the company disciplinary policy and the management. A classic case of this was described by the manager of the National Catering Company:

This chap Ahmed was stopped going to one of our units
and was found to be in possession of all sorts of things,
cheese and bacon, ham and bread and things, jars of
coffee, jars of tea, and of course he was charged with going
equipped to steal. And we were very surprised and
shattered in fact. He was found guilty at the Magistrates'
Court, but he did appeal and the appeal was upheld on
the basis that the judge ruled that it made no difference to
the customer whose sandwich he was buying, whether it
was the National Catering Company's sandwich or whether
it was Mr Ahmed's sandwich, as long as they got what they
wanted then it made no difference.

In short, then, the very interdependence of parts coupled with their semi-autonomous nature means that even in the case of the 'solitary' employee there are necessarily sufficient resources to enable some exercise of power over the structures that appear to be all pervasive in their domination.

In conclusion then, we can see how despite the hierarchical structure of the typical business enterprise or organisation, and regardless of the apparent managerial authority whereby discipline is dispensed, there exist a range of mutually interdependent parts of which the formal policy is only one. Simply because these parts are not described by the formal policy, does not and cannot remove them nor can it undermine their significance. Any analysis that ignores the mutual interaction and interdependence of the semi-autonomous parts that make up the totality of social control and takes for granted that disciplinary policy as the particular form, is likely to be grossly inadequate. Nor does the fact that some disciplinary policies formally recognise more of these semi-autonomous parts in their formal policy than others mean that their formal policy is somehow nearer to the reality of private justice. As we shall see in the next chapter, the same kinds of problems arise with those companies and organisations whose structure leads to them adopting a more overtly participatory approach.

5 The negotiated law of participatory justice:
accommodation, protection, legitimation and co-option

Introduction

As we saw in the last chapter, in the typical western industrial company, disciplinary policy is only one part of a range of interdependent, semi-autonomous parts which make up a continuum of social control extending both externally outside the factory and internally through formal and informal groups that make up the company. However, not all companies formalise the same elements from the range into their disciplinary policy. In particular, those companies and organisations that have a paternalistic or democratic tradition often adopt some form of joint management-union disciplinary tribunal for the purpose of administering private justice to rulebreakers. In this chapter, I shall look in depth at this approach and show that, even though the formal disciplinary policy adopted appears to be of a different form — 'participatory justice' as opposed to 'managerial justice', a range of semi-autonomous parts is drawn on and that this range is similar to that relied on by the disciplinary policy of more traditional hierarchically structured companies. Thus I shall show that although private justice is to some degree autonomous, with specific factories generating their own disciplinary forms as policy by having their own unique selection and combination of elements from the available range, there are nonetheless recurring elements that make up this range, such as state law, the economy, the unions, fellow employees and individual workers.

Whereas the material base for the previous chapter was

The negotiated law of participatory justice 133

drawn from interviews and survey data from a range of different companies, this chapter primarily draws on a depth study of one large (10,000 employees) food manufacturing company, Foodstuffs Ltd and in particular on interviews with managers, unionists and employees about the company's participatory approach to discipline (see Appendix).

Autonomy of private justice

As was clear from the last chapter, a company's disciplinary policy has its own historically specific autonomy, even though a part of that policy is both the outcome and the relations of other semi-autonomous parts of the totality of social control. Every company or organisation has an account of the emergence of its disciplinary policy and for many that history is seen as specific to its own peculiar and unique tradition, situation and circumstances. At Foodstuffs Ltd the joint management-union approach to discipline was described by Mike, a senior shop steward, as having, 'developed during a period of family business that operated with a great degree of paternalism'. For Don, a manager, Foodstuffs was,

> a paternalistic company, where the family bent over backwards to give the workers a say, within pretty closely defined limits. The PR was better than the doing, you might say. They created this impression that the elected members of the workforce mattered; they gave them jurisdiction; they gave them responsibility and that's a continuing tradition now.

This historical specificity means that the joint management-union disciplinary form cannot easily be transposed into another company, nor even borrowed as a model for others to copy. As Don explained:

> You're in a factory here which is full of tradition and full of a long period of mutual respect between management and shop floor . . . I think if you wanted to put the tribunal into a factory that didn't have that tradition it would be an absolute disaster. It's potentially so vulnerable

134 *The negotiated law of participatory justice*

to politicking and management self-interest and victimisation and to misuse, or what have you, that unless you've got the basis of respect the thing would never work.

Nor, indeed, would the Foodstuffs company be likely to adopt the same system itself if it were to begin trading under the present set of circumstances because these are necessarily different from those prevalent at the time when its own policy emerged. As Ann, the employment manager said, 'It's historical really. The basic idea for us now is to use it almost because it's there. Whether we, starting afresh, would have a similar thing is debatable.'

Perhaps the most important reason why the disciplinary policy could not be transposed is because it only works in relation to the specific semi-autonomous parts on which it relies and with which it has built up a symbiotic relationship. For the same reason it is difficult to replace one disciplinary policy with another, because only part of the disciplinary machinery, the formal, visible part is being substituted and the newly introduced policy has to build up the informal mutuality between itself and the already existing semi-autonomous parts. Clearly, then, there are likely to be problems when government intervention in discipline promotes a model based upon the disciplinary experiences of hierarchically organised companies which adopt a managerial form of justice rather than a participatory form.

Participatory justice and state law

As it is constituted, the participatory form of discipline operative at Foodstuffs Ltd is only one of a range of disciplinary forms, some of which are formally acknowledged and some of which are not. It is a multi-stage process, the first stage of which involves either management, security or a company detective, observing instances of rule-breaking, interviewing the suspected employee and submitting a report, often with an accompanying statement of admission, to the employment manager who decides whether the tribunal system or another of the available disciplinary forms is appropriate. Informally, as might be expected, there are other ways rule-breaking enters the formal tribunal system. One employee, Liz, explained that the detectives only get involved after they had been tipped off, 'When we see the detectives come into the room we always think somebody's told somebody because they only seem to come when you've got a suspicion that something's going on.'

If the tribunal is deemed appropriate, then the case, with all the evidence is brought before its members: three trade union shop stewards, a manager and an employment officer acting as secretary. The tribunal members may then themselves consider whether the case should be proceeded with further or whether to refer it back to management. The latter may invoke either a form of managerial justice or else bring in the state law, police and courts If the case is considered one worthy of processing by the tribunal then its members may discuss it and set a penalty, ranging from a reprimand to a week's suspension. As Ann, the employment manager, said:

> The tribunal members sit together in the first instance with an employment secretary and they look at the evidence and decide what they think is an appropriate penalty. They collectively decide, so that they are responsible for discipline; they can transfer somebody, give final warnings. In the case of dismissal, which we quaintly refer to as 'refer to management', then the trade union steps out and the management take effect.

The discussion and sanctions emerging at this 'informal' disciplinary tribunal stage are transmitted to the employee, who has not been present during its deliberations. The employee is told of the tribunal's decision in the presence of a non-management member of the company usually, though not necessarily, a trade union representative, and is asked if he wishes to accept its penalties. He has the choice of either doing so or of appealing. Any appeal goes to a 'formal disciplinary tribunal' which comprises the members of the 'informal' tribunal together with the employment manager as secretary and one of the senior managers, representing the factory director, as chairman. In addition, this second stage of the joint disciplinary tribunal includes the local section manager, the person who is supposed to have committed the offence and any colleague or representative that he or she might wish to bring, as well as any witnesses. Should they wish to do so, subsequent to the decision of the formal tribunal, the employee can further appeal to the factory director or contact a senior site shop steward or even appeal to an industrial tribunal.

The intervention of the state into the industrial disciplinary arena with the ACAS Code of Practice and the decisions of industrial tribunals, has meant that certain parts of the participatory disciplinary policy at Foodstuffs Ltd has been put under pressure. The employment manager spelled out the central issue:

> The problem is that against the ACAS Code of Practice we have actually decided the penalty which is appropriate before the accused person has had the opportunity to state his case. The advantage of our tribunal system is that where it is a 'fair cop' as it were, the employee doesn't want the embarrassment of public exposure to his crime and is only too willing to say 'Yes I did it, can I have my penalty and go away and forget about it?' The disadvantage is, of course, that the person who is said to have committed the offence does not have the opportunity to state his point of view before any judgement is made.

For Don, penetration of the state law via pressure to comply with the ACAS code would mean a fundamental change in the tribunal's operation: 'Giving the offender a chance to state his case wouldn't have much effect on the tribunal but to have him there would actually mean the end of it.'

However, when pressure was brought to bear on the disciplinary policy of the Tyre Company (employing 2,400 workers in the rubber industry) to change its joint management-union run disciplinary tribunal, the outcome was an endorsement and strengthening of the existing system. The industrial relations manager explained how, following the establishment of the employment protection legislation, an employee took the company to an industrial tribunal on the grounds that its 'misconduct committee was not right — the trade unions had no right to sit in judgement of their fellow workers'. He went on to describe what happened:

> The chairman of the industrial tribunal ruled that if a trade union mutually agreed to a system of tribunal, and one in which the man's trade union can say 'We don't agree' and therefore you've got a hung jury — you have to adjourn it and let the man go back to work, then it was fair. He said ours was clearly written up in an agreement which everybody had put their signature to.

At the same time, however, the chairman of the industrial court suggested that the company's joint participatory approach to discipline might be modified:

> He said 'I would like to point out that I think you should inform your employee of the offence he has committed in writing. You should spell out his rights under the law and his right to appeal. He should have his shop steward with him.' So we accepted all that. 'And having done that I think that your system is very good.'

The examples of state intervention in both Foodstuffs and the Tyre Company illustrate how state penetration is never total, since the company disciplinary policy always retains a substantial proportion of that which was autonomously generated, despite the forcefulness of the pressure to change. Moreover, as we shall see below, because the formal disciplinary policy of a company is only one component of the overall control package, then any policy changes that are a result of state penetration are even less significant than they seem. There are, however, other ways in which state law and private participatory justice are interdependent and these ways have a significant contribution to make to the legitimation of the overall control package.

As with managerial justice, participatory justice is also penetrated by general legal concepts. These operate to legitimate aspects of the private system by making them appear to be as 'just' as formal courts of law seem to be. This can be seen in the account of Andy, a senior shop steward and tribunal member, who compared some aspects of the working of Foodstuffs' joint tribunal to the work of the courts:

We could have access to interview people but we don't see that as part of our role. I mean, the JPs who sit in the courts don't do the investigating and the policework do they? They don't meet their customers until they come face to face with them in the dock. Then they have to make their judgement on the evidence by the authorities. We see ourselves in a similar role. Management and worker are like jurymen and women: they retire to consider the verdict; they get into a debate on the evidence and argue amongst themselves until they come up with a solution.

This penetration of state law goes further than mere legal concepts as Andy points out when discussing who becomes a tribunal member: 'some of our members have a bit of experience of this sort of thing because they've been JPs. Mr Pennison's a JP and Mrs Wilson who was on it was a JP.' An interchange of personnel between the private form and the state form is also reflected in Foodstuffs Ltd's investigation department, which is the first and crucial stage in their whole disciplinary process, and is staffed by ex-police officers. Mike, a senior union shop steward, points out the significance of this:

When the investigations department find anybody ... they must submit a report to us, stating what exactly took place: what time and where; whether there were any witnesses and what was said — very much like a court. And that forms the basis really for the complaint against the individual. Usually they try and obtain a signed statement. The people in the investigations department are former members of the police force, or many of them are; they know how to take statements, they know how to give reports and that influences our judgment considerably ... Their integrity has never really been challenged.

So, not only does the state penetrate disciplinary policy via its law concepts and the interchange of its personnel, but in doing so it conveys state law methods and practices which carry considerable influence in determining the case against the individual before the tribunal has even considered it. The dangers of this practice for the individual employee are described well by John, a senior shop steward:

> If somebody is caught doing something then nine times out of ten the investigation department will take the individual into an interviewing room and take a statement from him ... But when you're caught doing something, like when you're outside with the policeman saying 'I'll take a statement from you', your mind is all whizzing round — you may say certain things and then think later 'Oh Christ I didn't really mean that.' But you've signed it and he presents that as evidence and it's too late.

Indeed, for Colin, a senior union representative on the tribunal, these dangers needed to be checked as the autonomy of the investigator sometimes goes beyond the formal rights that an individual might have outside the factory:

> We've got three ex-police people here — their whole lifestyle had been catching criminals and ... they have got a wonderful technique of questioning people ... see this is what we've got to watch because we are only amateurs. I've been there when they've been interviewing people to try and prove a case and sometimes you've got to say 'oi, enough's enough! You're infringing his legal rights — even the police couldn't do this!' You've got to be a bit of a watchdog.

Mike agreed with the importance of this union role:

> We've let people off purely on the basis that the investigations department have gone about it the wrong way ... as a court would if they found that the police hadn't carried out their responsibilities and procedures correctly. If they don't stick to the letter of the law, then ... there's no case to answer.

Ironically, then, the legitimation deriving from the interdependence and exchange of state law concepts and personnel is ultimately limited by the trade union representatives to the tribunal who themselves draw on state law concepts.

State law can also be relied upon by the company as an extension to its own internal systems of disciplinary control. For example, although designed to protect the individual employee, management might utilise state law in order to outflank individual protections that have been built into the internal system. The device of selecting which approach to adopt is especially powerful against individual trade union shop stewards. Colin, a senior union representative at Foodstuffs, explained how this device was used:

> They'd done a shop steward and they sacked him. Had he been an ordinary employee he would have had to go through the tribunal system and I am 99 per cent certain he would have still been working here. But they had fixed opinions of this guy . . . That was it — instant dismissal. Now, when I walked in the room with the management, there in front of me was an open copy of the ACAS Code of Practice which says 'a union representative can be seen in front of the senior steward and dealt with by the company.' It stinks to me! The firm are now saying 'Well we'll now put on the tribunal who we want to and those that we don't we'll see to ourselves because we will use outside words . . . the legislation.' *In other words the company will use ACAS when it suits their purpose, which completely invalidates a local factory tribunal.* (My emphasis)

So, as in the case of managerial justice, the state law can be drawn on as an extension of the internal form of private justice. But it is not the case that state law penetrates in only one way. Just as the company can draw on the state law to extend its disciplinary control, so the state relies on private justice to administer some of its social control. The relations of private justice are therefore also some of the relations of state justice. Grahame, an employee at Foodstuffs, illustrated how this occurs:

> I think the police prefer it that the firm deals with it. It's only petty thieving really . . . not the big time. I mean, if they dragged the police in every time they caught somebody pinching a few bits and pieces then I don't think the police could cope. If the firm pushed it then they would have to take it, obviously. But the police have got more serious things to do than deal with petty thieving like that.

Now clearly any pilfering cases could be prosecuted through

the formal courts, but not only do the courts rely on companies to handle such crimes, the companies themselves prefer to do so. As Mike, a senior steward, says, there is an economic incentive: otherwise, 'the company would be in and out of the courts almost daily dealing with these trivialities'. For Tony, another employee, formal court appearances would bring the company bad publicity:

> Mostly they try to keep things, how would you put it, within the confines of the company — within its own framework. One would have to put your own logic to the reason — the image of the company, bad publicity. It keeps the firm out of the limelight doesn't it? I mean, publicity can do a lot of damage that way.

But the reliance by the state on private justice, also reciprocally concedes to that dimension of social control a certain accommodation to its autonomy. It is not the case that private justice administers a part of state law without at the same time penetrating that law with its own concepts, definitions and levels of tolerance. A particularly significant way this occurs is where private justice imposes its own concepts of theft upon state law.

Reconstructing concepts of crime

Private justice has its own criteria for what counts as theft. Important among these seems to be from whom the property is taken, the amount taken, the frequency with which it is taken, the context under which the taking occurs and the history of the individual concerned. Peter, an employee at Foodstuffs distinguishes between: occasional pilferage which is the result of opportunity; persistent taking of company property or time; and what he sees as the theft of fellow employees' property:

> An odd packet of them . . . I suppose a lot of people have done it over the years, haven't they, especially when they're working amongst them. But in cases where they've persistently fiddled the clock I think they deserve all they get. I have rather strong views here. I think anybody that

fiddles like that ... is robbing — how can I put it? It's not actually theft but it's dishonest. But I don't think you'd report your own people, would you? Unless you'd actual proof of someone stealing your property ... If you've had somebody go in your pocket and stealing your wallet that's different. It's much worse stealing off your own colleagues.

Other employees share these distinctions but have different priorities. Nick, a shop steward at Foodstuffs, is against deliberate theft of company property and clocking offences:

Petty pilfering — everybody does it right from the top to the bottom. All they say is 'it's a bit of bad luck they caught me'. It's something different to stealing — where somebody decides they are going to have something and try and get it through the gate — or to a clock fiddle ... You've got to draw the line because obviously it is criminal. Say you're being paid 8 hours for doing nothing. It's different than doing a quick pilfer as you're going through — that's just temptation.

Wil, an employee, confirms Peter's priority that the most serious offence is theft against the person:

I am bitter against anybody who is caught stealing their workmates' property. That's the only time I think they ought to be handed over to the police. But when it comes to company goods, I think that's fair enough.

These distinctions are also held by the union members on the Foodstuffs' tribunal. Andy, for example, a senior steward on the tribunal, makes a definite distinction between pilfering and theft and shows how this is reflected in the scale of punishments:

Let's take pilfering or theft. The question is the volume and the value of the goods that have been stolen. If it's say minor, one packet, we very often say to the management 'Give him a good ticking off and tell him not to do it again,' because it's not worthy of anything more. Then as the volume increases, some people do it on a big scale, then it's going to warrant more and more ... you will go

The negotiated law of participatory justice 143

from say a day's suspension up, depending on the value of goods stolen, to as much as two week's suspension, if the offence is very grave.

Therefore, the internal handling of cases which break state theft laws results in a certain proportion of employees being protected, for the most that can happen is that they lose their job. They do not get a criminal record. A very accommodative attitude to the offence is adopted. Indeed, for Colin, one of the tribunal representatives, Don, a manager and employees David and Trevor, the importance of participatory justice is in the way in which it *understands* the specific situation of temptation and pressure that often provides the context to an offence — an understanding which they felt would be absent from more formal court settings:

> Now there's a difference between when somebody goes along with a crowbar, yanks the bloody lock open, forces the lock off the door, walks in and comes out with armfuls of it and where a bloke walks through the stock room and walks past a load of stuff, nicely laid out and takes two or three packets. You can say to the company 'Look, you contributed 25 per cent . . . If you hadn't put temptation in his way he probably wouldn't have done it. There's a difference in someone intentionally going to steal it and succumbing to temptation. No way would I ever defend anybody that's walking out with half a dozen packets of it. (Colin)

> I think our understanding of what is a 'fair cop' as opposed to what the outside courts might say, is totally different. We would understand that it is relatively easy to pilfer but that someone would have to deliberately go out of their way to amass a large bedwrapper full of different sorts of biscuits and chocolates. Whereas to the courts a bag full of one sort would be indistinguishable from a bag full of another sort. They wouldn't know the fact that the chap had to go out of his way to round his stuff up. I think you do actually temper what goes on by your knowledge of the site and your knowledge of the working conditions. Which stuff gets left around for several days without being moved — that sort of thing. (Don)

> I wouldn't say the tribunal members were more competent than courts but they know what's going on in the factory, the lay-out and this sort of thing. If you go to a court they've never been here and they don't know the run of the place, they don't know how things work. I think in court, if they knew more about it they'd see things in a different light. (Trevor)
>
> Outside people deal with different crimes everyday and it's just another one. They don't understand the nature of the offence really. It's one in a line. Whereas here they know the details exactly; what the crimes are, what's going on, where it took place — they've had to experience it themselves — and they judge the crime on what they know. (David)

The same expression of the importance of the participatory tribunal in understanding the context and circumstances of the less serious offence can be found in other companies adopting the participatory form. This was expressed well by the industrial relations manager of the Tyre Company:

> When the law becomes involved it's difficult because the judiciary is involved in something that they don't really understand; the feelings on the shop floor, what motivates people. But, that chairman, those three union fellows, that manager who had come up through the shop floor himself, knew what it was like out there, what could have aggravated the situation. Perhaps someone down the line said 'That man is not responsible for that rotten building. It's that man over there that produced that rotten material for him.' You need someone who's in tune with the shop floor. You must know the way people feel or what aggravates them. Temperatures in the summer. Sometimes they are working in temperatures of 230°. A hot summer's evening, sticky, you know, somebody comes along and doesn't bring you the right tyres up. You swear at him. He takes offence — you know shop floor language is shop floor language. I well remember a manager coming to me and saying 'I'm going to fire him — he swore at me.' I said 'Well you swear all the time! What do you mean? Don't you come that with me. You've got no case there.

The negotiated law of participatory justice 145

> If you swear at him he's entitled to swear back at you . . . Well I don't say he's entitled to swear *at* you but in the course of conversation he can swear.'

In short then, the autonomy of private justice is relied on by the state to exercise some of its control and in the course of doing so it necessarily has some of its concepts of law penetrated. But the accommodation of crime by the disciplinary process itself suggests that, relative to the perceived notion of the operation of formal law, the employee is actually getting fairer treatment. This comparison then serves to legitimate the internal process, making it seem acceptable. Indeed, the most significant feature of this mutuality between state law and private justice is the legitimation of the private form as a direct result of presenting either/or options.

The duality of state law and factory law in the process of legitimation

The existence of an externally autonomous form of justice (state law) which is conceptualised as more punitive and potentially invocable, exercises considerable influence over whether the decisions of the internal system of private discipline are acceptable. In its crudest manifestation this is the interdependence between power and authority, between coercive and ideological domination, and it is the basis of legitimating all social control. A manager of the Tyre Company illustrates the point very clearly:

> In order to impose something you've got to have an alternative which is even stronger. 'Please stop doing that.' 'No.' 'Please stop doing that or I'll knock your bloody head off.' Unless you add that you've just got 'No'. So in a social democracy it's a very delicate balance all the time as to which way you are moving. If it was Nazi Germany or the Soviet Union it would be very simple. You could bring up a troop of MKVD and shoot a couple of dozen . . . Now you can run your society like that if you've got the SS or the KGB running the show behind you, but we haven't. So it goes by consent.

The 'consent' to private justice, because of the existence of something stronger, was clearly displayed in the comments of the employees of Foodstuffs. The important point is not so much the accuracy of the reports about what goes on in the formal legal system, or in the internal tribunal, but that in contrasting the two as alternative forms of justice, the disciplinary policy as a whole is rendered acceptable. Clearly a major criterion of comparison is in the softer penalties imposed by the internal tribunal which stem from the more understanding attitude taken to some rule-breaking. Trevor, for example, believes that the courts impose much harsher penalties than would be imposed by the internal tribunal:

> I think the majority of people get away a lot lighter than they would if it went to outsiders. See they might get a week's suspension — say they lose a week's money. Whereas if you went to the court outside you'd probably get a stiff fine which would come to more than a week's wages. They'd lose a lot more that way.

Ian argues that this stiffer punishment is inevitable because unlike the internal tribunal, outside courts see the offence as separate from the employee's circumstances and life history and do not consider his service to the company:

> It's better than prosecution in a court. The management consider your work record, how long you've been here, or if you might have done it before. In court they've got too much to do to consider all that. They just take you as another case. In the joint tribunal you don't know what sentence you're going to get, but the chances are it will be considered fairly.

However, not everyone takes the view that the sentences of the tribunal are less severe than those of the outside courts. Mike, a senior steward, for example, says:

> The only part of it that disturbs me a little is whether or not the penalties that we impose are not more severe than perhaps the court would impose. I can remember a case of a woman working here who was caught shoplifting outside. Now as a result of that, the police visited her home and found there some of our roller towels. So then the police

came to the company and said 'Had she got authority for these towels?' — 'No, she'd been stealing them.' A tribunal met and decided on a week's suspension. So she lost a week's pay. For the shoplifting offence the court gave her a suspended sentence — which means nothing.

However, for John, another steward, although the court penalties may seem to be less severe than that of the tribunal, the stigma of a court appearance is far worse than the stigma that might surround an appearance before the internal disciplinary tribunal:

> It could be argued that some of the penalties dished out by the tribunal are more severe than if you went to a court, but on the other hand you see, once you've gone to a court of law you're a criminal! You're branded and it's difficult then to get another job anywhere. So at least we're preventing giving an individual a record.

Both Wil and Nick, for example, explain that the tribunal is acceptable to them because the public shaming consequences of the formal legal system are much worse:

> I've had over thirty years here and I've never known anyone crib about the tribunal. I mean if they hadn't got it here, they'd have the outside police in wouldn't they? And then your name and everything's gone. Here you might get two or three days' suspension ... which surely is better than having it plastered in all the papers. (Wil)

> It's more or less done for you here, isn't it? You know you've done something wrong and something's got to happen ... getting two days' suspension and saying 'I'll do it.' If you go to court you've got all the nonsense of appearing and goodness knows what and ... it's more clinical ... and the neighbours would say, 'Where's he going in his best suit?' and you walk into court and there's Mrs so and so, 'Oh I didn't know you worked there'. (Nick)

For Martin, a senior steward on the tribunal, the internal stigma is less because most people not only understand moderate pilfering of company property, but actually see it as a means of status enhancement:

> What's the greater shame: half a dozen blokes you work with or printed in the *Mail* that you've been in court and fined £50 for stealing? The next door neighbour knows you've done it then! If it's in work — only your workmates know. And let's face it, there's an unwritten law that if you can do the company, then you're all right.

Wil too points out that there is the permanency of this stigma to consider, in the form of a record:

> If you go to an outside court, you've got a police record. If you wanted to start another job or anything, you've got that hanging over you. But if it's been dealt with here, you haven't.

Trevor, another employee, believes the police record is to be avoided at all costs:

> If I was stopped I would prefer to go to the firm's tribunal. You might get a black mark on your works record for so many years . . . but if you've got a black mark outside, you've always got a black mark.

Nick takes the same view:

> I think they probably tend to accept this inasmuch as it doesn't go on the records. They go for another job. They haven't been dismissed for stealing. In a court that would not happen. If I were caught doing something, I'd rather be called in here and have them say, 'Well you know you've been a naughty boy. You're going to get the chop anyway. How about resigning?' I'd resign and get out.

Ian an employee, and David, a shop steward, contrast the courts and the internal tribunal in terms of the anxiety created by the former, whereas this is minimised by the internal system which is much faster:

> The tribunal's better than the courts — it keeps it in the family. If a person's done some pilfering, at court they don't take anything else into consideration. It's just another case. Also it's a big waste of time . . . It might

The negotiated law of participatory justice 149

take five years for your sentence to come up. One of the main advantages here is that it's over and done with in a short time. (Ian)

Well the main advantage is that it doesn't go outside the works. When it starts going outside, that's when people start worrying. Because they are going to court aren't they? I think everybody prefers it to be settled here. It's over within a week — it might be over the next day. Whereas if you go to court you might have to wait months. It's what's going to happen in six months. (David)

Colin, a senior shop steward, maintains that the penalty of the court is actually a treble one involving stigma and a fine as well as automatic job loss. Internally, in contrast, not only is public knowledge of the offence restricted, it is also less traumatic:

To me, what is the ultimate sentence? If a bloke's working, the ultimate sentence is to be out of a job. If you go outside to court you can get fined £100 and the company ain't having you back.

As Martin said:

Some people say 'That's a bit steep for pinching a quid's worth of chocolate. If he'd have gone to court the magistrate wouldn't have fined him that much! But what they don't realise is that management would just dismiss him and if the case was considered serious enough they would prosecute him as well. You'd be prosecuted and you'd go to court and you'd be fined a sum of money, perhaps less than you'd lose by suspension, but you've got no job. You're on the dole so there is a big difference between the two you see.

Whether or not this extra coercion from unemployment is significant as a sanction depends in part upon the general availability of jobs. John pointed out that when unemployment was high, this source of control was obviously greater, although whether or not job non-availability can be relied on by managements as a coercive measure also depends upon an individual employee's attitudes and thereby their autonomy, as we shall see below (pp. 172-6).

In short then, the acceptability of private justice depends upon the creation of a conceptual comparison between the disciplinary policy and the more coercive state legal system. But the ideological process that we have described resulting in acceptability of the total system of control is also employed in rendering different aspects of that control acceptable. It is precisely for this reason that there is not one disciplinary form operative within participatory justice, but a number of inter-related parts, each offering a range of punishments and sanctions.

Diversification and legitimation

It should now be very apparent that a company's disciplinary policy is only one part of a range of semi-autonomous parts that make up the totality of social control operative on the members of that company. As we saw in the previous chapter, most companies have a formalised disciplinary policy while they informally rely on the range of other control elements. In this chapter we have seen that some companies incorporate more of those informal elements into their formal policy. They institutionalise a joint participatory approach to discipline as a part of the overall disciplinary policy. It is not the case, as is sometimes thought, that all aspects of discipline are participatory. Rather, the participatory component is used selectively and restricts union involvement to one narrow area. The Washing Machine Company, for example, while claiming a paternalistic development, formally incorporated participatory justice only in decisions on sick pay eligibility, where it was used principally to control false claims. Cases of rule-breaking at the factory were dealt with by traditional managerial justice. The Tyre Company's joint management-union misconduct committee excluded theft cases. Very illustrative of this diversification of internal disciplinary systems is that operative at Foodstuffs Ltd, where the formal disciplinary policy made reference to no less than four separate but interdependent elements, in addition to its reliance on state law and informally on both

The negotiated law of participatory justice 151

peer group pressure and employee self-discipline.

I described the two-stage disciplinary tribunal earlier in this chapter (p. 135). This handles offences such as pilferage, smoking, horse-play, etc. In addition to this though, there is a standard managerial disciplinary procedure, which covers late and absent time, work performance and some safety offences. Tony, a trade union shop steward, describes how this element of managerial justice works:

> There's a system which runs parallel to the tribunal. Take lateness and absence — the local line management in the firm would privately tell a person 'OK, don't let it happen again.' If in a short period of time they're late again or absent again then the management would have them and say 'This is the second warning I've given you.' The shop stewards would probably be in on that one and it would be recorded. The final warning he has from his line manager and if he persists he's given a written warning that the next instance will mean dismissal. A thing like that wouldn't have to go to the tribunal. It runs alongside it. You see, the whole system is interwoven — it's extremely fair.

Ann, the employment manager, explains how decisions are made about which internal or indeed, external discipline is appropriate for a particular case:

> The employment officer looks at the evidence submitted and decides in the first place whether there is anything to answer, whether it's suspicion or fact. And secondly whether it's sufficiently grave to call a tribunal. We run the two systems side by side. The company reserves the right, in all cases, to say this offence is either too major or too minor to go before the tribunal. If it's too major, we will either summarily dismiss it, or we will send it to the police.

However, the decision whether to opt for managerial justice, the joint tribunal, or to bring in the outside enforcement agencies, is neither automatic nor clear. The actual instances of rule-breaking are more difficult to disentangle as one of the managers, Don, explains:

> One of the areas which we don't define too clearly is this matter of actual shop floor rule-breaking. One thing is a

disciplinary offence and one isn't. I find myself somewhat unhappy about the distinctions. If, for example, you catch a bloke in the wrong department or loitering around or clearly asleep, say, is that something that you should deal with through the local management chain? — the local manager giving him a warning and putting it on his record card, which could ultimately lead to dismissal if he did it again — or is it something you bring to the disciplinary tribunal as somebody who was defrauding the company of money because they were not working and they were supposed to be? . . . There's the petty end of the range; minor clocking offences, stealing for personal use, smoking. And then there's the other end of the range where there's conspiracy to defraud the company by prolonged booking out of somebody an hour after they should have done, and stealing to supply a shop down in the market, or something like this. At that end of the range, someone who gets a fortnight's suspension or holiday gift withdrawn when they've been guilty of fairly massive defrauding of the company by prolonged claiming of overtime or something like that feels very lucky he wasn't handed over to the police. There is a debate around actually at what stage we should do that. Our security manager happens to think we should hand over everyone guilty of stealing goods as a matter of principle.

Given the apparent management dominated nature of the decision about which aspect of internal discipline to invoke it is surprising that this crucial decision is not more frequently the subject of dispute. But as Paul, a manager, says:

Once or twice where management chose not to involve the tribunal there have been cases of the union side saying it should have been taken through tribunal. But surprisingly enough it hasn't been particularly contentious.

The central reason for the acceptance of the managerial decision to invoke one rather than another type of discipline has to do with the very plurality of the variety of internal systems. The diversity of systems enables different semi-autonomous parts within the organisation to exploit the plurality for their own interests. At one level, for example, the unions can use the diversity of internal systems in order to maximise their power to defeat the company. As the shop steward, John, explains:

> I think the other systems complement the tribunal, not undermine it. I'm talking from a negotiator's point of view and as far as I am concerned I will try and find any way possible to reduce the effect of whatever is going to happen to a person. If I've got the disciplinary tribunal or if I've got the negotiation area or any other that I can think of where the amount of punishment would be less — then I'll use that. I'll take him through until the system is completely bare. You see the fiddling bits — health and safety at work, stealing, those things — have always been seen as an issue that should be taken up by the individual trade unions. There are occasions when we would wish to take things outside the tribunal. I'll give you an example. There was a chap who was trolleying loads and he found out that he could double-up — still doing the work quite legitimately, but he was getting two tabs for carrying one load. They wanted to take him to a discipline tribunal for fiddling the firm. But we said this is a person using his initiative to be able to work quicker. So there are occasions when we say quite clearly to the company that there's no way we see that going to a discipline tribunal.

This exploitation of the diversity of internal disciplinary systems is also undertaken by management, especially, as we saw in the account of Colin (see above, p. 140), to circumvent systems that might not work in the company's interests. John illustrates this further:

> I've had my outside official called in directly under the ACAS Code of Practice to discipline me. This was because of my activities as a senior shop steward. They never won it obviously, but they tried it on. I mean, they've done it with three of us up to now. They got rid of one — he got the sack. He was a trouble-maker, but he was good as far as we were concerned . . . We believe the company deliberately fabricated the issue so that they could get rid of him. He was a thorn in the company's back and in the end they got rid of him.

A further significant pointer to an understanding of the way in which the company's social control package is legitimated is the way in which the different parallel internal disciplinary systems are differentially ranked by employees as being of varying severity in terms of their punitive consequences. Irrespective of how severe the general level of punishment of the systems, if one system is perceived to be less severe than the others then it will gain a relative acceptance in the eyes of those who are subject to discipline. In other words, having the tribunal appear as the least severe form of discipline of the range of internal systems, renders it more acceptable to employees than would be the case if it existed alone as *the* disciplinary policy. As Mike explained:

> The workforce in general, respect the tribunal and are glad that it operates because I believe they think, and quite rightly so, that without it they would be subject to far sterner disciplinary measures.

The same ideological significance of diversity of control systems explains the usefulness of staging any one of them into a process where the subsequent stages are more severe than the previous ones. As Mike again says 'If he's guilty he thinks to himself "Well I've got away with it fairly light, it's not too bad. I'll accept that because the alternatives might be worse."' And although the individual has the option of taking his case from the informal to the formal tribunal, he does this only about one in fifty cases for, as Paul says:

> There is a feeling on the employee's part that if he goes to the formal tribunal he's as likely to have a more severe punishment than to get it reduced or removed altogether. I think that is the tendency. Therefore, unless you've got a dismissal when there is nothing else you can lose, people would be very loath indeed to go to a formal tribunal. And also the whole court-like connotations it has turns people off.

So far it has been implied that there are three disciplinary systems at Foodstuffs: one is to go to outside agencies such as the police or industrial courts; another is to use managerial justice; and a third is the joint disciplinary tribunal. It is also clear from earlier discussions that trade unionists might be considered as a special case and handled by a kind of managerial justice that draws heavily on the externally validated ACAS Code of Practice for shop stewards. But it is not only stewards as a group who are subject to a system of discipline that is separate from the rest. A fourth system of discipline is that operative for managers. But the effect of this is not exclusive to managers since it is used as part of the ideological process of rendering disciplinary forms for employees more acceptable. Thus the disciplinary system for managers, while seen to be different, is also presented as far harsher than the other systems, especially the tribunal system. Don, a manager, explains the reason for this:

> I am quite clear the management penalties are far higher than one actually would impose on the shop floor for a similar offence. I think that's right — if at any time we were seen to be trying to get a manager off lightly I think that would be fatal. It would be the 'old boy' network, etc. It's got to be seen to be above reproach and I think free from any suggestion that we try to protect management. The manager is normally disciplined. It's then our practice to see the three members of the shop floor tribunal and say to them 'We wish you to know that a manager was guilty of stealing and has been punished by such and such.' We don't mention the manager's name, and their normal procedure is to thank us for informing them, and on they go. But we do it deliberately so that if there's any rumours around they know what the actual facts were about the penalty and things like that.

That the 'correct' message is received about the relative unacceptability of management's own discipline to the merits of their tribunal is apparent from the employees' accounts. Those of Sue, Mike, and Nick, are illustrative:

> I don't think it matters because they really deal with their own differently, don't they? I'm not sure whether they do have a tribunal. They do get dealt with harshly. I have known of it — they do get dealt with very harshly. (Sue)

> I don't altogether accept that 'what's good for the goose

is good for the gander' and that a theft of say £1's goods is just as bad if it's done by a manager as if it's done by a cleaner ... I don't know, but I tend to believe that they are more hard on the management than they are on the workforce through the tribunal system. (Mike)

Well, from the general talk I've heard, I think that our system is better than theirs'. It's just talk I've heard. I think they tend to be more severe — saying you're in management, you've done wrong and you should know better. (Nick)

But this view is not taken by everyone. John, a shop steward, for example, believes that the unions ought to be on the managerial disciplinary body just as management are on their tribunal:

We've got a joint tribunal with management and workers sitting down to discipline the ordinary shop floor worker then if management are caught we should sit on their discipline tribunal to discipline them as well. They say, 'Well we'll take care of them.' And we say 'Well we don't agree with that because we don't know how you're taking care of them!' They've already got the ace you see. Whereas they've got control over us, we haven't got over them. They can sit in judgement on us but we can't on them. So that's their benefit within the tribunal system and our benefit is that we should look at ways in which we get the least possible inconvenience for our people.

In short, then, the diversification of internal systems of discipline, not only render the less severe option relatively acceptable, but in so far as this option is seen as *the* disciplinary policy, more harsh options are also carried as legitimate. We have seen that participatory justice maximises the use of ideological domination in terms of the way it structures its social control package. Rather than conceal the range of semi-autonomous parts which constitute the totality of social control, participatory justice acknowledges the existence of these and employs them in such a way as to render discipline acceptable to those upon whom it is exercised. We have seen how it does this by contrasting state law and its own

The negotiated law of participatory justice 157

participatory 'form': by presenting one marginally less punitive internal system of control as the best alternative amongst a range of internal systems; and by extending this diversification of control within any one system through the use of staging. But this by no means exhausts the ideological manifestations of the participatory form. Indeed, it can be argued that these reach a climax in the policy's explicit use of union participation in decision-making.

Co-opting the unions: participation without representation

We saw in the examination of managerial justice how most companies and organisations rely on the trade unions at certain stages of their disciplinary process, principally warnings and appeals, and how this dependence is instrumental to the achievement of legitimacy. We also saw how the disciplinary policy relied on informal union 'co-operation' to exercise part of its social control function. In the case of those companies that formally involve unions in a participatory role in decisions about private justice, this legitimation is even more secured. Examination of the way this operates at Foodstuffs suggests that a formal policy of sharing disciplinary responsibility among management and unions actually relies on the individual autonomy of union members to penetrate union collective interests. The formal sharing of responsibility for administering discipline between management and unions by the incorporation of individual and senior trade union representatives, paradoxically absolves the latter from their advocacy and representative role and temporarily and in a limited way imbues them with a managerial authority. It is almost as though the formal recognition of individual responsibility and autonomy, of itself, generates a management attitude. The employment manager of Foodstuffs, Ann, expressed the value of this participation and showed how it presented individual trade unionists with a conflict:

> It isn't as straightforward as management and union, because the purpose of a tribunal is to try and forget your

158 The negotiated law of participatory justice

station in life and that isn't always easy, for a trade union representative or for a manager. But if there's a conflict of interest they stay there in session until they sort it out . . . It's a bit like electing a pope you know! The only way you get away from that pressure is if the manager and the accused take on their traditional roles, with the shop steward brought in if the accused wishes. There is a very strong trade union view that they shouldn't be collectively responsible for the disciplining of their members but their role is that of representation against managerial discipline. I don't think the trade union have really reconciled that problem. Individual trade union representatives who happen to work within the tribunal have managed to reconcile that problem for themselves obviously, by sitting on it.

The reliance on individual unionists' autonomy is very apparent from the accounts of a senior representative on the tribunal, Colin:

When people come to me and say 'What shall I do?' You can only say 'Well, if you've done wrong admit it; just say so, don't try and argue and tell lies.' What can we do, really? To be very honest — very little because they've broken the law. 'Just admit it', I tell them, because I won't tell lies and 'it's no good coming to me and saying "so and so down the road is doing it." Don't throw mud at everybody because it's not going to make your sentence any lighter. All you're doing is upsetting what is nine times out of ten, a smooth running department.' Quite honestly I've got no time for people like that. I say 'Look pal, it's nothing to do with me you've been copped.' You know some people seem to think I'm Perry Mason in a wheelchair! I can't do a barrister's job . . . You've got to keep discipline. One can't use the tribunal to do away with any discipline — it's not used to undermine it.

A further point about the co-option of unions is that the joint tribunal channels an individual's autonomy away from conflict with management, which might frustrate its exercise of discipline, into a debate about which is the most appropriate punishment for the offence concerned. The issue is

The negotiated law of participatory justice

not so much why the offence was committed but whether the reason why it was committed can provide grounds for a more lenient response. Indeed, as we saw earlier, since the employee's guilt is 'convincingly' established outside the hearing by the investigation department, the tribunal members' energies are invested in a debate about what the appropriate disciplinary response should be. As Don, a manager, says:

> We generally have little problem in agreeing whether someone is guilty or not. If there is a problem it's what the appropriate sentence should be. We get hung up between the need to be consistent, like pinching a quid's worth of goods is a day's suspension, and between making the punishment fit the crime or particularly making the punishment fit the offender

Similarly, Trevor, an employee, says:

> The thing is both management and unions have got the same interests at heart . . . he's done something wrong so he's got to be punished — but what punishment to give? . . . The workers' representatives know he's got to have a punishment of some description.

In order to preserve this focus rather than one addressing collective issues with management, any procedures which would divide management and union members on the tribunal are strictly avoided. As Ann said:

> I think voting is counterproductive to what you're trying to achieve. It evades the issue and it helps you to hide, somewhat anonymously, behind solving the problem. Conflict of interest is not an admissible solution . . . You do not come out of the room until you've got an agreement — you can't walk away and pretend the problem isn't yours. Once you know that, you're on your metal to try and come to some conclusion . . . If you know that it's got to be done by consensus rather than voting it actually draws your attention to the evidence . . . to ensure that the penalty that you're trying to impose is a fair one. It makes you leave your traditional roles.

A further device which enables the co-option of the individual unionist away from his collectivist commitment is to ensure that those members who are appointed to the tribunal are senior representatives. That senior representatives are already seen as detached from, and hierarchically superior to, ordinary trade union members eases their transition into the quasi-managerial role that shared disciplinary decision-making imposes upon them. Paul, a manager at Foodstuffs, recognises the value of the appointment of senior stewards:

> Because they are the senior stewards they take a slightly more dispassionate view. I suppose the reason why that's apparent is because the senior steward involved in the tribunal system is operating from a factory-wide point of view, whereas the shop steward coming as an observer or as an advocate is from the same area, department, the same sort of work area, a chum quite possibly, of the guy who is coming up. So there's a different sense of loyalty. The employee doesn't know that the shop steward might actually be making the bullets for him as much as the manager making the bullets in the tribunal situation.

Thus even though trade unions are participating in disciplinary decisions, the extent of their involvement in these as trade unionists or employee representatives, is limited to that of a subordinate role in which their mere presence is seen as a privilege. A senior manager, Don, says:

> You start from the premise that it's the manager's job to manage the factory and in order to do that they have an accepted set of conditions of employment — a set of rules ... which are formally agreed with the trade unions on site and which every employee has a copy of ... Through the tribunal the managers are effectively sharing or inviting the shop floor to see that justice is done in terms of administration of those rules ... Management actually execute their duty by taking the advice of three senior stewards who are there to see that the system is fair ... The senior steward on the tribunal feels very responsible for discipline. If he and his two trade union colleagues are allowing the informal tribunal system to fall into disrepute, they've lost any say in how the discipline is run. It might be an envisaged privilege that they've got.

The negotiated law of participatory justice 161

> At times they probably say 'how on earth did we get landed with this?' because it faces them with some pretty embarrassing dilemmas. But at the end of the day they would recognise that that's the price they've got to pay for being treated as a senior steward in a responsible way.

The advantages of the participatory role granted to trade unions is summarised by Ann:

> For all the hiccups, the concerns, the difficulties, the system is accepted and that's got to be an advantage. It makes management's job easier in one respect and it makes representatives' jobs easier as well because since it is not really right for any individual to feel that they have to represent an employee come hell or high water, the tribunal allows the shop stewards not to do that. It makes management's job easier in that there is seen to be fairness and you don't always find yourself challenged having taken disciplinary action.

Nor is this assertion of the acceptability of the tribunal simply wishful thinking by management. Many employees see formal involvement by unions in discipline as being in their interests. They fail to see that, at the same time, such involvement also means losing the representative role. The accounts of Trevor, an employee, Andy, a senior shop steward and tribunal member and Nick, another steward, are illustrative:

> We've got manager and worker participating together, that's the thing. Everybody's happy because you've got both sides of the fence. They're together. Although the workers' representatives know that you've got to have some punishment — they can also hold the reins a bit if they think it's going too far . . . And employees know that if they've got some union reps. or worker reps. there, they'll get a fairer deal . . . that somebody there will try to look after their interests. (Trevor)

> The fact that they have been sentenced by their own people means they accept the rules — they know they are wrong and they are expecting suspension because they've been conditioned to it . . . The reps. feel bound

to look after their own and see that the sentence isn't too severe ... You feel there is somebody on your side — the management is seen as 'them' and 'us'. (Nick)

I believe that they know it's not just a question of them against the investigation department who represent the company or the management. They know there is an element of their own organisation, jointly with the management, who'll deal with them as well and that is something which they can't ignore ... They know that the people who are on the tribunal are there mainly for the reason that people trust them to do a job without prejudice or bias. It's become accepted and that's why there are very few cases where a person will deny it or attempt to talk their way out of it. They say, 'it's a fair cop'. (Andy)

Indeed, some employees do not realise that the union involvement goes as far as joint decision-making, believing that it is merely a forum for the traditional management-union collective bargaining. Tony, for example, says:

I didn't believe the trade union took part in the result. Well I wouldn't like to think that, because I'm a trade unionist and I pay them to look after my conditions of employment and to look after my wages. Now having said that, if I'm going to go in there, where my trade union colleagues are sitting, I believe that they should be there for my defence. Whether I was in the right or in the wrong I would expect my trade union to stand by me. That's what they are elected for. Now if they are going to be a party to a decision by that tribunal then they are not there for my protection. I don't believe the trade union should be a party to a decision on their own member who pays dues for his protection. I would rather take a friend in who would speak on my behalf and definitely defend me at the trial.

In contrast a minority of employees are aware of the co-option that participatory justice implies and as a result are suspicious of it:

There isn't many union members is there? And I mean

The negotiated law of participatory justice 163

they aren't low enough on the shop floor to be able to influence anybody else . . . Oh yes they're union but they're the top union. They're not your shop floor union. They're your little 'uns at the top, you know, get all the perks. Those are the one's that sit on the tribunal. (Liz)

I don't think sometimes the union are all for you. I think they are sometimes on the management's side . . . You get a feeling that you've got nobody on your side if you've done anything wrong . . . The union here that I belong to, I just don't trust them. (Sue)

I know that there are some people that I definitely would not like to judge me. I wouldn't trust them with a pair of socks. It depends on how you get on with a person. If you know some of the people on the tribunal you've got to be careful because they might be prejudiced against you. I've got the back up of one or two people here — I wouldn't like to go in front of them. (Ian)

Yet others are aware that the co-option of the unions within the joint tribunal can extend beyond its formally constituted limits and thereby be used as a means whereby management can informally penetrate employee groups. Grahame illustrates the point well:

If the management want to get across to anybody that they've got their eye on, they can just have a word in the union rep.'s ear — 'so and so was seen up in the moulding He's been in the office two or three times for not doing the job. Now what's he doing up there? Tell him he's been seen, so the next time he'll be in the office.' The bloke thinks the union rep.'s on his side when he does this . . . but it's a stepping stone between the management and the worker. It might be enough to deter them — just a word in their ear.

As with all interdependent, semi-autonomous parts, however, it is not the case that penetration only goes one way. It is not, for example, only employees that are penetrated by the managerial co-option of unions through the company disciplinary policy. At the same time the union involvement gives some genuine protection to individual employees against over-zealous managers. As Colin says, managers can build up cases against individuals:

> There's nothing to stop my gaffer having his own notebook in his desk. He can put it on my record and rub it off but he's got his own dossier on me. And let's face it, every manager has got people he would like to get rid of . . . I think especially modern day management would like the tribunal removed because they see it as undermining their position. They would like the right to hire and fire which has never been the right of any manager here.

Indeed, from the employee's point of view, it is the protection against victimisation that is seen to be the most important aspect of the joint tribunal. This is particularly well brought out in the following views of employees and trade unionists:

> Even if the boss had got something in for you, I don't think he could use the tribunal because of the fact that the union is there. (Wil)

> I think you might get a case where the manager doesn't like the particular person and he could be victimised, whereas if you've got a committee, a lot of those people are impartial and they judge the case on its merits which I think is a very good system rather than depending on the judgement of one man. (Peter)

> I think if it was management on their own they would tend to bully you but with the union there they've got to lay it on the line . . . So the union bloke is there to see they don't overstep the mark. He isn't defending the person. He's only there to see that justice is done. (Grahame)

> If we didn't have a tribunal system the people would say, 'He can get away with it, because the manager likes him. I can't because he doesn't like me.' Whereas I think the workforce know that the people who represent them will be fair so therefore they know that these people will protect them when they are right but not protect them when they are wrong. (Martin)

> I don't think the company would use a back door way of

getting rid of anybody. I don't think they would victimise them . . . I think they would take them to task and try and do it via the rules . . . You see the one chap who did go was a steward and he was a bit of a thorn in the side but he was really caught going home with stuff. I think when he was caught he knew what he was in for and he resigned there and then. (Nick)

However, as with other aspects of the social control package, the perception of a better deal through union involvement is another way in which the tribunal system is legitimated. As David says:

I think you get a fairer deal because you've got your own representatives. If you just had management, people would be more inclined to think that they would got more punishment. The union are working with the men on the shop floor and they know what's going on so they are more understanding . . . It doesn't actually cut down the sentence . . . but I think people are much happier going knowing they've got representatives on there. They'll accept the punishment easier from 50/50 rather than from complete management. If it was all management they would think they were being picked on.

Therefore, although some general protection exists through union involvement in many cases it would seem that management were able to impose their own views on what should happen. Union involvement meant that protection from such managerial penetration was less possible. As Tony says, 'you are protected all the way along the line but I believe management have a hand in this sort of thing. If your face didn't fit you'd get the banger'. As Nick pointed out above, the victimisation may be achieved by sticking to the rules. Bob, another employee, explains how sometimes the protections of the formal tribunal can be circumvented:

I don't think they drum up cases but I think they do watch certain people. There are certain people that have to be careful. These tribunals are all very well, everything's supposedly brought out in the open and written down, but there are a lot of little things that don't go through.

Some people can remember a lot of things from a long time ago and bring them up in a situation like that any time they like. Well I've had personal experience of my manager saying 'That fellow, I know he smokes. I know where he goes and he wants to be careful because I could use him.' It's a weapon.

Grahame, another employee, describes further how this informal pressure by management can be brought to bear on certain individuals without any need to go through the joint tribunal:

There are ways and means that management can get rid of people that they don't particularly like or who don't do their jobs well. They can use the disciplinary code as a threat. Sometimes this works; sometimes it doesn't. They could pick them up for smoking. As you know we're not supposed to smoke in the factory and they would deliberately look out for them if they go smoking and have them that way. But it's difficult to deliberately have them for pilfering . . . If a person's blotted their record and they are not good workers and they are usually a bad influence on the remainder of their mates — management make it difficult for them. They don't give them a permanent job. They move them about here, there and everywhere and they get restless.

A similar illustration was given by Ian:

It's not the tribunal that's used to single out people but certainly if you're in dispute they'll watch you more than they might watch other people. If people are taking a lot, their eyes are on them . . . Detectives might be told to watch people who have been active in the union. We've lost one or two recently. One union secretary got done on a clocking offence. If they want, they could get rid of anyone for taking stuff. They're not too strict but they can pick it up if they want to. If they've got a reason . . . It's there if they need it.

Ian, like Grahame, also points out that it is not necessary for a person whom the management might want to dismiss to be

The negotiated law of participatory justice 167

disciplined through formal or even informal pressure. The same effect can be brought about by other, more subtle means:

> They might be put in a position where they have to leave. They might be put on a job that they don't want to do and that's what's happened to me before now ... They just get bored of doing a job or say, 'Oh there's no money in this' and they'll get fed up with being moved around so they'll go and get a job somewhere else. It looks good because the company don't have to lay anyone off.

However, it is not the case that management will always use every means at their disposal to eliminate those unionists or employees whom they find objectionable, even when to do so would be supported by the workforce. Nick, for example, described the case of a shop steward who was,

> an awful thorn in their side, and he was causing a hell of a lot of trouble and he survived right the way through. In fact there were times when the shop floor — how can I put this? — were considering ways and means to get rid of him. He was such a blasted nuisance to everybody. Had the company, at that time, actually done it, there would have been absolutely no resistance at all from the shop floor. But they didn't.

Nor is it the case that only the management penetrate the joint disciplinary policy. The same is true of the unions, whose own semi-autonomy enables them to penetrate the policy on behalf of the members and themselves. Indeed, that this can happen is seen by management as one of the greatest disadvantages of the joint tribunal system. Ann, for example, says:

> I have seen the tribunal so affected once when a trade union representative who happened to be a tribunal member used his position to represent his member and prevent a case achieving a verdict. And as our tribunal is currently constituted, that facility is there. It's open to corruption and abuse ... His opening remark before the case was 'I am convinced this man is innocent' and throughout the whole proceedings he never changed his position ... His two trade union colleagues found

themselves in a very difficult position, because it brought in the trade union representative role, as opposed to the collective disciplinary role . . . In the end one of the other representatives sat on the fence and refused to decide and the verdict was 'not proven'. See he avoided the responsibilities the tribunal put upon him and if that happens the tribunal is completely valueless.

Don described a similar case of

a shop steward who used to go to great lengths to lecture to all the new night employees about the iniquities of smoking — that if they got caught they deserved what they got. It was very interesting that he regarded anyone who got caught smoking on nights in a very personal manner. Like they'd let him down. He was a very powerful and autocratic shop steward. If somebody had been here a fortnight and they got caught smoking, he was the devil's own bloke not to actually insist on the chap being dismissed. He was influencing the whole thing . . . If you get the wrong person who's in it for personal gain, stature or whatever, you'll get the 'little Hitler' come up through the system and God help them if they get that. That's the one thing that would be death to any system based on our lines.

So far then, we have examined the interpenetration of different semi-autonomous parts as these are formally constituted within the joint disciplinary tribunal. However, as was the case with managerial justice, participatory justice also relies on the existence of an informally constituted set of semi-autonomous parts. Of major importance is the reliance on employee peer group pressure. The other, no less significant, is the reliance on employee self-discipline. I shall look at each of these in turn.

Co-opting the workers: reliance on the just community

That the formal joint disciplinary tribunal at Foodstuffs imposes sanctions of an economic nature, such as suspensions, fines and transfers, does not mean that these are the only consequences of participatory justice. At one level, for example, the very fact of having fellow workers, albeit trade union officials, judging and sanctioning their colleagues can have a considerable impact on those so processed. In an earlier section we saw how employees seemed to prefer this internal shaming to that which might have emanated from state law. But that does not mean that the shaming effect of the internal tribunal is negligible. Indeed, as Ann, the employment manager recognised, employee judgements can have a considerable impact on the individual rule-breaker and as such can operate as an effective and forceful deterrent:

> The essence of the tribunal procedure is collective and if the individual is embarrassed by facing so many people publicly and having the question of his supposed guilt exposed, that pressure is there inherently ... A collective system does not allow for sensitivity by an employee. However much you might try in your tribunal hearings to help them, which the tribunal members do, it's a very awe inspiring situation. The majority of employees only go through the system once.

Bob, an employee, confirmed Ann's observation when recounting how his appearance fifteen years ago before the tribunal had deterred him from committing future offences:

> It deterred me — put it that way! To walk into a room and see four men sat there who could literally say 'out'. It was frightening and I think it lived with me.

It is not just the tribunal itself that is relied on to deter employee rule-breakers, but additionally, the community of employees. Employees get to know about tribunal decisions and talk about them; about the sanctions for a particular offence; whether it was too tough or too lenient; and about how deserving the individual employee is of the punishment. This penetration of the community of employees by the disciplinary policy is short-lived and consequently is of questionable importance if being relied on as a general deterrent. Indeed, as an issue or talking point, tribunal decisions are generally believed to be topical for a day or two and certainly for no more than a week:

> As soon as the person comes back from the tribunal everybody wants to know exactly what went on . . . They say 'Ere. Come here. What went on? What did they say to you?' And then everybody goes away and they're talking about it in little groups (Grahame)
>
> In a couple of days it's over isn't it? People do talk but it's only in passing, like. (Liz)
>
> Well everybody knows. But it would be a one day talking point then that's it. He'd get his two days' suspension and when he comes back somebody would say, 'Have you enjoyed your holiday?' (David)
>
> It gets about anyway, even though it's a big factory. The effect of it doesn't last. It's a five day wonder — like the budget — then something else comes along and then they are on to that. But I imagine with the person concerned it lingers on for some time. (Ian)

However, in so far as the autonomy of the community of employees is being relied on to exercise, indeed, to convey the shaming component of the sanction, then the mutuality of the interdependence means that the disciplinary policy is also penetrated by the employee groups. Thus there are degrees of peer-group pressure, depending upon whether the employee in question is deemed to have deserved the punishment. Those individual rule-breakers who are thought to have gone beyond the taken for granted limits informally set by the community of employees are both ridiculed and rejected by their fellows. The sanctions imposed by the joint tribunal will be endorsed as 'deserved' and sometimes seen as not going far enough:

> From what I've heard I think they are over lenient . . .
> The people that are taking it out aren't eating it themselves are they? They have obviously got friends who are getting it . . . There are a couple of people in the section taking, filling their bags full. It's almost like a drama. Everyone's waiting for them to get copped . . . The general opinion is that they ought to get copped. I think people are more honest than they give them credit for. You know it's just a few. (Liz)

There are certain people who go out of the gate for doing certain things and the men say 'well so he should have done'. They agree with a lot more than they disagree with, let's put it that way ... They are quite happy for them chaps to go outside more than they are for people who've been unlucky ... What they're doing is, sometimes they're trouble makers, you know fighters ... they've done something or picked on somebody in the wrong way. They go too far you know. When it gets to that stage everybody says, 'well if they find him out we'd really like to see him out the gate'. It's the general view. It's when it starts getting personal that they change their attitude and have got no time for the person. (David)

The autonomy of employee groups also means that fellow workers sanction those of their colleagues seen to be going beyond the accepted levels and do so without even the need for a tribunal, although clearly the possibility of such sanctioning provides the broader context for this action. Nick explained how such informal control might operate:

Like you might go into a room. You're working there and somebody's got all the stuff out and you think, 'Oh blimey. All that stuff going. They'll think I've had it.' You can't very well shop your own mates. So you've got to say to the man, 'I'd move that lot, because I'm not having it.' Put the onus on him to come and do something about it.

In contrast, there are those rule-breakers who are seen as 'unlucky' to get caught. Such employees, rather than being further sanctioned by the community are actually protected from any shame or embarrassment that the sanctions might have invoked. This is accomplished by the provision of various verbal escape routes:

I told the chaps I was working with. I thought they were bound to know so I told them in any case. All they said was 'stupid bugger. Fancy getting caught with that. Why didn't you take a big piece! ... Get caught for a penny may as well get caught for a £1.' (Bob)

> If they get two days' or a week's suspension they just take no notice ... For the minor cases, like two days for smoking, they sort of think 'Well it's two days off without pay. I'll get on with some decorating' ... Other people rarely take it out of them. They might sort of joke and say 'It serves you right' ... But as far as their workmates shunning them — I don't think they'd do that. They wouldn't labour the point with them or literally run them down for it. (David)

In short, then the employee's semi-autonomy imposes its own control over whether and by how much a person should be sanctioned by regulating the amount of shame that the individual concerned will experience. However, just as the management cannot wholly rely on the employees to support their sanctioning in a way that would confirm their disciplinary decisions, neither is the expression of collective sanctioning completely free to penetrate the individual employee, since each has his own autonomy. In the next section, we can see how this autonomy is itself both relied upon by the disciplinary policy and how, in turn, it penetrates the other semi-autonomous parts such as the management, union and community of employees.

Reliance on employee self-discipline

Whether an individual employee feels the shame stemming from fellow employees' 'talk' and ridicule, or even whether the employees can provide sufficient protection from self-disciplining, depends upon the particular individual's own background and history. Employees distinguish between two kinds of people: those who care and who are likely to be considerably affected by the shame and public knowledge of their offence, and those who do not care and on whom there is little effect:

> You get different kinds of people — some people couldn't care less what other people think, and then there's the people who do. (Sue)

> Some who do commit petty thefts, would probably do it in any case. But it depends on what type of person they are. Some persons don't trouble do they? (Peter)

The kind of person one is seen to be depends upon one's family background, age, responsibilities and circumstances:

> If you give say two days' suspension to a young trolley boy, particularly this time of the year before the end of the tax year, he'd actually thank you. He'd lay in bed for two mornings and get the tax rebate. Whereas if you give it to a married bloke with four kids who's been here twenty years, who's very responsible, two nights' suspension could actually be like the end of the world. He would feel it personally — let his family down. We have great debates about whether you should be consistent or whether you should try and fit the punishment to that particular offender's situation. (Don)

> You get such a lot of the young lads now who joke about it. I mean, where I worked we used to have about twelve of them and they used to talk about it and show us letters — you know 'This is your final warning for being late, timekeeping, your final warning . . . your final warning . . . your final warning.' They used to get six or seven of these and they ignored them — they joked about them. Showed off with them. So, I think it depends on the individual whether these tribunals are deterrents or not. (Bob)

> Well, I think they must be hardened. I do honestly because nothing stops them, does it? They come back to work, bold as brass and they even expect the same job back in the same department . . . And nothing's said to them. Apart from 'Oh it's a shame she was copped!' No shame. I reckon they just don't care. (Liz)

> It depends who you're married to, what reaction they'd take against you, and things like that. It would deter quite a lot of people. I couldn't imagine telling my husband. I think I'd be a little bit ashamed, you know. But, of course, we've been brought up different. Our childhood, if you can understand, we were dealt with quite

strictly — the policemen could cuff your earhole and tell you to go home. (Carol)

From the last section we saw that for some individual employees the effects of sanctioning from both the tribunal and colleagues is no more than a temporary embarrassment which soon subsides:

> In my view it doesn't have a deterrent effect though it's an awful embarrassment at the time for the chap concerned. There's no doubt that there's a sort of stigma about it . . . because although we're all criminals together, if one gets caught and named then he gets embarrassed and he feels sort of 'unclean' for a couple of days. But it soon wears off. (Nick)

> They usually come back from the tribunal laughing, because I suppose it's relief, and say 'I have got a couple or three days' suspension starting from Monday.' They're laughing, all red faced and a bit embarrassed about it you see. If the message has got through, they won't do it again and I suppose it's worth it isn't it? (Grahame)

Ironically, though, the most dramatic effect is on those who are more sensitive to peer group shaming, who care and who would probably be deterred anyway. Such individuals are more penetrated by the company disciplinary policy than penetrate it. A good illustration of how devastating can be the shame from peer group pressure is given by Sue, an employee:

> I know someone who had an egg drop into her bag accidentally — she didn't know that egg was there. She'd gone to the toilet and left her bag by the clock. The detectives looked in and there it was, on the top . . . She had to go to a sort of mini-tribunal to put her case. A union rep. was with her . . . he fought for her and she got off with it because it was an accident. But she got branded for it. It was awful for her because a lot of people were saying that she'd took it. You hear them say 'Oh, so and so's been caught. So and so's got to go to a tribunal' . . . People who worked with her understood. I know she wouldn't have taken it . . . She went through hell that

week. She said 'I shall have to give my job up if I don't
get off.' Her husband wanted her to leave. He said, 'Just
leave and forget it.' But she said 'No, I've got to face up to
it because I know I haven't done anything wrong' . . .
She seemed to change that week, she looked ever so
poorly. When she found she had won her case, she felt
better. But she said to me 'girls from other rooms still
say "Oh look, there's the one who stole that egg." '
She was ever so cut up about it. Even though she had
won her case she was still branded. She said 'I've got a
sister that works here and if it ever gets back to her, and
if she thinks I've taken the egg.' You see in a big firm like
this rumours get round and a little bit's added here and a
little bit's added there, and then by the time you're
finished the girl stole the egg and she's probably been
sacked and all that. Ever so wrong that is. Some take
three or four and they don't care anyway, but the one
girl who's done it and it's an accident — she gets branded
the same. It seems a lot to do through an accident and
we all knew that it was, because it can happen.

In spite of this seemingly dramatic effect on Sue's 'friend'
she did not leave the company. Indeed, as can be seen from
the following accounts, it seems that employees rarely
do leave:

> They might feel ashamed when they stand there before
> the tribunal but I've never heard one of them say they'll
> never come back to the factory. They've all come back
> and faced it. (Liz)

> Well, I've never heard of anybody who's not accepted it.
> They don't usually leave the company. I think the only
> ones who leave are the ones who get dismissed. (Wil)

> They only leave the company if they get sacked, or they
> get a better job elsewhere. They wouldn't leave just for
> the sake of the tribunal . . . very few. (David)

> They are ashamed when it's put on their records for so
> many years. But I've never heard of anybody feeling that
> embarrassed that they wanted to change jobs or anything.
> (Trevor)

Very, very rarely do they hand in their notice as a result of the tribunal. They may at some later stage decide to leave, but it would be for another reason. (Andy)

Clearly, however, some do feel the shame is too much to take, and as a result leave of their own volition:

I think someone left the company. It was so embarrassing. This girl was caught with a couple of toilet rolls (taken from the loo) and it was really terrible. I think she would rather have been caught with a big tin of biscuits! You could buy these toilet rolls in the shop for about five pence each. It was a shame for her. She felt so embarrassed. She did leave in the end — got suspended and then left. I don't know if it was over that, but I presume it was. (Val)

Ultimately, of course, it is the individual's autonomy and agreement to accept formal rules and conditions, which sets the context for the overall disciplinary effect:

You join the company and the company's got the rules in the first place. But if you don't like them, you don't have to work there. (Ian)

Well, I've never been involved in these rules and regulations — the making of them. We sign to accept them when we come here. So, if somebody drops on you for taking the firm's goods or pilfering, whatever they like to call it ... then you have to take it. As I said, there's a set of rules everybody agrees to and it's like playing a game really. Like playing cricket or something — if you're out, you're out. That is that. If you do well and win you get a round of applause. People say poor old so and so got caught. (Nick)

Let me ask you a question. Has anybody come here and said they don't agree with the court? No, well this is it you see, people have accepted it. You come to a firm and they offer you a job and a certain wage, and they give you a rule book — 'These are the company's rules. If you come here for a job and you accept them, then you accept the conditions.' And people do accept. (Grahame)

In conclusion, then, it can be seen that although a company may operate a disciplinary policy, which formally

The negotiated law of participatory justice 177

acknowledges the joint decision-making role of trade union representatives, this is only a surface difference in policy from managerial discipline, since the underlying reality is the interpenetration of mutually dependent semi-autonomous parts. We have seen in this chapter how the interdependent relationship between state law and private justice, for example, means that while the state has some of its control functions carried out by private justice, private justice also penetrates into state law, determining to some extent what is to count as acceptable behaviour and what appropriate sanction. Indeed, it is precisely because of this accommodation and protection from the state that private justice is legitimated as an acceptable form of discipline and thereby through this acceptance that it is able to effect some of the state's social control functions. In other words it has been shown that private justice is rendered acceptable because it is *contrasted* to state law which by comparison is seen as a more severe and formidable option. For that to be the case we have seen that some concession was necessary and was demanded in the form of the imposition of a measure of the autonomous definitions of the private form; while this protects, it also implies reciprocal penetration by the state, albeit in a modified form.

A similar process of mutuality and interpenetration was shown to occur between the participatory policy and other semi-autonomous parts such as the unions or the community of workers. It was argued that having a disciplinary policy which formally acknowledged the existence of a complementary and diverse semi-autonomous control system further legitimates the form of private justice as a whole, since as with the comparison between state law and private justice, that between a joint tribunal and managerial justice, gives the illusion that the 'dominant' sub-system is the one employees 'choose' as the 'fairest' option.

A third level of legitimation was that in which worker representatives accept responsibility for administering disciplinary policy, rather than simply taking part as advocates or observers, and thereby formally recognise the role of acting and being relied on as an extension to the management's own disciplinary action. But it was found that even this formal incorporation does not make the reliance on other internal semi-autonomous parts redundant. The same reliance and mutual penetration is found between the participatory policy and informal employee groups described in the previous chapter. Thus, although the community of employees is relied upon as a hidden arm of the company disciplinary policy, at the same time it is afforded the opportunity of imposing a measure of its own community definitions as to what counts as rule-breaking, and how this is prioritised and sanctioned.

Now it may be argued that the reason why the same interdependent semi-autonomous parts recur in participatory justice as in managerial justice, is because the former is just a more ideologically sophisticated version of the latter. Overall, it may be felt that both organisational types and both forms of formal disciplinary policy are shaped by the same basically similar hierarchical command structure. I think the evidence drawn on so far shows that such a view would not do justice to the differing ways in which semi-autonomous parts develop and interrelate. However, in the next chapter we see how, even co-operative organisations, which are explicitly opposed to hierarchical structures, property ownership and capitalism, develop and rely on a similar range of interdependent semi-autonomous parts as their overall social control package, and that these parts are used in very similar ways to their use in organisations whose disciplinary policy we examined above.

6 Celebration, co-operation and contamination:

the collective law of community justice

Introduction

In the previous two chapters we have seen how social control in capitalist companies involves much more than that expressed in their formal disciplinary policies. Irrespective of the kind of discipline formally adopted, we have seen that social control is crucially dependent on the interpenetration of this policy with the various internal and external semi-autonomous parts which together make up the company and the wider society. We have seen how, at one level, all factory law relies on state law and how at another it relies on the semi-autonomy of both informal peer-group sanctioning and individual self-discipline. That this is not recognised might be understood as part of the ideology of legitimation under capitalism.

It might reasonably be thought that companies and organisations which reject the aims and structures of capitalism, replacing hierarchy, specialisation, competition and profit with democracy, interchangeability, co-operation and relationships would have a disciplinary policy which transcended the need for such legitimation. Indeed, co-operative organisations which are quite explicit about their reliance on informal social control as a disciplinary device might be perceived as having liberated themselves from the need to use a diversified range of disciplinary systems like those adopted under less democratic structures. However, what emerges from the following analysis of co-operative discipline is the surprising finding that despite their ostensibly different policy, co-operatives remain interdependent with a similar range of semi-autonomous parts to those relied on by capitalist companies. The surprise is not that informal networks are acknowledged as central to the co-operative social control policy, but that reliance on elite decision-making and even state law occurs and is not similarly acknowledged.

One possible reading of these findings is that the mechanisms of social control might be universal irrespective of whether they occur under capitalism or socialism. In other words, it suggests that social control comprises a combination of ideological and coercive domination in which one of the less punitive forms is thrown into relief as *the* disciplinary policy to be legitimated by the existence of 'worse' options. A further possibility is that reliance on a diverse range of co-existing disciplinary forms reflects a human tendency towards the development of a hierarchically differentiated division of labour.

Both of these explanations raise serious questions for those who believe that social control may be different in a future society organised along socialist principles. Such theorists might find more favour in the explanation that these 'contradictions of co-operation' imply that capitalism is so pervasive that it is impossible to break from its grasp without a change in the total social structure. Only then would there be sufficient correspondence between the semi-autonomous parts relied upon by a co-operative and the internal disciplinary policy to avoid the latter being contaminated by the former.

In moving towards a conclusion, this chapter asserts that freedom from capitalist social control is not to be found in an embrace with socialist forms since these are no more directed towards the central issue. This has less to do with implementing idealised structures than to do with recognising the existence of ideological processes. This in itself requires revelation rather than revolution. It requires us to become aware that in order to transcend the ideological domination of social control under capitalism or socialism, we need to be impregnated with integrated theorising; to be consistently aware that the parts in which we live and work are both autonomous and constraining; that they make up a totality whose very power to shape and coerce depends on the relative ease with which our attention is focused on the particular; and that this is thereby separated from the totality leaving it adrift as an apparent reality. It is this ideology of diversification with its powers of mystification which stifles the possibility of liberation.

Co-operative disciplinary policy

It is not insignificant that the majority of delegates to a conference on employment law in co-operatives held in London during March 1979 said their co-ops had no formal policy on discipline or dismissals procedures. The reason they were there was to learn from other delegates' experiences. This lack of formal procedure in co-operative discipline is not simply a feature of the co-op's relatively recent life, nor of their small size, though clearly these are factors making its adoption less likely. Rather, the lack of formal procedure reflects a positive decision by many co-operatives to adopt a policy that is humanistic, informal and substantive. Indeed, many co-operatives report that they have no policy on discipline. Each case is handled informally in the course of everyday co-operative working, the latter imposing its own discipline. Stan, a member of Habit Housing Co-operative explained how this operated:

> The co-operative spirit is actually doing the right thing without the formality. In a sense, there's a lot of coercion. Well, perhaps it's not as strong as coercion — it's less formal than that. It's just co-operation between small groups of people. We agree to get something done in the best way possible and that sometimes means that you have to put yourself out.

For Clive of the Electronics Commune this took the form of a continual exchange of critical appraisal:

> I think to a large extent we seem to have evolved mechanisms of preventing disciplinary problems . . . All the time I'm asking them what they think about the standard of what I'm doing. There's a group feeling that we should do this . . . You've got constantly to be working

together. I don't think we tend to get upset by criticism, but we have a much tighter group feeling.

A similar informal approach is described by Kevin of the Plastic Community:

We have no supervision as such and find that the best form of control is by our fellow workmates in the same group and through open discussion, with criticism of each other in as constructive a way as possible. Everyone sees themselves as a member of a team and after all it's their company and if things go well they are the only people to benefit.

This approach toward discipline can be explained in terms of the co-op expectation that because members share a commitment to the same principles, there will be virtually no rule-breaking and that even if some deviance occurs it will not be serious. This co-operative spirit is particularly strong at the formation of a new co-operative, as Linda of Habit Housing Co-operative says:

When we first got together it was naturally a co-op. There was no debate as to whether or not it would be a co-op, because we were all in the same boat, we all wanted to get out of the situation we were in and do something about it. Everybody wanted to have a say and everybody had something to say at the time. We were a small group. And because we were into self-help and mutual advancements naturally there was no question about it, we actually needed people's skills. We wanted to maintain it on a self-help basis and we couldn't do that unless we knew which people had skills and we knew who we could call on. And if we couldn't call on them, then what were we supposed to do in a crisis situation?

A further explanation is that co-op members are in relationships with one another beyond simply those to do with work, and are therefore afforded a greater opportunity for the continuous process of influence. As Clive of the Electronics Commune pointed out:

Most of us are working and living together, so it doesn't

Celebration, co-operation and contamination

happen that we have anybody who is socially isolated to any extent. Because of that it is much easier to discuss problems outside of meetings.

The value of this network of intimacy is well expressed by Kirsty of Co-operative Life:

> We have all known each other for quite a long time, and all of us also live together in a co-operative situation. It's our close relationship, I think, that largely accounts for our commitment and our lack of serious disagreement. Because we know, trust and respect one another's perhaps differing feelings about a situation, we take each other into consideration, and make as much effort as possible to accommodate one another in most situations; swapping around work notes, looking after kids, etc., and making allowances for domestic situations and commitments which might well be ignored in a different work situation. As a consequence of this, real disagreement rarely occurs.

One consequence of this sustained form of social control is that it does not work in only one direction. Just as we saw in the previous chapters, the individual whose behaviour is subject to social control can penetrate the co-operative structure to impose some of his own standards and levels of tolerance. Penetration can occur in such a way that the co-op accommodates its structure and definitions of rule-breaking to incorporate the individual diversity without repressing it. Eric of Share and Care explained how one employee made incursions into the co-op's policy to such an extent that members were forced to respond:

> She was turning up when she felt like it. It was because she was working here that she thought she could get away with it. Well, we put up with her to a substantial extent. We thought maybe it's a temporary problem and she'll get over it. But, in the end, we had people within the organisation saying '. . . We are bloody here at 9 a.m. and she turns up at 11 a.m., and you don't do anything about it. Why are you putting up with it?' The point is, to a large extent we accept a degree of failure. If it is that bad that it is going to affect the achievements of our goals then we

might have to talk to the person concerned and say, as in this case, 'If you are not able to do the job it may be the wrong one for you' or 'If you are able to do the job, what are the problems?'

Some individual members of the collective exploit this accommodative attitude to serve their own interests. One member of Habit Housing Co-operative, for example, was renowned for leaning heavily on the co-operative's toleration of personal and emotional difficulties. As Linda explained:

> Peter is a special case. People think 'Oh he's got a lot of problems.' But it's only because we know about his problems, because he's made damn sure everybody knows about them, whereas other people in the co-op don't do that. There may be people who've got into rent arrears difficulties, who've got really serious problems, but they haven't made it their business to try and say to us 'Well, I have got these problems.'

In some cases, however, this penetration of co-operative principles by an individual can be seriously disruptive to the extent that the co-op members might be held to ransom. Gerry of the Big Bag Wholefood Co-op explained how his co-op's accommodative attitude led to serious problems of the kind that would not be encountered by capitalist companies:

> If a capitalist company needed to recruit five people, they'd put an ad in the paper. They've got clear terms of reference: 'Right, we pay you this much, you work these hours, these are your holidays.' And if they do the job right they keep them and if they don't they sack them, and it's all very straightforward. In a co-operative — oh no! For recruiting you've got to have somebody who's totally tuned in to what is happening. If they are not you can pick four good people and then one bad person, and because everybody believes in being nice to everyone and all that, one person could put a complete spanner in the works. You've got this sort of democratic structure and you've only got to have one person keeping on asking awkward questions and you've got trouble.

Gerry went on to illustrate precisely how individual penetration combined with an accommodative disciplinary policy can disrupt co-op work:

> This guy came along for an interview and he seemed all right. He was quite friendly. I spoke to him for a bit, we had a meeting and then he came back in. We all had a chat to him for about an hour and we decided that we'd employ him on a trial basis. Well, almost from the word go it was a total disaster because his idea, that wasn't clearly stated at the time, but it became clear, was that he saw a co-operative as a very supportive environment which would be doing something for him. He saw himself as being sensitive, and I think he was in a way. He tended to be very easily offended and used to react to things that weren't really happening. He'd walk in and if he thought the atmosphere was bad he would start getting in a mood about it and come up here and sit around saying how depressed he was and things like that. But he wasn't very sensitive really to what was happening all around him or to other people. He had actually upset, or was upsetting a number of the other younger workers because of his manner — he started telling them 'Don't do this, don't do that' in a fairly aggressive way. He'd only been here a couple of weeks! He also had a sort of unfortunate manner with customers. He'd be standing by the counter and if there was a queue of people he would yell 'next!' All stupid sorts of things like that and he was upsetting quite a lot of people and he was upsetting me because I was finding it very frustrating. He used to come in and say things like 'I don't feel like lifting that stuff today. I don't think I'm going to be doing much . . .'. I said 'Look, there's therapeutic communities, things like this, there's places that can offer you help but this isn't it.' It's a question of priorities. If you've got somebody who's draining the morale of the place it can have a number of effects. Apart from being bad for the sort of financial side of the business it can have a very very negative effect on all the other people. This is what happened with this guy.

Now there are a number of responses to a situation where an

individual or group of individuals are persistently penetrating the co-operative policy. A celebratory response, especially important where there is a group of offenders, is to divide and grow into two or more co-operatives. As Gary of Computer Collective says:

> I think in a sense that's why we only vaguely talk about strategies for discipline. Because the ideal solution is to split. You know, find some sort of equilibrium size which might be 7, might be 10, 15 or something, anything bigger than that and problems start to arise. So, the best thing is to split.

This is particularly likely to be a solution in widespread housing co-operatives such as Living Space who explained how:

> As the co-op grew many members began to feel less a part of it and to regard it much as they regarded the council. The houses were widely dispersed over a large area and the meetings were always very big. Then Living Space made the decision to break down into area groups, for each group to have its own meeting and control over its own affairs. As a result there has been much more interest shown by the members in the co-op's affairs and some of those who had lost interest began to get involved again.

Where individual penetration is more isolated the response is often an informal collective one which might build up over time. Clive of the Electronics Commune told how some members had left as a result of resisting the co-op's principles:

> I can think of three people who left, and in each case it was because they had trouble in fitting in with the way the rest of us worked. They didn't take enough responsibility for the work they did and didn't have the feeling of needing to present it all the time so that we could see how good it was. What happened was that as often as they failed to present their work they were told in the normal course of the way the rest of us are always criticising each other. This hurt their pride too much and they left.

A similar build up of informal peer group pressure was

Celebration, co-operation and contamination

described by Julian of the Big Brick Housing Co-op:

> The members actually booted out one or two people who had really caused a lot of difficulty. There was a fairly vigorous sort of warfare. These people came to committee particularly when they wanted to control something and when it came to a business affair — transfer from one property into another. Then, they decided, right, you know, we'll come and get what we want. But, they didn't get it. People had just had enough of them because they were obnoxious sort of dominant figures, never articulate . . . and people decided to give them the boot by no other way than making them feel unwelcome at committee meetings. First of all this person was replaced in office, so they got reduction of control there. Then, they came less often to committee . . . So it didn't happen at once, it was a gradual process over quite a long time.

In other cases the effect of an individual's behaviour on fellow co-op members is felt to be in need of more certain and specific action. One response is for the co-op members to rely on self-discipline. Eric of Share and Care describes how his criticism of a fellow member resulted in the member in question leaving the organisation:

> In the end I challenged him and said one or two things about what was happening. He got fed up and blew his top — he was that kind of person; stress case and very objectionable —, swore at me and said 'Stuff your job! I'm going out.' We just accepted that. We didn't have to take any action in that case.

This approach has additional benefits, as Gary of the Computer Collective says:

> If you are going to run into hassles with employment legislation then obviously the thing to try and do is to heavy people so much that they resign rather than you fire them — make them an offer they can't refuse.

The same informal peer group sanctioning, relying on self-discipline, need not result in a member leaving the co-op. Phil of the arts collective, Troupe Together, explained how, rather than call the police in when they had a theft, they asked for the action to stop by making those responsible feel guilty:

> We had wage packets disappearing ... this, that and the other disappearing and we coped with it by saying whoever was doing it should go and talk to Rob Rich, who is the financial director, and explain the problem ... What was happening stopped.

Gerry of Big Bag described how rather than sanction one member who was repeatedly late for work, they asked him to sanction himself:

> We said 'We think you need some strong incentive to stop you. What do you think? If you were working at Whitmans, down the road, you'd be losing a quarter of an hour's money, wouldn't you? We don't really want to do things like that, but why should you be less conscientious here than you would there?' And he said 'I think maybe financial incentive would have some effect.' So we said 'All right then, what do you suggest?' He replied 'If I'm up to a quarter of an hour late, lose a quarter of an hour's wages.' So I said 'All right!'

But in most cases the persistent deviance of some members, together with their continued presence in the co-op and their resistance to informal pressure, leads to the adoption of a more formalised collective response. The type this takes varies, but for many co-ops the meeting of the collective provides one appropriate forum. This is seen to have certain advantages over the use of informal group pressure. Some co-op members, for example, take the view that it provides a vehicle for the collective to express problems openly and prevent them building up into more serious issues. As Polly from the Electronics Commune explained:

> Well, I think it was good when we started to have meetings every week because that solved a lot of problems. People were able to air their feelings a bit more and, although others suffered a lot of anguish as a result sometimes, at least it was out in the open. We do have times where people come in here on their own and bring a problem

up because they obviously want to solve it. That helps to throw light on discussion at the next meeting, or sometimes it's resolved outside a meeting.

It is believed also that the formality depersonalises the issue, making it more easy to discuss and resolve. Others, however, suggest that the very fact that fellow workers are judging each other means that a level of formality is necessary to prevent the occurrence of arbitrariness and viciousness. Julian of Big Brick says the formal policy is,

> not a highly personalised thing. It isn't just individual kangaroo courts ... If groups are sitting down and making judgement on a fellow, structure and policy as a way of doing things are very important. If you are following a policy which has some sense to it, then you are taking some of the personal viciousness out of it. That seems to me to be a valuable structure for dealing with things.

The main purpose of the formal meeting, however, is not so much to provide a legitimation of the disciplinary action, but to remind the rule-breaker of his duties and responsibilities to the co-operative by focusing his attention on the collective sentiment. At the same time this brings the behaviour in question to the attention of the other members of the co-operative. Members of the Habit Housing Co-operative explained how rent arrears were symbolic of a breakdown of the co-operative spirit and how formal meetings provided the forum to express this collective consciousness:

> If they are not put in a situation where they have to discuss it they might just think 'Oh, I've got rent arrears, I'll get around to solving them sometime' and they don't think what the implications are for the other co-op members and what it means for them personally. Whereas if they are in a meeting they can see the implications for the organisation and they can see the implications for themselves. (Linda)

> People who would normally act in a very responsible co-operative way sometimes forget what the co-op system is and don't use it properly. They fail in their duty to pay rent, which is most fundamental I suppose. If you can

remind people of their duties, talk to them on a friendly
basis, then they think 'Oh, of course,' and they'll sort of
act in a co-operative way. It's no more complicated than
that. (Stan)

I think it's also a lot to do with friends. I'm not sure but
... at a meeting if there are friends there and they find
out that you are not paying rent then there's much more
pressure on you to pay. It's group pressure, but I don't
know exactly how it works. People might be cut off from
their friends if they don't pay. (Robin)

Clearly this formal collective policy can only work where attending co-op meetings is an inevitable part of co-op life. In some co-operatives, where the membership is geographically dispersed, members might be more able to avoid formal meetings. In such cases one response is to force absent members to attend meetings or insist that they become involved in other ways. This is attempted by enacting 'legislation' to ensure minimum participation. Linda and Robin of Habit Housing Co-operative describe their attempt to enforce participation:

If they won't come to meetings and won't get involved
then I think we should get rid of them because those of us
who believe that we should stay a co-operative and strive
to be a real co-operative can't carry that kind of membership. I mean, apart from anything else, if we want to be a
co-op we have to have a mandate from the membership to
do the things we do, and you won't have a mandate if
people aren't there to say 'yes' or 'no'. So, we put together
this motion. 'Every member of the co-op shall assign
themselves to one pre-determined area of work in 'List A'
within which their skills may lie, and can be called upon
to utilise their skills and assist in the running of the co-op.
Anyone who persistently fails to help when asked will
have their membership questioned by the participation
sub-committee (which was intended to be set up if the
motion got through). In addition no member shall be
exempt from assisting in any area of activity in List B.'
(Linda)

> But what happened was, it was amended. Someone got up and said 'I will support anything as long as there is no compulsion in it.' He was a very good speaker. The part about the compulsion and about being checked up on by a participation committee got fought against and we lost it. It was dropped. (Robin)

Stan of Habit points out the difficulties of this kind of formal collective approach:

> I can see no sense in people attending meetings which they are not interested in. It makes it difficult to run the meeting because if people are not interested in a particular issue, which is the business of a meeting, they will talk about other things and thereby divert the course of the meeting. I think if you were going to try and get people to go who don't want to, or even if they do want to, you insist that they go, they would take offence and it would alienate. I saw this, actually, at the general meeting, where on precisely this motion people just happened to be wandering out. You know, they were going home to their tea or something and the finger was pointed — 'These people are leaving the meeting, isn't it a disgrace.' Well, there was no evidence to suggest that they were acting in the wrong way, so they took offence. They said 'Fuck you!'

An equally dramatic response, designed to make deviant members feel the weight of the collective voice, is that which takes the 'meeting' to the member. One way this is accomplished in housing co-operatives is to have a system of 'visits'. These are undertaken by sub-groups of the collective meeting with the brief of finding those deviant members who have not attended the formal meeting in order to discuss with them 'their problems'. Clearly there are difficulties with this approach. Whether the collective action takes the form of a group meeting or a visit, it can be highly counter-productive. This is because, from the point of view of the co-operative, a formal collective disciplinary policy is very vulnerable to incursions by the individual who is being controlled. Members are so sensitive to the accusation of pushing out minority interests that rather than a 'gang of heavies' they appear more often as an apologetic 'gaggle of softies'. Stan of Habit Housing describes how this occurs:

> The idea behind the 'visits' was not to bludgeon the rent out of people. You don't go along as a sort of threatening mob. It's more of a visit to try and find out whether there are any mitigating circumstances and to sort out a means of payment, but not in a lump sum.

At a regular co-op meeting of Habit, volunteers were invited to go on a visit and there was a lot of humour and joking expressing a consciousness of how seriously their visit might be viewed. One member asked 'What is it going to be then? Knee job?' Another replied 'They're not going to break his legs, just bruise him a little — where it can't be seen.' 'Come out with your hands up or your rent book', said another. Indeed, a further reason why this approach is vulnerable is because co-op members do not enjoy taking responsibility for discipline since this can be an unpleasant experience. Stan of Habit reflected on his experiences:

> I was on one of these early visits. That's why I didn't go the second time — because it freaked me out. We went in a group of six and stood round shuffling our feet, feeling very uncomfortable. We went along to a house in Galena Drive, a large house, with large debts . . . I went along to 'visit' one girl in particular and she was obviously taken aback and abusive.

Another housing co-operative, Home Time, had similar experiences with 'visits'. Brian, a member, described how the visiting committee were subject to personal abuse which carried over to their relations with other co-op members:

> Some members are quite happy to go and visit others and to take them to task on their rent arrears but others don't like doing it because they find it unpleasant. They will try and shirk that responsibility. There is no doubt about that . . . Members of the committee had to get quite heavily involved and were caused a lot of distress and a certain amount of aggravation because they were having to apply the rules. In one case a person was in quite serious rent arrears who was fairly good friends with a number of

people on the committee. That friendship was soured because those people had to take part in telling her that she'd got to sort out her rent arrears. Whichever way the committee made a decision it would alienate somebody and there was unpleasantness outside the co-op meeting because the co-op doesn't just stop when you go outside the door . . . They got people stopping them in the street and saying, 'I think that was really unfair what you did about such and such,'. Then there's people from the co-op at the school where you take your kids, when you go into the local shops, the playgroup that you go to and things like that.

Indeed, because of the close relationship between co-op members there is a tendency for any formal collective response to be seen by the individuals subject to discipline as the outcome of personal vindictiveness. Brian of Home Time, for example, says of one member:

> She felt it wasn't fair that her private affairs should be discussed at a committee. What she thought should happen is that Toby should see the rent arrears and that he should visit people privately, you know it should be confidential. Even though her name hadn't been mentioned, I think she worried about the idea of her next door neighbours knowing that she was in rent arrears . . . We've had some problems when that sort of thing has gone wrong. The individuals concerned almost expect to be taken to task, but they are surprised and resentful when they find a person they see as a comrade knocking on the door. Quite a lot of them react aggressively saying that our calculations of rent arrears are wrong or that there was something wrong with their house and it hadn't been attended to for sometime. They sort of feel that they have to hit back. People think they are being victimised.

But even without this particular attribution of motive, the very fact that the personal details of some members are being discussed by others can be disturbing as Kevin of Habit said when questioned at a meeting about why he had showed an aggravated response to the co-op's handling of his own arrears:

> Look I'm shit scared. It's sheer hell to stand up and explain your financial expenses to a meeting of twenty or thirty people. This co-op policy is a peculiar way to collect rent. It just frightens people who are already in a state about their inability to pay, who are unemployed and on social security.

It would appear, then, that the close-knit nature of co-op life makes personality conflict of one sort or another inevitable where formal peer group pressure of this type is used. It seems that the effect of collective justice is, indeed, quite the reverse of what is required by the co-operative. It can result in alienation of the member rather than in his further integration, as he is provoked into defensive hostility. Eric of Share and Care desribed how his co-operative's group meetings failed to solve the problems created by one disruptive member who was ultimately able to penetrate the disciplinary policy:

> The first group meeting she didn't turn up to. The second one, she came in sat in the office but didn't come into the group. The third one she sat there like a dummy and didn't say a bloody thing. So in other words, she was not relating to the group situation.

Similarly Stan of Habit Housing Co-operative said,

> If there isn't hostility then the person who is being visited is bound to get overwhelmed. It is rather intimidating when six people suddenly descend on you with no prior notice at all. It's not a good forum to discuss personal things like 'Are you going to pay your rent?', and 'Why are you not paying it?'.

The essence of the problem was captured by Donna of Habit who said:

> If they came along to the meeting, they would get a warning and we'd be very nice to them and make an arrangement for them to pay. None of us wants to get our fingers burned or be seen to be heavy so what happens? We start feeling sorry for them. 'Ah poor dears. They've got all these problems. Let's make it easier for them.'

Perhaps we ought to reorganise and restructure the co-op to make it more accessible' . . . But on the receiving end, when people in arrears come to meetings it puts them on edge to be strong about it. It's incredibly humiliating and I think it's a cheek to make people come along and be humiliated because I don't think it's going to make them want to be more co-operative. It's just going to put their backs up.

This individual penetration of the formal collective response is made even more potent by those individual members who exploit the situation in order to absolve themselves from co-operative responsibilities. Brian of Home Time said,

> Another problem with members sorting out disciplinary problems among themselves is that it has actually resulted in some people dropping out of co-op activities altogether following an unpleasant experience. Some people have said to me that those individuals just use it as an excuse to drop their responsibilities. It's just an indication of laziness. They can't be bothered . . . whereas some people shirk their personal responsibilities. One co-op member came to a general meeting and, without warning, stood up and said that the person who lived upstairs from him never washed her curtains! Could something be done about it? I think there's a danger if individuals see the co-op as a way in which they can get out of the responsibility of approaching people individually, that they can get away with it because the co-op offers a listening ear.

The penetration of formal collective disciplinary policy by the individual member and how it moves through various stages, from accommodation and informality to formality and ultimately a reliance on self-discipline, is illustrated by Gerry of the Big Bag Wholefood Collective in his account of how one disruptive member was dealt with:

> First of all we asked him, 'How do you think you're getting on?' And he came up with a few non-committal things. And we said, 'Well look from our point of view there seems to be a number of problems' and we mentioned the fact that he'd upset a number of people

and told him who they were. We also said we thought he had an unfortunate manner with customers and we thought he over-reacted to things. We told him of a number of things that we thought were causing problems and his reaction was a sort of mixture of saying that it wasn't true and that what we were telling him was upsetting him very much. So we had this meeting and in the end I just got angry. I said, 'Look we're trying to help you because unless something changes . . .' I didn't actually say, 'we're going to kick you out', I said, 'We are going to have big trouble. We are trying to talk to you in an adult way. This is the way we see it and if you've got about five people telling you something, you ought to listen to it' . . . The next day he arrived very late and he just sort of looked terrible. He said, 'I didn't get any sleep last night.' We said, 'Why was that then?' And he said, 'Well I did find it pretty devastating what happened last night.' I said, 'Well it might be a bit of a shock but it's not the end of the world. Something can be done about it.' He just sat up here for about an hour doing something, with his face down to the floor and then said, 'I'm really feeling very bad, I think I'll have to go home.' And that point I felt like sacking him. I thought 'This is not on.' We could not go on like that. I just couldn't and didn't feel sympathetic to him . . . I believed that the right way of doing these things was to be direct, not to butter him up and say, 'You're not doing bad' and give him a load of old crap. I just thought 'There are so many things that I can't even bother to mention: his behaviour; things that were causing problems that were clearly his responsibility, that he had to do something about; and which he had not been completely up-front with when he came for his interview . . .' Well we had another meeting without him being there and decided that we were going to have to get rid of him. We said, 'Should we?', because he'd go through a day where he seemed to be trying quite hard and then although there were still problems it was slightly better. But then there were days which would be just disastrous. We didn't want to say, 'Well we think it's best if you leave at the end of the month', because we thought, 'If he gets totally depressed by just telling him that there are a few things wrong, what's his reaction if we tell him he's got to go?' What happened was, since we'd had this earlier meeting with him, he'd just got more and more into his sort of bag of self-pity and depression. So we decided to do something about it fairly soon because he was really having a bad effect on the morale of everyone involved. The atmosphere in the shop was so bad. In actual fact we gave him a week's notice . . . So we called him along and basically, without actually saying, 'Look we are going to kick you out', we said, 'Look this is a dead end situation with no possibility of resolving the problem and we want to do something about it. What do you think?' And he turned round and said 'Well basically I've been thinking the same myself.' So that was it he left.

Thus in spite of the co-ops' explicit policy to avoid formal discipline, many clearly resort to this when the semi-autonomy of individual rule-breakers is sufficiently persistent and penetrating to be disruptive. But of itself, the formal policy is no more resistant to individuals' penetration. The ideological trick which ultimately defeats the individual, is that both formal and informal exist together, and the power to decide which system to use at any point rests with the collective. This flexibility to move from informal to formal and back again clinches the individual's subordination to collective justice. As such it differs from capitalist discipline only in its emphasis on one side of this duality rather than the other. As Mandy of Troupe Together recognises, the two sides are mutually interdependent:

> I'm aware of it but I hadn't really thought about it much. We are actually struggling with two systems and the fact that we have two systems means we never fully commit ourselves to either. There are the two different wheels. They will always step in if you want them to. They will always say, 'I'll wield the big stick.' It's always there in the background. I mean to that extent we are not using one or the other.

Contradictions of collective justice

In the previous section we saw how collective justice, whether formal or informal, is someway penetrable by those individuals who are subject to discipline. Indeed, such policy explicitly recognises that to a degree this should be the case and also that every other member of the co-operative should contribute toward the formulation and application of discipline. What is not acknowledged, however, is that: (1) certain individuals should be able to penetrate the disciplinary policy more than others; (2) that elite groups or cliques should form with more power than the rest of the collective; and that (3) the collective should rely on state law enforcement agencies to back up its disciplinary policy.

Penetration by individual co-op members may occur at either the informal or formal levels of disciplinary policy in such a way that shapes disciplinary practice differently from disciplinary policy. At the informal level, some individuals will simply enforce their own selection of standards as Phil of Troupe Together explained:

> Take rules like 'no smoking' that exist in various areas. We have that rule because of the insurance, the obvious fire risk. And those rules are enforced by confrontation. Individuals handle that sort of thing to the level that they think appropriate. I enforce them in the audio room because *I* dislike smoking.

At the formal level, individuals may penetrate the disciplinary policy simply because they enjoy and rise to the 'public' nature of the occasion. Stan of Habit Housing Co-operative observes that,

> People don't act too co-operatively in some of the meetings. There's an element of listening to the sound of your own voice. There's the joy of getting a point over and the feeling that you're getting something done.

Others may claim, or indeed be allowed, to assert their individual position because they appear to do so very competently relative to the other co-op members. Dario of Face to Face theatre collective illustrates the point well:

If we look at a meeting which is deciding an ideological move someone inside will be able to say 'Yeah, Cliff is the one who usually speaks about these things.' We often find ourselves agreeing with him. Of course all sorts of factors operate upon it: people who have been in the company more recently are predisposed to be more hesitant about things from their lack of experience; competency in speaking; and social skills in manipulating situations, which I have for instance. All these things are going to predetermine the decision in a particular direction and usually it works in Cliff's favour.

The same point was made more directly by Clive of the Electronics Commune:

Even if you think you've got a consensus system it's possible to find that people with the strongest personalities so often carry everyone else with them that it's almost as if they are able to control the direction in which we go.

As Julian of Big Brick Housing Co-operative points out, under certain conditions, this is especially likely to occur, such as where there is a failure by members to take collective responsibility:

You get some very strange people wanting to do certain things and if there is a power vacuum they will jump in and fill it. It's as if you're stepping back and saying, 'We the workers don't control. The unions don't control. There's nothing here. Here it is.' Well you just get one or two powerful characters and they can have a field day.

Perhaps the most serious of these individual incursions is the kind where the committee is being manipulated by an individual for his own personal interests. Some members become skilled at this practice. Phil of Troupe Together admits that although the formal collective disciplinary policy of his co-operative, the committee of three, is used on the whole constructively, some members,

just go out of their way to freak the individual out. They rely on a kind of rule of fear. In two and a half years I've learnt how to manipulate these meetings. I've learnt how to do lots of horrible things.

Thus through the inevitability of their involvement, some individuals find that manipulative skills alone or in conjunction with others can be employed in securing their own personal or even political interests. A good illustration of this can be seen from the account of Cathy, who was expelled from Troupe Together:

> Now this woman, Judy, had been running it previously but I was supposed to be running it as the co-ordinator. Still, she kept coming back in and telling me how to do things. Then she came back part time and I began to get the feeling that she didn't like me because . . . I had seen and heard little things. This goat's girl, Rita, they were very much hand in glove and I'd caught things. You know when something is going on around you — you catch a little glimpse . . . If someone is behind your back doing something, you can tell, and once or twice I caught her doing something — a sort of gesture to Judy, then Judy would laugh, or I'd suddenly look up and her face was a picture of innocence. She was just picking me to pieces and looking for things that were wrong. Rita just jumped down my throat every time I said anything to her. So, I said 'Well, what's the matter then? Why are you like this?' And she said 'Quite honestly because I don't like you. I wouldn't choose you for a friend or to work with.' So I said 'Well I'm sorry Rita, there's nothing I can do about that situation, is there.' Then I spoke to this Judy about Rita's attitude. I said 'Rita's making things difficult, I can't seem to get through, I've tried to be pleasant but she just will not accept it.' She said 'Well Kathy, if you must know, I've not been talking to you either.' I knew her and Rita had been talking together in little huddles, but that was a bit of a blow. Well, this was all in the first few months you see before I had my committee of three. That's the review committee. There was a Chairman, a director and the representative of the division. But, he was the husband of this Judy woman. When the personnel told me that he was on the review committee I said 'Can I change him?' She said 'Well why? He is your divisional representative.' I said 'Because he is Judy's husband and I

think she is trying to get rid of me.' She said 'Oh no, it can't be. You must be imagining things.' I said 'I don't think I am.' And she said 'No, you can't change him he must be on the committee.' So I thought at that point, 'I don't stand a great deal of chance.' Then she told me that an independent person would be there from another division. It didn't occur to me then that this person knew Judy and her husband very well — but of course she must have done. At a later date she said she did. Anyway, I went to this committee of three. They went through the routine things first. Then they mentioned some conflict — I knew this might come up — and started talking to me and asking me questions. I said 'Well look, I've already written this out because I knew there had been personality conflict.' So I handed these sheets out that I'd had duplicated. We talked over how Kate had given me advice or what she called advice — she expected me to act on it. In other words she was giving me a directive, or as I said at a later stage advice is something one gives freely, you can't enforce it. I said I had tried to resolve the conflict but couldn't. Then they said 'Well, we ought to have Judy in on this.' They postponed it for 24 hours, unfortunately, and gave her time to prepare her attack — really prepare it. And she just tore into me, absolutely ripped to shreds the whole of the four months I'd been there. Of course, they voted against me. The vote was that I was not suitable for the job. So I appealed. I was told I could appeal to the main policy committee — which I did and again I asked for Judy's husband not to be there. They said 'He's got to be there, he's your divisional representative.' The next meeting was in a fortnight when one of the founder members, Tom, should be back from America. I thought 'Right, that's fine.' I sent a letter off to him in America asking him if he would write a report on my behalf for this next meeting. I don't even know if he ever got that. The courier who went doesn't know whether he took it or not. Anyway the person who had been Chairman of that management committee the previous day came round to me and said 'I'm sorry but Scott (Judy's husband) has called an emergency meeting of the main policy committee.'

And I said 'That's totally unfair because everyone knows
that Tom won't be back from America.' So I objected. I
felt it was done deliberately. I had nobody on my side.
So he said 'Well you can't go on objecting like this.' But I
said 'Look, I object to this, I objected to Scott and I am
objecting now to you that he is able to call this emergency
meeting. It doesn't give me any hope whatsoever of a fair
hearing, does it?' She said 'You make it sound like a court.'
I said 'Yes it does, doesn't it?' She said that Judy's
husband was not influenced by her. 'Isn't this influence?'
I said. Normally I'm a person that gets on with everyone
but I was livid. For one person like this to attack somebody and be determined to get them out and to make up
all sorts of fabrications in order to do it. She said 'I don't
think that is so'. I said, 'It is. It jolly well is!' Anyway I
couldn't do anything about it so they called an emergency
meeting for that Friday before Tom came back from
America. All those who were there had a vote and it was
4:3 against me, with one abstention. But it was even
minuted wrongly. It said there were 5 against me and no
abstentions. But I counted them carefully. I was there and
I wrote them down . . . Well it seemed to me that it was
rigged all the way through by these people — this
particular woman who wanted me out. She'd got a lever
through her husband to every committee and he was very
definite in the end. He wanted me out too.

It would be possible to dismiss this account as at least a
distortion if it were not for the fact that other members of
the co-op identified the same problem of penetration and
manipulation. Indeed, even the worker responsible for
personnel admitted that personal interest was a significant
factor in not only this case but in co-op discipline generally:

> The woman didn't want her rep to be on the committee
> because she thought he was unduly influenced by his wife.
> I maintained that nonetheless he was the divisional rep
> and as such he was one of the only people on the main
> policy committee who knew her work and the work of
> the division. I was going to say it's an unlikely situation,
> but given the nature of the organisation it's more likely

than you might imagine. In the size of organisation we are talking about, co-operatives, it's going to be a problem. The committee you get is possibly going to be influenced in that kind of way.

The same penetration into the collective disciplinary policy can occur when small groups develop an autonomy and identity that is separate from the rest of the co-operative membership. We saw in the previous section how those who exercise discipline on behalf of the membership can provoke hostility against themselves as individuals. Indeed this very situation is enhanced where collective support is not sought and where there is no rotation of the disciplinary function among the membership. Such a situation is self-fuelling because the very act of disciplining drives a further wedge between those who are on the disciplining body and the rest of the collective. Thus if some members persistently fail to become involved in co-op activities or act counter to them, a formal disciplinary response may occur. But the lack of participation and especially willingness to assume unpopular responsibility means only a certain group do the disciplining. They then build up an expert knowledge of disciplinary policy and take action which itself separates them from the membership. This results in an escalation of the problem: even less feeling of involvement, less participation and thereby more need to discipline. For example, Murial of the English Word Language School described how in her housing co-operative:

> A lot of resentment built up against the committee of management because it was felt that they formed a little clique who did not make any attempt to consult other members of the co-operative. And resentment by the committee of management against other members of the co-operative occurred because it was felt they were not taking any part in it or showing any interest.

The same separation of an elite group was described by Stan of Habit Housing co-operative:

> On the old management committee people were building up expertise which only they had. Some of the members

outside of the management committee thought that what was going on was wrong, that because the management committee had become a bunch of experts, perhaps they were corrupt as well, you know, power. And there's always been a lot of allegations about people bringing in their friends, fiddling here and there, that sort of business, which of course may go on . . . So the allegation was that the management committee had become very centralised, very tight and alienating to the members.

While some of these problems may be an inevitable consequence of co-operatives expanding in size, and taking on new members who do not share in either the original pioneering spirit of the more long-standing members or in the knowledge and expertise that has grown with experience, the response to them seems almost certainly to make matters worse as can be seen from the account of Linda, also of Habit:

Last year we got very big, very quickly and a lot of people are either very ignorant of what is going on or who would otherwise get involved, are intimidated by the organisation. They come along to meetings, and don't like to say 'I don't understand', because of the whole kind of social taboo about not being 'in with the scene' . . . I suppose it is intimidating if you don't know anything about the organisation — you are a new member — or somebody who hasn't been involved because they came in last year and haven't been called upon to be involved. Then they come along to a meeting and a lot of discussion takes place. There's clearly a lot more going on at meetings than meets the eye, and they don't know the background and then everyone else gets fed up going over old ground and unless you can grab someone in the pub and ask them what's going on, you know it's difficult to get involved . . . It's all very well them complaining but they should make more effort. If the members think something's wrong, if they feel they are being subjected to something they don't like, the opportunity has always been there for them to devise a different system. But if they have not participated, what right have they got to complain? There are so many people in this co-operative who only acknowledge it's a co-operative when they've got something to complain about. So if they haven't helped to devise a different system and if they then accumulate rent arrears, I've really got no sympathy with them.

The same response was expressed by Brian of Home Time:

If somebody never comes to meetings and then moans to me about something which has resulted from a decision taken at a meeting, I just say to them, 'Well that's tough! The decision was made at the general meeting and you should have raised it then if you were worried about it!' I would argue that that's a sanction on those people who don't know what's going on.

In its extreme form the penetration of collective justice by elite groups can escalate to the degree that a formal collective response is inadequate since it lacks the legitimacy of collective sentiment owing to the separation of the group from the membership as a whole. In such a situation, rather than dispersing the responsibility from the administrative centre by dissolving the elite, some co-operatives further entrench the problem of going outside the collective and relying on state law to enforce the expulsion of some of their more unco-operative members. Donna of Habit, for example, says that they were forced to move to a reliance on formal law because neither the informal group pressure, nor the formal collective policy was enough to solve the problem of rent arrears:

We reached a stage then when we sent out eviction notices and nobody believed we'd carry them out, because basically, up to then, nobody had carried them out. There were no possession orders and people just saw it as an empty threat. They said, 'Oh yes, here we go again, send in a couple of quid.' And meetings just delayed things further. We invited them to come along and explain. But I mean you can talk until you're blue in the arse and still nothing gets done about it. Then, the visits were a bloody disaster. There was a rumpus which was totally over personal things, it had sod all to do with rent. I mean the reason for people getting at each other's throats about those visiting and calling them the 'heavy mob', was because of their own personal feelings towards those people that came. And also you try and get six people together that will go on a visit . . . See the people who advocate policies and the people who come to meetings are human beings and most human beings are unstable in the sense that they don't want to be disliked. But if you are going to lay on someone, you're not going to be liked. So people won't go. As far as I'm concerned if it can't be done there's no point in even attempting it . . . You see the problem when you're trying to use discipline or just logic is that people get in the way, because people aren't disciplined and they aren't logical, right? To run an efficient rent system you've got to get the human element out as much as possible because that is what messes the whole thing up — people's emotions and whatever. I know it sounds daft trying to get the human element out, but a system where you don't have to go and explain why you haven't paid and involve yourself in totally irrelevant personal problems, has to be preferable, as long as you pay it. I mean if there is a good rent system I don't see why anybody should be intimidated, humiliated. There's no reason. As far as I'm concerned it's cut and dried. So that's why we introduced the new system . . . Now, if they are four weeks behind with their rent they get a warning letter; if they're eight weeks behind they get a notice to quit, and when that expires we take court proceedings. Of course the main objection we have from people is, if you send them a notice to quit, they say, 'Oh that's a bit heavy isn't it?' or if it's a possession order, 'getting the law involved'. But, number one, if the law wasn't involved, people wouldn't be secure in their short-life housing, they would be in squats, because all short-life housing is official squats. So the law is already involved. Number two, they tell us that it's a bloody cheek that we send them eviction notices, but of course it's not a bloody cheek that they don't pay their rent . . . Well I'm afraid you just have to kick them out. I mean I feel that a co-op is a very important and a good way of living — good for the people. And because of that you've got to treat it like a bloody baby. You've got to wrap it in cotton wool. If anybody comes near to strike it down, then you go for them, go for their throats. Oh that sounds really heavy but you've got to protect it . . . I'd much rather not get the law involved. But if there isn't another way then you've got to do it. I think it's a drag giving credibility to the law in this sense because the law doesn't particularly like co-ops or people who are in them. There are a lot of funny people in co-ops and they'd love to get hold of all that. We are allowing the police to harass our members, more or less, which is very heavy but there's no option. You see you can't do evictions yourself it's illegal. But that's what I'd like to see, co-op members doing their own evictions, because it would scare the shit out of all of them if they had to do it themselves. It would work if people would do it but they won't. I know from working here that it's just pie in the sky. How many people do we get to meetings? Ten? Well occasionally if there's a house going we get loads of people. People only come when they've got a vested interest. If the members were really co-operative, you wouldn't have to do anything like that. They would pay their rent. They would want to come to the meetings because they would be involved . . . A co-operative should be a joint effort by every member. You shouldn't need a single person keeping it together because the idea of a co-op is that everyone knows what's going on and is involved. But I think because we're so big and the members aren't involved and don't want to be involved, then you can't run it like a proper co-op. It's running now like a housing association, especially on the rents side. That's all you can do if you want the money.

So far, then, we have seen that in addition to contradicting their explicit policy, or at most adopting only informal social control, co-operatives, like traditional capitalist companies, are penetrated by other disciplinary systems on which they also rely, ranging from individual and elite decision making, to most surprisingly formal state justice. The crucial question is why do these contradictions occur? One explanation might be that, just as under capitalist discipline, it is necessary to diversify in order to present one form of discipline as relatively less coercive than the other possibilities. But this explanation has little credibility here, because, in the first place co-operatives are ideally supposed to be opposed to capitalism and its institutions, so that the 'option' of drawing on state justice or elite groups would be more alienating of co-op members than it would be legitimating. Furthermore, in many cases greater coercive power exists within the collective policy and its peer group sanctioning, than exists by drawing on external systems. Clearly the research material on co-operative discipline suggests that a different explanation is required. Such an explanation may itself give us greater insight into why there exist a range of parallel interpenetrating systems in the private justice of capitalist institutions.

Intrinsic human differentiation or extraneous capitalist contamination

There are two broadly opposing explanations for why collective justice in co-operatives co-exists with a range of other semi-autonomous forms of private justice and state law. The first of these is to adopt a micro-analytical perspective and to relate the existence of multiplex disciplinary systems to the inevitability of intrinsic differentiation, specialisation and hierarchicalisation which occurs whenever human agency is organised towards accomplishing a collective goal. Thus although many co-operatives explicitly reject differentiation or hierarchy as natural, they find an inevitable tendency for it to recur which is reflected in their attempts to redefine it or justify it. This can be seen in the account of Gerry of the Big Bag Wholefood Collective, who believes that division of responsibility would actually benefit co-ops:

> Most of the sort of alternative society people that I've got sympathy for, and we associate ourselves a lot with, think that the essential thing about a co-operative is that nobody really tells anybody else what to do: that every decision is not just collective but sort of consensus; that

you don't vote on anything; you are all able to do everything. But these to me aren't essential ingredients of a co-operative . . . I'm beginning to question whether they are even realistic or feasible, whether or not it's not better to say, 'Look what are the aims of a co-operative enterprise? A democratic structure, but not necessarily a structure in which every single person has exactly equal responsibilities; a structure in which everyone is accountable where any profits that are made are distributed amongst the workers or used for outside aims, but that one person isn't creaming all the profit.' Those are the sort of things that to me are the actual, real crucial things about a co-operative.

So some co-op members explain the tendency towards specialisation and differentiation as a desirable reflection of human individuality. Clive of the Electronics Commune, for example, says,

> Although in theory we are very much a co-op of equals, I do think we inevitably move away from this ideal. But only within limits that are quite acceptable because we are all different people, with different levels of confidence to work. Particularly in certain areas, some people have almost unlimited confidence that they can gather information extremely readily and think things through carefully in their spare time. As a result there is an imbalance in that decision-making process which reflects that justifiably.

Similarly, Gary of the Computer Collective says,

> I think a division of labour has to be inevitable in some fields doesn't it? There's going to be some things that I might find interesting that say Bob or Ken or somebody else doesn't find interesting. So if this co-op isn't satisfying me then I'm going to develop in my sort of areas and they are going to develop in their sort of areas. There are tasks that should be shared that aren't being shared, like book-keeping, or filing or whatever. We all hate dull tasks and so nobody really wants to take any particular one of them over.

Others, in contrast, explain specialisation and differentiation in terms, not of some natural inner force but in terms of the all-pervasive nature of a hierarchically differentiated capitalist society. Dario of Face to Face is aware of this issue:

> I think specialisation is exactly the sort of contradiction that happens when you try and behave in a way that is contradicted by life. You know, by the particular form of our society. I'm not surprised it's like that. You can't avoid it.

Indeed, some aspects of co-operative organisation can be directly attributed to member's expectations, that themselves have emerged in a hierarchical setting. Eric of Share and Care was adamant about the importance of this problem:

> They take the view that it is your company; 'you are the boss, you employ us and tell us what to do.' We find it's very difficult for them to change their attitude. A chap downstairs who is responsible for the clearing work has, to say the least, an establishment line. He wants everything drawn out in straight lines. 'Tell me what's required? I don't understand what's required of me. I don't understand the situation.' And even though you say 'the opportunity is there for you to express your point of view' we find he doesn't let himself go. He doesn't open up and say what the problems are.

Sheila of Talk About said this was particularly difficult where the co-operative had been created out of a former hierarchical company:

> When we turned it into a co-op we got problems because some members were much happier in a hierarchical setting. The co-op's not an easy setting to work in if you are used to a hierarchy. I mean, who's going to do everything. You haven't got anybody in particular that you can go and complain to. People often got stuck because of this. That is why we had to set up a complaints' person.

Nor is the problem any less for housing co-operatives. Here, the tendency to specialisation and hierarchy occurs in the form of co-op members taking on the role of tenant, putting pressure on the formal co-op meeting to take the role of landlord. Brian of Home Time says,

> I think it's almost conditioning. I mean they have always had to be aggressive with their landlords. So they might sort of come stomping in here and say that they've got a burst pipe or something. I think that is where their background is always being on the receiving end, they only really do see how things have changed when they are actually required to play the role of landlord. And some of them are reluctant to do that. It's a question of people having been traditionally in a very, very weak position, suddenly they are in a position of power but not aware of it. Like going to a general meeting and asking for a decision to serve a notice to quit — a lot of people can't really believe that by putting their hands up that is actually going to result in somebody being kicked out of their home. People find it difficult. They can't comprehend how Joe and Mabel from up the road are going to be able to kick them out of their home.

Other aspects of the collective structure also reflect the existing divisions within the capitalist society. Particularly interesting here is the way role differentiation is generally accepted and leads to some functions being performed more by men than women and some organisational processes being more appropriate to men's forms of communication than women's. Clive of Electronics Commune explained:

> At the moment it happens that it's mostly the men in the co-op who show the most interest in sort of continually acquiring skills in the policy areas. And the women are more generally concerned with continually updating their skills in the manufacturing areas. I should hardly talk about men and women because we are small enough that we are all individuals. But there is that slight split between the sexes which makes us wonder whether these things are being channelled in a way that we are not very conscious of at the moment — a sexist way. And I think in the light of that one could postulate that meetings themselves are sexist . . . The men seem to enjoy meetings as a sort of social interaction, a bit like being down the

pub together, or boys in the back room, and you know it's quite a strong interaction for them. Whereas, to a slightly greater extent, the women are stronger in terms of one to one interaction during the course of their ordinary productive process of talking, just sort of chatting over the shoulder and so on. Both are methods really for achieving the same thing, which is, you find out what other people are thinking about, express your own opinions, interact and through that you could make decisions. But if you then are going to say meetings are how this co-op makes its decisions it may be that there is a slight sexual bias to it . . . I'll give you an example. 'Who would like to join the sub-committee?', four of the men say 'Yes' and none of the women. So we all thought we are becoming terribly sexist . . . it mustn't just be the men who are involved in these normally male-orientated things. But then as soon as the meeting is over and you're outside the women show as much interest.

A similar sexist penetration from the wider society was illustrated by Brian of Home Time when describing how the 'visits' aspect of their disciplinary policy was penetrated by culturally determined sexist attitudes:

It happens our co-op is women dominated. But most of the women are not sort of radical. In their home lives most of them are still very much under the thumb of the husband. There are lots of examples where the women will be at a committee meeting making very important decisions and then they will say 'Sorry, I've got to get my husband's supper ready for when he gets home from the pub' or something like that. I remember one West Indian tenant saying to me 'If I'm ever in rent arrears I don't mind if you come round and tell me about it, but I don't want any of the women off the committee coming round. If they come and start telling me what to do then they'll be out in the street before they know what has happened.' And I think those are the sort of cultural problems that the group faces.

It is for this reason that Linda of Habit Housing Co-operative believes that enforced discipline is a necessity if co-ops are ever to break away from the influence of the wider society:

> It's like belief in a way. And how do you persuade someone to change their beliefs? From believing in elitist institutions to believing in collective groups and self-discipline. I mean, you have to persuade them or control them into it first, especially if they have got no experience.

But, Clive of the Electronics Commune does not think this is the answer:

> The only way to change that would be either to smother somebody who was feeling very confident about an area or to insist that others without confidence should in some way be forced to stand forward and make decisions. Both of which I think would be a shame and almost immediately against what co-ops stand for.

Undoubtedly the most significant way in which the capitalist society penetrates the collective ideal is that co-operatives have necessarily to deal with capitalist organisations whose system of working then contaminates their attempts to remain alternative and autonomous. A very good illustration of how the hard economic facts of being a co-operative under capitalism can affect the co-operative ideal is revealed in the account of Gerry of Big Bag:

> You see this is where I get very annoyed when people in the sort of alternative co-operative movement come out with statements to me like 'You're not a proper co-operative. You're just capitalistic.' A lot of co-operatives say that the style or administrative system, even the authority systems of capitalist organisations, are completely incompatible with a co-operative structure. Some of them even say that if you aim to pay reasonable wages or if you aim to make a profit you are not a real co-operative. To me it's not whether you make profit, it's what you do with it that counts. In actual fact profit just means making more money than it costs you to . . . you know it means having a surplus at the end of the year rather than a deficit. And if you keep having a deficit you go bankrupt. Also you've got to make enough money to replace your equipment. We've got a van that's depreciated

a certain amount, 25 per cent, every year and so I mean just to cover those costs you have to, at least on paper, make something . . . Basically I'm a socialist and a militant socialist — if anything ever happened I'd be out there on the streets. I've been involved in struggles like that. It's just that I'm not keen on the idea that the image is more important than the content, if you like. I see a lot of co-operatives very concerned with the superficial image of whether or not they are a kind of far-out place. You know, they have no authority structure, everybody just does their own thing, and they're not actually concerned with building something up that is strong, that is actually going to be able to generate some money and take on capitalists at their own game . . . Also the attitude of many of the alternative groups we deal with is that big shops should help small shops and so you should be prepared to pay more. To me this sort of thing was totally cock-eyed — all it means is we're all going to go broke. Although we might have a much bigger turnover it doesn't mean that we're making a load of money. It just means that we were selling more stuff. But, your costs are higher. Also we were trying to pay proper wages and most of the other shops aren't. A lot of them are run on a voluntary basis and things like this . . . We were a member of a co-op warehouse but we left because it meant that we were spending about £800 a fortnight compared to most other co-ops' £100. Now our buying powers meant that we could have gone down to the London wholesalers and got considerable discount, you see. They were inefficient and we thought *they* acted unco-operatively. Also we were the only people who had any money because we had a bank overdraft. We were the only people who tended to pay on time or one of the few. And they used to do things like, if they had a cash problem, phone up and ask us to pay for our order before we got it, and then the order wouldn't arrive. And I sort of thought this is really just not on . . . So the way I'm coming round to seeing things is, although we try very hard to run things in a fully democratic way, what's happened is I'm the one who's been here longest. So, I've got far more experience of the organisation, not because I've wanted to monopolise it but because of the way people have come and gone. Those who knew most have gradually gone and we've recruited a lot of younger people ... I think personally, I'm getting more autocratic. I'm getting more and more of the opinion that you've really got to make being a full member of the co-operative — if that involves having a total say in the way that most crucial decisions of the shop are made — means people have got to put themselves out quite a lot — You've got the people who've got a variety of different understandings of the workings of the business. What to me is ordinary business sense, the way you operate, isn't that easy to everybody. A lot of people, particularly the new ones, don't understand the most simple things of cash flow, how you price stuff, and why you price something higher than something else. But, you are talking about pretty crucial decisions. For example, whether you can afford to take on a new shop in town ... I think you need a core group of preferably three or four people with at least more than one who is a founder member. And I would favour those people having more authority and responsibility than ordinary co-op members in some ways. I mean we are fairly small, but if we got this bigger shop and there was ten or eleven people, you'd need a co-ordinator, call them a director or whatever. That would be very sensible. A lot of people then immediately say 'Ah, hierarchists' but I don't think so.

In conclusion, if the explanation which posits differentiation, specialisation and hierarchy as products of micro processes of human individuality is credible, then collective justice is simply an ideal that cannot be met; a framework whose reality is present only at the point of its creation, and which time, growth and action will ultimately undermine. The conclusion to such an interpretation is that collective justice as a pure form is unstable.

In contrast, if the other explanation is credible and differentiation and hierarchy is the result of macro forces of the wider society, then only a total revolution will bring about a stable form of collective justice, since anything less will result in contamination of the alternative form by the dominant structure and its institutions.

There is, however, a third explanation which transcends this familiar dichotomy.

Towards integrated justice

It is not necessary that the two explanations given above are mutually exclusive. Throughout this book we have seen how theories which are located solely at the level of individual interaction are as inadequate as those which absorb this interaction into an adjunct of macro-structural forces. It has been forcefully argued that an adequate theory of law must address both the macro and the micro without losing the autonomy of either. So it is with explanations for the contradictions of collective justice. While micro processes of human agency produce differentiation and specialisation which delivers a hierarchical capitalist society, it is also the case that the capitalist society is more than simply an aggregate of these micro processes and one which has sufficient autonomy to act back on the agents of its production, to draw out and shape emergent action in a process of reproduction. But this seemingly perpetual process only takes on the particular form it does because those agents whose action creates and at the same time is shaped by capitalism, lose sight of the connection between themselves and the totality. To break free from the constraints of this particular dialectical process it is not enough to imagine and enact new forms of structure, new patterns of organisation or new models of justice. Rather, what is required is to recognise and emphasise the partiality of any particular form and the interdependence of it with the totality. Paradoxically, therefore, co-operatives which seek to contrast themselves with capitalism are perpetuating the ideology which produces the appearance of one particular structure rather than another. Socialist forms are not different from capitalist forms but are contained already within them. Capitalism depends upon collective justice just as socialism depends upon hierarchical elite group decision-making. The fundamental issue, then, is not to create idealistic alternatives but to reflect upon how human experience is related to the totality of which it is a part. Fortunately, some co-op members are well aware of this perspective, as can be seen from the account of Dario from Face to Face:

> The main problem is how do you change things. There's a belief that things change when people get sick of them, and if you organise society in an inefficient enough way, and basically a free enterprise system is a highly inefficient way, eventually a sufficient number of people get sick of it and want to change things ... Then there's those who believe the western capitalist system is so irrational, so extraordinarily unbalanced and catastrophically unstable, with the experience of people within it so out of phase with the experience of other people in the world, that social change is going to come from economic processes that are way beyond this country ... But the big debate of the left is between changing things by moving through a centralised state — which is in danger of fixing itself — or by trying to glimpse what you're aiming at in the present world. It's really the second of these two things that we're doing. We are trying to glimpse possible relationships in the present outside world. Unless you know what it would be like to have a society where people co-operate, unless you've got some glimpse of it, I really don't see what you're doing trying to get it. Or even if you manage to get it, what on earth you are going to do with it ... The only way things change, in my experience — all the things I'm referring to are a very intricate set of relationships ranging from personal ones to huge ones involving organisations — is in an imaginative, co-operative, creative way, where someone offers a possibility with a degree of conviction, energy and forethought about how that possibility will be organised, so that it becomes evident to the other people that that's what happens. I really want to make it mundane, because I think it's very important to make it mundane. I don't want to end up talking about mass party organisation. I'm not convinced that someone running a socialist centre,

however au fait he is with contemporary political ideas, is going to be able to handle society better than Sue Smith, who's 19, because she's doing it now. You know, she's actually trying to work out what happens when she's got a better idea than someone who is older than her, or apparently usually knows better, and how to explain to them without causing an argument and wasted time . . . Like lots of co-operatives we started with the assumption that everybody does everything. That's a philosophical idea, but not an idea that works out as soon as you start doing something complicated. Now no more do I believe we operate as perfectly as a collective could operate. Obviously it's contradicted by lots of things in the outside world. We are on one level a co-operative experimenting with new ways of doing things and on another level we are a small company. The company is concerned with developing plays as a method of expressing ideas and with the experience of taking them out. Now the one thing beyond anything else that makes that possible is economic survival. If you want to eat and do community theatre it's necessary to earn money and that means making endless concessions and of course they are real concessions . . . In order to exist legally there are certain accounting skills which you must have and to train people would take months, in which time you couldn't do anything. So it's better to use people's capacities and to build them into the idea of the co-op. For Greg, who is learning about performing, to interest himself in the details of the administration would destroy his ability to perform. Everything would numb out into a vague blandness. Geoffrey is a far more interesting artist than me and I think I could say that I've set myself quite a lot of things to learn without wanting to learn artistic skills. Therefore Geoffrey is much more the obvious choice to do the posters. It is important that we have posters that are good, rather than posters which I've learnt a lot doing. The basic job a poster does is it brings people to the show and it confers a guise of respectability which attracts money which allows us to exist . . . It's clearly a division of labour and I believe that society functions through a division of labour. But I don't think a division of labour necessarily means a division of experience, nor does it imply a hierarchy. Now the posters are interesting in themselves but they are not the essential experience; these skills are being operated by people in the company to the end which all of us together have decided. I think that if you work in a factory and you experience a division of labour organised for profits, then you experience an irrational set of experiences. The experiences you're offered don't explain it. But I think you can divide labour so that people select a group of experiences that are meaningful and do explain life, and thereby get the maximum productive creative life out of it. I think that the number of experiences that you can have with people, objects, processes, are infinite. Anyone anywhere who lives is involved in a selection of experiences. Now I think to experience a process in a real way is to experience an intelligent selection of those little experiences. Then the essential experience is the one which is built up to, in our case, creating a show and the experience of getting it out on the road . . . I don't believe that the job we do operates as it could do in a better world, but it's developing a kind of tool and learning how to use it and it's very clumsy. What happens is that a lot of people's emotions and ideas and paths of behaviour aren't tuned to it. But all of the workers in the company sense that most of the arguments that rage for a few hours or perhaps simmer for a few weeks are always followed by people apologising or giving in or accepting that the problem was in them adapting to what needed to be done. It's like we're being sucked forwards. People groan at their incapacity to fit but they don't hesitate at the direction they are going . . . The only really important question in my mind is 'Will the existence of co-ops prevent society changing for the better?' Now I think that's a much more legitimate criticism, actually, to level at liberal education and the social services.

Conclusion

The original assumption on which the research for this book was based was that different types of organisational structure have their own corresponding systems of discipline. This did not seem unreasonable, especially since considerable literature in the sociology and anthropology of law suggested that particular social structures have corresponding types of law (see chapter 1). The major conclusion and indeed the most overriding of the study, was that this assumption was wrong. *The findings analysed in the second half of this book demonstrate clearly that different kinds of organisational structure accommodate aspects of the whole range of theoretically identifiable forms of private justice.* Quite unexpectedly, it was found that as well as having managerial discipline, companies and organisations with hierarchical decision-making structures also had a form of collective peer-group discipline among employees which involved sanctions taken by workers, or their representatives, on fellow workers (see chapter 4). In contrast, worker co-operatives, although having a policy of collective decision-making in justice, and formally conferring equal status on their members, exhibited, in addition, executive-elite decision-making of the kind found in hierarchically organised companies. Perhaps most surprisingly, these co-operatives also relied on state law in spite of their professed independence and 'alternative' approach (see chapter 6). In short, then, each type of discipline was found to operate in different kinds of organisation at the informal level, despite an explicit formal policy which appeared to express and conform to the overall organisational policy, and actual disciplinary types seem to be composites which use different disciplinary forms at different stages of this procedure.

Now had the evidence been examined from conventional macro- or micro-theoretical perspectives, it would not have been difficult to explain away these 'anomalies'. Thus the forms of private justice might have been depicted as 'ideal types' simply aiding the understanding of the complexity of social reality. Alternatively, it might have been possible to explain away the 'anomalies' as by-products of change. In so far as structures might have appeared to have been changing in an evolutionary way, then discrepancies would become merely evidence of residual forms or vanguards of emerging forms. Had the micro approach been taken, the 'anomalies' would represent no more than the reality as opposed to the theory, but then this would leave unexplained why structures and law forms *appeared* to be different and why it was that some of these appearances were more profuse than others.

As should now be clear, my research findings indicate that conventional approaches to explaining private justice are inadequate. Neither the totalising macro theory nor the partial micro theory provides an explanation sufficiently comprehensive to capture the complexity of private justice and its relationship to state law and the wider social structure. The macro theory denies the autonomy of private justice, explaining this in terms of its function to the totality. This does not account for the way in which private justice contradicts and often undermines the very social structures on whose behalf it is supposed to be operating. Private justice does not simply support capitalism, nor does it merely serve to legitimate the existing social order, but it also claims some of its territory, imposing its own definitions and designs. As such, the relations of private justice exist actively and creatively as some of the relations of the totality. Private justice cannot be reduced or subordinated to social structure.

But neither does this mean that a micro-analytical approach, which acknowledges autonomy and independence from structure, is better placed to account for the phenomenon. It blatantly fails to address the way structure shapes and constrains, limits and channels the autonomy of the private form. While private justice is not completely constrained neither is it completely free. Conventional macro and micro approaches either absorb the reality and autonomy of private justice or else they ignore the totality of social control. As we have seen, however, an integrated approach to theorising allows us to transcend the limitations of this dichotomy. We have seen how there is an interaction and mutuality between the structure and the action that constitutes it. As a result, not only does the totality rely on the autonomy of private justice but it also intervenes to strengthen, refine and redefine it. At the same time, private justice acts on the totality, in particular on the state law, and penetrates into its construction and formulation.

Now such a conclusion has serious implications for socio-legal change. It means that any attempt to change society through merely changing formal laws must fail because formal law is only one part of an interrelated set of semi-autonomous constituent parts. Such is the force of the existing mutuality of relations between these parts that rather than bringing about change new laws are more likely to be absorbed into the pre-existing relations. This is because the only way the new form can function is to integrate with those relations of the existing form which includes both the already established relations of private justice and the range of other semi-autonomous parts making up the totality. The same is true for any changes made to private justice. Any attempt to substitute a new form for the existing form will result in a selection of only those aspects of the new form which are relevant to the existing relations of social control.

In conclusion, the implications of integrated theorising for the sociology of law are that any changes that fail to acknowledge both the formal state law *and* the 'informal' relations of private justice will bring no change at all. Only by simultaneously changing both the formal and the informal is it possible to change the totality. But such change first requires a consciousness that those who act in institutions of social control exercise power both for themselves and on behalf of others. Real change will not occur until the power that they exercise is exercised on their own behalf. Such change requires revelation not revolution.

Appendix

Background to the research project and methods used

The research for this book was undertaken as an SSRC funded project (HR5907/2) which attempted to describe and compare the range of internal private disciplinary procedures used by different organisations in their handling of internal rule-breaking behaviour. A number of organisations were selected for depth examination and others for supporting information. These were chosen to enable comparison between collective disciplinary procedures, in which offenders are brought before their colleagues for sanctioning (community courts), and other more hierarchical disciplinary procedures (managerial justice; joint disciplinary tribunals), at both the formal and informal levels of operation within different organisational structures.

My previous research had shown that some internal rule-breaking activities such as pilfering, fiddling and amateur trading had a different motivational structure from conventional rule-breaking — that it was a *socially* motivated form of deviance and as such would require a model of discipline and justice suitably responsive to its nature (Henry, 1978). Studies I had conducted into self-help showed how peer-group control could be an effective force in limiting extreme forms of certain deviant behaviour, such as alcoholism and mental illness, being sufficiently flexible to accommodate minor deviations without being too oppressive or alienating (Robinson and Henry, 1977; Henry and Robinson, 1978a; 1978b). Thus, a form of self-help justice which would allow moral boundaries to be flexible enough to accommodate inevitable minor offences, while being sufficiently forceful to control more serious and more universally accepted moral departures from the rules, seemed an appropriate model to adopt in the context of factory deviance (Henry and Mars, 1978; Henry, 1979).

At the time of the original proposal it was widely believed that although self-help justice in the form of workers' courts, comrades' courts and people's courts was a feature of most socialist societies (Henry, 1981b) there were few actual examples of 'community courts' in Britain. Although the British industrial context provides more autonomy from the state than is the case in socialist countries, allowing individual factories to operate their own institutions of private discipline, previous research suggested that the typical model of discipline adopted in practice was either a hierarchical punitive-authoritarian kind or more recently, a corrective-representative form. Indeed, the latter model was recommended by the ACAS Code of Practice and has been shown by more recent work to have been adopted, even if not as completely as some believed (see chapters 3 and 4 above).

However, my own previous work and that of others, had confirmed the existence of what appeared to be an exceptional but long-established 'participatory' form of disciplinary procedure, known as the joint disciplinary tribunal (Henry, 1978, pp. 160-73; Wedderburn and Davis, 1969; Plumridge, 1964). This had certain similarities with the 'community court' and was established in a few companies whose own peculiar 'paternalistic' history had led them to find this a useful form of dispute resolution where disciplinary issues were concerned. In addition, the little work that had been done on producer co-operatives suggested that these might have a form of community court for handling in discipline and so too might voluntary societies and professional associations.

The original proposal, then, was to investigate one of the longest established of the joint disciplinary procedures in depth, and to compare this with a depth study of examples from each of the other types: conventional managerial justice, in its punitive-authoritarian or corrective-representative forms, as found in small non-unionised enterprises and large private and public companies; 'collective' justice as found in co-operative organisations, and some voluntary societies.

Strategy and methods

The original proposal sought to achieve the objectives of the project via a comparative depth study of four British companies which were selected because each appeared to operate a different disciplinary procedure, and together reflected the range of disciplinary models under investigation. Crucial to the project was Foodstuffs Ltd, which operated the quasi-community court in its joint disciplinary tribunal. Also included were a conventional manufacturing company, a co-ownership company and a co-operative.

It was thought desirable to undertake five levels of research at each of the four companies: (1) tape-recorded interviews with those responsible for discipline (2) semi-structured interviewer-administered questionnaires with employees (3) observation of actual disciplinary proceedings (4) interviews with employees who had been subject to discipline (5) examination of company records or disciplinary cases. As the research progressed two problems became apparent. The first stemmed from an initial difficulty of gaining access to any company other than Foodstuffs and the second, requiring a clarification in structure, arose from the action taken to remedy the first.

Apart from Foodstuffs, negotiations with each of the other selected companies failed to secure access. A number of reasons were given, from an unwillingness to have employees diverted from production, change of directorship, 'Irish Postal Strike', being over-researched, seeing no benefits to the company, through to the sensitive nature of the area of investigation, and a willingness to protect individuals from exposure as a result of past misdemeanours. In order to overcome these difficulties it was decided to revise the strategy to incorporate two tiers of information gathering. One tier, designated as the 'core research' involved gaining access as deeply as possible into the disciplinary procedure of one company from each type. A second tier, called 'support research', involved obtaining information from a number of similar type companies via whatever means possible: postal questionnaire, interviews, observation, letter requesting information. This was successful in securing enough material to achieve adequately the objectives of the research project, but, since it brought in material wider than the original proposal, it revealed that the original criteria for classifying types of disciplinary procedure, according to type of company, based loosely on whether it was co-operative, paternalistic or traditional managerial, was inadequate. The result was a clarification of the structure of the project and an adjustment to the strategy, principally involving a reduction in some projected areas of inquiry and an extension in others.

The clarification of structure stemmed from trying to make sense of the different kinds of disciplinary procedure in relationship to corresponding types of organisational structure as found in different companies. Ongoing analysis of the preliminary findings suggested that the kind of disciplinary procedure a company had, depended upon the organisational features of the 'community' in which discipline occurs. Two criteria seemed to be important. These were the relative status of the membership within the company's community and the type of decision-making adopted. Membership status was either equal or unequal while the decision-making process was either hierarchical, joint or collective. This gave the theoretical possibilities of six types of organisation, each with its own distinctive type of internal disciplinary procedure. These were: *managerial discipline*, thought to occur in conventional capitalist companies having a hierarchical decision-making process and an unequal membership status; *joint disciplinary tribunal*, thought to be peculiar to paternalistic or democratic companies which have unequal membership status but decentralise some decision-making to employee representatives; *community discipline*, which is a theoretical possibility that might occur where companies have an unequal membership structure but which adopt a collective decision-making process in certain areas, such as health and safety at work; *community courts*, thought to occur in small collectives such as co-operatives or communes, where membership is equal and decision-making is shared among the membership of the collective; *joint elite panel*, is a possibility among equal membership organisations which adopt a joint elite decision-making process because their size renders collective meetings inefficient and the elected committee becomes divorced from the other members to a degree that new representatives have to be elected to deal with the first; and *disciplinary council or board* is thought to occur when an equal membership organisation elects an elite committee to manage itself. This typology, while useful as a heuristic device, had certain fundamental weaknesses, not least of which was that the membership status of individuals within an organisation was partly dependent on their power to make decisions, so that some of the theoretical possibilities were absent in practice. Also problematic was how easily organisations could be distinguished as pure types. These difficulties were not overcome, but subsequently acknowledged as reflecting an important characteristic about the nature of organisational structure and discipline. At the preliminary stages, however, the framework was adequate to enable collection of material to proceed.

Thus having apparently clarified the relationship between the type of discipline and the organisational structure in which it was likely to occur, it seemed possible to conduct research into both core and support examples of each of the six types. But, not only was this attempt frustrated by the virtual non-existence of certain of the types, it was also limited in the information that it was possible to obtain, since the very disciplinary process often precluded access to some areas of inquiry. For example, no interviews with employees were possible in those companies using managerial discipline since the management who made the decisions did not see such interviews as relevant. But since unions took part in some stages of the procedure, they were allowed to be interviewed. In contrast, where employees were directly involved in disciplinary decision-making it was sometimes possible to obtain, not only interviews, but access to observe procedures as well. However, while not obtaining the same depth of information from each individual company, the utilisation of a broader approach using different methods has led to it being possible to obtain a comparable body of material from each of the types of disciplinary procedure under study. In the following summary of research conducted, I give details of the quality and amount of material obtained.

Research material gathered

The bulk of the research material was collected in 1979 and 1980. All the names of companies, organisations and individuals mentioned either below or in the main body of the text are fictitious and have no relationship to any actual company or individual who might bear the same name.

Managerial discipline

Eleven tape-recorded interviews with representatives of management at different levels of seniority of the following companies: Public Transport; National Catering Company; Paper Products Ltd; Paper Distribution Ltd; Public Security Ltd and the Rex Rubber Company. A one in twenty postal questionnaire survey of the top 1,000 UK industrial companies produced a 23 per cent response rate resulting in 40 questionnaires from an original sample size of 174. The average size of respondent companies in the survey was 2,623 employees, with a median company size of 1,500 employees and with 77 per cent of respondents being between 500 and 10,000 in size.

Joint disciplinary tribunal

Ten tape-recorded interviews with different levels of management from Foodstuffs Ltd, the Tyre Company, the Motal Manufactures and the Washing Machine Company. In addition four trade union members and eighteen employees were interviewed from Foodstuffs and the company provided documentary information of its disciplinary records over the past twenty years. The Washing Machine Company allowed observation of three actual tribunal hearings.

Community discipline

No examples researched or found to exist in practice since this form seemed to operate in practice as a joint-tribunal.

Community courts

Twenty-seven tape-recorded interviews conducted with members of both producer and housing co-operatives: thirteen of these interviews were with members of the following housing co-operatives; Habit, Living Space, Big Brick, Home Time, and fourteen were with members of the following producer co-operatives; Electronics Commune, Big Bag Wholefood Co-operative, Computer Collective, Share and Care, Troupe Together, Talk About, Face to Face and English Words. In addition, I attended nineteen disciplinary meetings of the Habit Housing Co-operative over a four month period and received correspondence from eighty-one housing co-operatives and twenty other producer co-operatives.

Joint elite panel

No examples of this found, although to some extent the arts co-operative

Troupe Together could be classified in this category as could the disablement workers' group Share and Care.

Disciplinary council or board

Twelve tape-recorded interviews with major professional associations and trade unions and thirty-seven written replies from other associations and trade unions. This material was not included in the analysis.

In summary then, a total of twenty-three disciplinary hearings were attended over five months; seventy-seven interviews were recorded totalling over one hundred hours and producing 800 pages of transcript material; and replies to 138 letters of correspondence and forty questionnaires were received.

Bibliography

Abel, R. (1981), 'Conservative conflict and the reproduction of capitalism: the role of informal justice', *International Journal of the Sociology of Law*, vol. 9, pp. 245-67.
Abel, R. (ed.) (1982), *The Politics of Informal Justice*, 2 vols, New York, Academic Press.
ACAS (Advisory Conciliation and Arbitration Service) (1977), *Disciplinary Practice and Procedures in Employment*, London, HMSO.
Anderman, S. D. (1972), *Voluntary Dismissals Procedures and the Industrial Relations Act*, London, PEP.
Archer, M. S. (1982), 'Morphogenesis versus structuration: on combining structure and action', *British Journal of Sociology*, vol. 33, pp. 455-83.
Ashdown, R. T., and Baker, K. H. (1973), *In Working Order: A Study of Industrial Discipline*, London, HMSO.
Austin, J. (1832), *Lectures on Jurisprudence*, London, John Murray.
Bailey, F. G. (1960), *Tribe Caste and Nation: A Study of Political Activity and Political Change in Highland Orissa*, Manchester University Press.
Baldwin, J., and McConville, M. (1977), *Negotiated Justice*, Oxford, Martin Robertson.
Bendall, R. D. (1981), '"Legal" pluralism: a critique of holistic conceptions of law', mimeo, University of Kent.
Bendall, R. D. (1982), 'Towards an integrative approach to the study of law', mimeo, University of Kent.
Berman, H. J., and Spindler, J. W. (1963), 'Soviet comrades' courts', *Washington Law Review*, vol. 38, pp. 842-910.
Berndt, R. M. (1962), *Excess and Constraint: Social Control Among a New Guinea Mountain People*, Chicago University Press.
Blumberg, A. S. (1967), *Criminal Justice*, Chicago, Quadrangle Books.
Bohannon, P. (1957), *Justice and Judgement Among the Tiv*, London, Oxford University Press.
Bosserman, P. (1968), *Dialectical Sociology: An Analysis of the*

Sociology of Georges Gurvitch, Boston, Mass., Porter Sargent.
Bottomley, A. K. (1979), *Criminology in Focus*, Oxford, Martin Robertson.
Bottoms, A. E., and McClean, J. D. (1976), *Defendants in the Criminal Process*, London, Routledge & Kegan Paul.
Brady, J. P. (1981), 'Sorting out the exile's confusion: or a dialogue on popular justice', *Contemporary Crisis*, vol. 5, pp. 31-8.
Brinton, C. (1953), *The Anatomy of Revolution*, London, Cape.
Cappelletti, M., and Garth, B. (eds) (1978), *Access to Justice: A World Survey*, 4 vols, Milan, Sijthoff Giuffre.
Carson, W. G. (1974), 'The sociology of crime and the emergence of criminal laws', in P. Rock and M. McIntosh (eds), *Deviance and Social Control*, London, Tavistock, pp. 67-90.
Christie, N. (1976), *Conflicts as Property*, Sheffield University Centre for Criminology.
Cicourel, A. V. (1981), 'Notes on the integration of micro- and macro-levels of analysis' in K. Knorr-Cetina and A. V. Cicourel (eds) (1981), pp. 51-80.
Collins, R. (1981a), 'On the Microfoundations of Macrosociology' *American Journal of Sociology*, vol. 86, pp. 984-1014.
Collins, R. (1981b), 'Micro-translation as a theory-building strategy', in K. Knorr-Cetina and A. V. Cicourel (eds) (1981), pp. 81-108.
Colson, E. (1953), 'Social control and vengeance in plateau Tonga society', *Africa*, vol. 23, pp. 199-212.
Comaroff, J. L., and Roberts, S. (1981), *Rules and Processes: The Cultural Logic of Dispute in an African Context*, University of Chicago Press.
Dalton, M. (1959), *Men Who Manage*, New York, John Wiley & Sons.
Daniel, W. W., and Stilgoe, E. (1978), *The Impact of Employment Protection Laws*, London, Policy Studies Institute.
Danzig, R. (1973), 'Towards the creation of a complementary decentralised system of criminal justice', *Stanford Law Review*, vol. 26, pp. 1-54.
Dawson, S. J. (1969), 'Disciplinary and dismissals practice and procedures', unpublished government social survey.
Dell, S. (1971), *Silent in Court*, London, Bell.
Department of Employment (1972), *The Code of Industrial Relations Practice*, London, HMSO.
Dickens, L. *et al.* (1979), 'A response to the government working papers on amendments to employment protection legislation' mimeo, Coventry, University of Warwick, Industrial Relations Unit.
Durkheim, E. (1893), *The Division of Labour in Society*, Chicago, The Free Press, 1964.
Durkheim, E. (1969), 'Types of law in relation to types of social solidarity', in V. Aubert (ed.), *Sociology of Law*, Harmondsworth, Penguin, pp. 17-29.
Eckhoff, T. (1966), 'The mediator, the judge and the administrator in conflict-resolution', *Acta Sociologica*, vol. 10, pp. 148-72.

Ehrlich, E. (1913), *Fundamental Principles of the Sociology of Law*, Cambridge, Mass., Harvard University Press.
Ehrlich, E. (1979), 'Living law', in C. Campbell and P. Wiles (eds), *Law and Society*, Oxford, Martin Robertson, pp. 121-5.
Eldridge, J. (1970), *Max Weber: The Interpretation of Social Reality*, London, Michael Joseph.
Evans Pritchard, E. E. (1940), *The Nuer*, Oxford, Clarendon Press.
Fallers, L. (1969), *Law Without Precedent*, University of Chicago Press.
Ferdinand, T. N. (1977), 'Criminal justice in America: from colonial intimacy to bureaucratic formality', mimeo, Northern Illinois University.
Fisher, E. A. (1975), 'Community courts: an alternative to conventional criminal adjudication', *American University Law Review*, vol. 24, pp. 1253-91.
Fitzpatrick, P. (1981), 'Law, Plurality and Underdevelopment', mimeo, University of Kent, as cited in Bendall (1982), p. 14.
Fitzpatrick, P. (1982), 'The dissolution and persistence of law', mimeo, University of Kent, as cited in Bendall (1982), p. 11.
Freund, J. (1965), *The Sociology of Max Weber*, New York, Random House.
Garfinkel, H. (1956), 'Conditions of successful degradation ceremonies', *American Journal of Sociology*, vol. 6, pp. 420-4.
Giddens, A. (1979), *Central Problems in Social Theory: Action, Structure and Contradiction in Social Analysis*, London, Macmillan.
Giddens, A. (1981), 'Agency, institution and time-space analysis', in K. Knorr-Cetina and A. V. Cicourel (eds) (1981), pp. 161-74.
Glazer, B., and Strauss, A. (1971), *Status Passage*, London, Routledge & Kegan Paul.
Gluckman, M. (1955), *The Judicial Process Among the Barotse*, Manchester University Press.
Gouldner, A. (1954), *Patterns of Industrial Bureaucracy*, New York, Free Press.
Grace, C., and Wilkinson, P. (1978), *Sociological Inquiry and Legal Phenomena*, London, Collier-Macmillan.
Gulliver, P. H. (1963), *Social Control in African Society*, London, Routledge & Kegan Paul.
Gurvitch, G. (1947), *Sociology of Law*, London, Routledge & Kegan Paul, 1973.
Hamnett, I. (1975), *Chieftainship and Legitimacy: An Anthropological Study of Executive Law in Lesotho*, London, Routledge & Kegan Paul.
Harré, R. (1981), 'Philosophical aspects of the micro-macro problem', in K. Knorr-Cetina and A. V. Cicourel (eds) (1981), pp. 139-60.
Hart, H. L. A. (1961), *The Concept of Law*, London, Clarendon Press.
Henry, S. (1978), *The Hidden Economy: The Context and Control of Borderline Crime*, Oxford, Martin Robertson.
Henry, S. (1979), 'Controlling the hidden economy', *Employee Relations*, vol. 1, pp. 17-22.

Henry, S. (1981a), 'Discipline at work: basic results from a survey', mimeo, Enfield, Middlesex Polytechnic, Centre for Occupational and Community Research.
Henry, S. (1981b), 'Decentralised justice: private v democratic informality', in S. Henry (ed.), *Informal Institutions: Alternative Networks in the Corporate State*, New York, St. Martin's Press, pp. 179-91.
Henry, S. (1982), 'Factory law: the changing disciplinary technology of industrial social control', *International Journal of the Sociology of Law*, vol. 10, pp. 365-84.
Henry, S., and Mars, G. (1978), 'Crime at work: the social construction of amateur property theft', *Sociology*, vol. 12, pp. 245-63.
Henry, S., and Robinson, D. (1978a), 'Understanding Alcoholics Anonymous: results from a survey in England and Wales', *Lancet*, 18 February, pp. 372-5.
Henry, S., and Robinson, D. (1978b), 'Talking out of alcoholism: results from a survey in England and Wales', *The Journal of the Royal College of General Practitioners*, vol. 28, pp. 414-19.
Hoebel, E. A. (1954), *The Law of Primitive Man*, Cambridge, Mass., Harvard University Press.
Horning, D. (1970), 'Blue-collar theft: conceptions of property and attitudes toward pilfering and work group norms in a modern plant', in E. Smigel and H. Ross (eds), *Crimes Against Bureaucracy*, New York, van Nostrand Reinhold, pp. 46-64.
Hudson, K. (1970), *Working to Rule*, London, Adams & Dart.
Hunt, A. (1978), *The Sociological Movement in Law*, London, Macmillan.
Hunt, A. (1981), 'Dichotomy and contradiction in the sociology of law', *British Journal of Law and Society*, vol. 8, pp. 47-77.
Industrial Relations Review and Report (1978), 'Company disciplinary procedures', Part 1 in no. 169 (Feb.), pp. 2-6; part 2 in no. 171 (March), pp. 8-10; part 3 in no. 184 (Sept.), pp. 8-11.
Industrial Relations Review and Report (1980), 'Dismissal for dishonesty', Part 1 in no. 236, pp. 2-13; part 2 in no. 237, pp. 2-12.
IPM (Institute of Personnel Management) (1979), *Disciplinary Procedures and Practice*, London, Institute of Personnel Management.
Jones, D. L. (1961), *Arbitration and Industrial Discipline*, Ann Arbor, University of Michigan.
Kamenka, E., and Tay, A. E.-S. (1975), 'Beyond bourgeois individualism: the contemporary crisis in law and legal ideology', in E. Kamenka and R. S. Neale (eds), *Feudalism, Capitalism and Beyond*, London, Edward Arnold.
Kamenka, E., and Tay, A. E.-S. (1978), 'Socialism, anarchism and law', in E. Kamenka, R. Brown and A. Tay (eds), *Law and Society: The Crisis in Legal Ideals*, London, Edward Arnold, pp. 48-80.
Kamenka, E., and Tay, A. E.-S. (1980), 'Social traditions, legal traditions', in E. Kamenka and A. Tay (eds), *Law and Social Control*, London, Edward Arnold, pp. 3-26.

Kelsen, H. (1934), 'The pure theory of law: its methods and fundamental concepts' *The Law Quarterly Review*, vol. 50, pp. 474-535.
Kelsen, H. (1945), *General Theory of Law and State*, Cambridge, Mass., Harvard University Press.
King, M. (1981), *The Framework of Criminal Justice*, London, Croom Helm.
Kinsey, R. (1979), 'Despotism and legality', in B. Fine *et al.* (eds), *Capitalism and the Rule of Law*, London, Hutchinson, pp. 76-89.
Knorr-Cetina, K. (1981), 'Introduction: The micro-sociological challenge of macro-sociology: towards a reconstruction of social theory and methodology' in K. Knorr-Cetina and A. V. Cicourel (eds) (1981), pp. 1-47.
Knorr-Cetina, K., and Cicourel, A. V. (1981), *Advances in Social Theory and Methodology: Toward an Integration of Micro- and Macro-Sociologies*, London, Routledge & Kegan Paul.
Koch, K. F. (1974), *War and Peace in Jalemo: The Management of Conflict in Highland New Guinea*, Cambridge, Mass., Harvard University Press.
Kuhn, T. (1970), *The Structure of Scientific Revolutions*, University of Chicago Press.
Lapenna, I. (1968), *Soviet Penal Policy*, London, The Bodley Head.
Lea, J. (1979), 'Discipline and capitalist development', in B. Fine *et al.* (eds), *Capitalism and the Rule of Law*, London, Hutchinson, pp. 46-64.
Lidz, V. (1981), 'Transformational theory and the internal environment of action systems', in K. Knorr-Cetina and A. V. Cicourel (eds) (1981), pp. 205-33.
Llewellyn, K. (1930), 'A realistic jurisprudence — the next step', *Columbia Law Review*, vol. 30.
Llewellyn, K. (1931), 'Some realism about realism', *Harvard Law Review*, vol. 44, pp. 1222-60.
Llewellyn, K. (1960), *The Common Law Tradition: Deciding Appeals*, Boston, Little, Brown.
Llewellyn, K., and Hoebel, E. A. (1941), *The Cheyenne Way*, Norman, University of Oklahoma Press.
Longmire, D. R. (1981), 'A popular justice system: a radical alternative to the traditional criminal justice system', *Contemporary Crisis*, vol. 5, pp. 15-30.
Luhmann, N. (1981), 'Communication about law in interaction systems', in K. Knorr-Cetina and A. V. Cicourel (eds), (1981), pp. 234-56.
McCabe, S., and Purves, R. (1972), *By-passing the Jury*, Oxford, Blackwell.
Maine, H. S. (1861), *Ancient Law*, London, John Murray, 1912.
Maine, H. S. (1979), 'Law in progressive societies', in C. Campbell and P. Wiles (eds), *Law and Society*, Oxford, Martin Robertson, pp. 18-23.

Malinowski, B. (1926), *Crime and Custom in Savage Society*, London, Kegan Paul Trench Trubner.
Malinowski, B. (1979), 'Law and custom', in C. Campbell and P. Wiles (eds), *Law and Society*, Oxford, Martin Robertson, pp. 93-6.
Mars, G. (1974), 'Dock pilferage', in P. Rock and M. McIntosh (eds), *Deviance and Social Control*, London, Tavistock, pp. 209-28.
Martin, J. P. (1962), *Offenders as Employees*, London, Macmillan.
Marx, K., and Engels, F. (1965), *The German Ideology*, London, Lawrence & Wishart.
Marx, K., and Engels, F. (1848), *The Communist Manifesto*, in *Selected Works*, vol. 1, London, Lawrence & Wishart.
Mellish, M., and Collis-Squires, N. (1976), 'Legal and social norms in discipline and dismissal', *Industrial Law Journal*, vol. 5, pp. 164-77.
Moore, S. F. (1978), *Law as Process*, London, Routledge & Kegan Paul.
Newman, D. J. (1966), *Convictions: The Determination of Guilt or Innocence Without Trial*, Boston, Little, Brown.
NJAC (National Joint Advisory Council) (1967), *Dismissal Procedure: Report of a Committee*, London, HMSO.
Packer, H. L. (1969), *The Limits of the Criminal Sanction*, Stamford University Press.
Parsons, T. (1937), *The Structure of Social Action*, New York, McGraw-Hill.
Parsons, T. (1962), 'The law and social control', in W. M. Evan (ed.), *Law and Sociology*, Chicago, Free Press, pp. 64-9.
Pashukanis, E. B. (1929), *Law and Marxism: A General Theory*, London, Ink Links, 1978.
Plumridge, M. D. (1964), 'Disciplinary practice in industry', unpublished PhD thesis, University of Manchester.
Pound, R. (1903), *Outlines of Lectures on Jurisprudence*, Cambridge, Mass., Harvard University Press, 1943.
Pound, R. (1942), *Social Control Through Law*, New Haven, Yale University Press.
Pound, R. (1959), *Jurisprudence*, 5 vols, St. Paul, Minn. West Publishing.
Radcliffe-Brown, A. R. (1952), *Structure and Function in Primitive Society*, London, Cohen & West.
Ramundo, B. A. (1965), 'The comrades' court: molder and keeper of socialist morality', *George Washington Law Review*, vol. 33, pp. 692-727.
Renner, K. (1904), *The Institutions of Private Law and Their Social Functions*, London, Routledge & Kegan Paul, 1949.
Rich, R. (1979), *The Sociology of Criminal Law*, Toronto, Butterworths.
Ritzer, G. (1975), *Sociology: A Multiple Paradigm Science*, Boston, Allyn & Bacon.
Roberts, S. (1979), *Order and Dispute: An Introduction to Legal Anthropology*, Harmondsworth, Penguin.
Robinson, D., and Henry, S. (1977), *Self-help and Health: Mutual*

Aid for Modern Problems, Oxford, Martin Robertson.
Rogovin, E. B. (1961), 'Socialist conformity and the comradely courts in the Soviet Union', *Crime and Delinquency*, vol. 7, pp. 303-11.
Ross, E. A. (1901), *Social Control: A Study of the Foundations of Order*, New York, Macmillan, 1910.
Santos, B. S. (1980), 'Law and community: the changing nature of state power in late capitalism', *International Journal of the Sociology of Law*, vol. 8, pp. 379-97.
Schur, E. M. (1968), *Law and Society*, New York, Random House.
Shapera, I. (1938), *A Handbook of Tswana Law and Custom*, Oxford University Press.
South, N., and Scraton, P. (1981), 'Capitalist discipline, private justice and the hidden economy', mimeo, Enfield, Middlesex Polytechnic.
Statsky, W. P. (1974), 'Community courts: decentralising juvenile jurisprudence', *Capital University Law Review*, vol. 3, pp. 1-26.
Thompson, E. P. (1968), *The Making of the English Working Class*, Harmondsworth, Penguin.
Tönnies, F. (1912), *Gemeinschaft and Gesellschaft*, C. P. Loomis (trans.), East Lansing Mich., Michigan State University Press, 1957.
Toulemont, R. (1955), *Sociologie et pluralisme dialectique*, Louvain, Belgium, Editions Nauwelaerts.
Turner, V. W. (1957), *Schism and Continuity in an African Society: A Study of Ndembu Village Life*, Manchester University Press.
Unger, R. M. (1976), *Law in Modern Society*, New York, Free Press.
Versele, S. C. (1969), 'Public participation in administration of criminal justice', *International Review of Criminal Policy*, vol. 27, pp. 9-17.
Walton, P. (1976), 'Max Weber's sociology of law', in P. Carlen (ed.), *The Sociology of Law*, Keele, Sociological Review Monographs.
Weber, M. (1922), *The Theory of Social and Economic Organisation*, Chicago, Free Press, 1947.
Wedderburn, K. W., and Davis, P. L. (1969), *Employment Grievances and Disputes Procedure in Britain*, Berkeley, University of California Press.
Whelan, C. J. (1981), 'Informalising Judicial Procedures', in S. Henry (ed.), *Informal Institutions: Alternative Networks in the Corporate State*, New York, St. Martin's Press, pp. 166-78.
Young, J. (1981), 'Thinking seriously about crime: some models of criminology', in M. Fitzgerald *et al.* (eds), *Crime and Society*, London, Routledge & Kegan Paul, pp. 248-309.
Young, M. (1971), *Fighting with Food*, Cambridge Mass., Harvard University Press.

Index

Abel, R., 44-6, 230
accommodative-participative model of discipline, 85-92, 93, 132-78, *see* participation in justice
accountability, 36-7, 38
acephalous societies, 8, 20
Advisory, Conciliation and Arbitration Service (ACAS), 102-8, 136, 140, 153, 155, 224, 230
aggregation hypothesis, 64, 65, 216
alliances, *see* interpenetration of semi-autonomous parts
alternative courts, 40-6, 93-6, 223-4
analytical dualism, 62, 65
Anderman, S., 77, 229
anxiety reduction, 148-9
appeals, 73, 75, 77, 79, 81, 91, 104, 109, 135-6, 201-2
arbitrary justice, 72-3, 77, 80, 102
arbitration, 38, 40, 45, 50, 58
Archer, M., 63-4, 65, 229
Ashdown, R., 72, 73, 77, 80, 103, 229
Austin, J., 1, 2, 229
authority and power, 2, 3, 8, 72, 73, 82-3, 84, 89, 92, 117-23, 145-50, 153, 190-1, 203-7
autonomy and semi-autonomy, 23, 47-57, 60-1, 64, 84, 92-3, 96-7, 98-100, 133-4; externally generated, 97, 99, 100-15; internally generated, 97, 99, 116-26; source in individual, 77, 99, 126-31, *see* penetration

Baker, K., 72, 73, 77, 80, 103, 229
Baldwin, J., 36, 229
Bendall, R., 229, 231
Blumberg, A., 17, 36, 229
Bosserman, P., 55, 229
Bottomley, A., 17, 36-7, 230
Brady, J., 43-4, 230
Brinton, C., 9, 230
bureaucratic administrative regulation, 14-17, 19, 23, 24-6, 67
bureaucratic model of justice, 15-17, 27, 28, 33, 38, 119-23, 136, *see* accommodative-participative model of discipline
bureaucratic structures, 14-17, 19, 78

capitalist contamination, 180, 210-19
capitalist organisation of society, 11-14, 70, 71-3, 82-5, 92, 93, 179-80, 184-5, 207-8, 210-19
Christie, N., 39-40, 230

Cicourel, A., 64, 65, 230, 231, 233
classicist model of justice, *see* due process model of justice
cliques and elite groups, 199-207, 213-15
collective bargaining, 85-92, 119-23, 162
collective conflict, 74, 76, 78, 82, 85-92, 102, 111; defusing of, 157-66, 181-2, 188-9
collective justice, 6-9, 42-3, 89, 90, 93-6, 123-6, 169-76, 179-219, 220, 223, *see* community justice
Collins, R., 64, 230
Collis-Squires, N., 85, 86, 87, 88, 234
Comaroff, J., 57, 58-9, 61, 68, 230
community courts, 25-6, 39-46, 224-5, 225, 227
community justice, 6-11, 25-6, 37, 38-46, 123-6, 129, 168-76, 179-219, 220, 223-4, 225, 227; manipulation of, 198-207
community justice reformers, 38-42
community structures, 5-11, 19, 225
company detectives, 134-5
comrades' courts, 42-3, 223
conciliation, 39, 40, 45, 58
consensus theorising, 44-5, 62-3, 64, 66, 67, 70, 71-81, 84, 86
conservatism, 5-6
conservative conflict, 44-5
conservative theorising, 44-5, 62-3
contract, 12-13, 18, 78, 83, 90, 115, 127, 160
contradictions of co-operation, 180, 198, 219
co-operatives, 93-6, 179-219, 220, 224

co-option, 43-6, 74, 76, 84, 86, 117-23, 125, 157-66
corporations, 15, 78, 99, 115
corrective-representative model of discipline, 73, 76-81, 93, 96, 100-31, 224, *see* due process model of justice
courts, 9, 10-11, 13-14, 16, 21, 34, 35, 36-7, 39, 46, 57, 58, 102, 108-11, 135, 137, 138, 139, 140, 143, 144, 146-50; as an alternative to private justice, 102, 108-9, 135, 146-50, 223-4
crime and deviance, 5, 12, 15-16, 42, 43, 60, 72, 73, 74, 76-7, 78, 94, 96, 102, 111, 115, 116, 141-5, 151-2, 182, 188, 189, 223; accommodation to, 183-5; celebration of, 95, 96, 180-3, 186; disobedience, 72, 73, 74, 77, 78; incompetence and poor performance, 72, 74, 77, 78, 106, 196-7; lateness and absence, 127-8, 151, 183-4, 188; non-participation, 190-1; property damage, 74, 78; rent arrears, 184, 189-90, 192-5, 205-7; smoking, 87, 151, 166, 168, 172, 198; unco-operativeness, 189-90, 195, 198; *see* theft; pilfering; fiddling
crime control model of justice, 10, 27-8, 72-3, 74-5, 155-6

Danzig, R., 39, 40, 230
Dawson, S., 100-1, 102, 230
decentralised justice, 33, 38-46, 93, *see* community justice
demotion, 19, 80, 91, 101
despotism, 70, 72-3, 82-3
deterrence, 6-7, 10-11, 14, 72, 73, 75, 80-1, 163, 169-76
deviance, *see* crime and deviance
dialectical relationships, 55, 56, 57, 59, 60-9
Dickens, L., 100, 101, 230

disciplinary boards, 40, 50, 226-8
disciplinary change, 72-3, 77, 80 81, 82-3, 85-6, 86-9, 96-7, 100-6, 134, 137, 222
disciplinary diversity and social control, 106-9, 139-41, *see* ideological processes; legitimation
disciplinary policy, 71-97, 98-9, 100-1, 102-12, 126-8, 132, 133, 137, 176-7, 181-97, 198; as a semi-autonomous part, 97, 99, 102-12, 121, 134, 137
disciplinary procedures, 73, 75, 77, 79, 88, 91, 95, 100-1, 102-12, 226-8
discipline and industrialisation, 72-3
discipline as a management prerogative, 72, 74-5, 77-81, 82-4, 106-7, 118-19, *see* managerial justice; punitive-authoritarian model of discipline; corrective-representative model of discipline
discretionary decision making, 33, 35, 36-7, 38, 110, 121-3
dismissal, 74, 79, 80, 83, 85, 91, 101, 103, 106-7, 108, 113-14, 124, 135, 140, 143, 148, 149, 152, 166, 175, 196-7, 202, 205-7
dispute processing, 8, 20-1, 33, 39, 40, 42-3, 46, 57-62, 67, 111-12, *see* community justice
division of labour, *see* hierarchy, differentiation and specialisation
duality of structure, 63, 65, 104-5
due process model of justice, 10, 13-14, 16, 17, 23, 24, 25, 27, 73, 76-81, 102, 109-11, 137, 189, *see* corrective-representative model of discipline
Durkheim, E., 1, 5, 6, 7-8, 11, 12-13, 18, 19, 56, 57, 230

Eckhoff, T., 39, 40, 231
economy, as a semi-autonomous part, 99, 112-16
Ehrlich, E., 2, 35, 49-50, 56, 231
employees, 72, 76, 82-3, 85-92, 105, 118-19, 123-31; as a semi-autonomous part, 123-26; *see* participation in justice
employment protection legislation, 103, 107, 136, 181, 187
Engels, F., 19, 234

factory law, 69, 70-97, *see* rule creation
Ferdinand, T., 9, 231
fiddling, 75, 87, 112, 114, 115, 125, 129-30, 141-2, 152, 153, 166, 204, 223, *see* theft
fines, 79, 80, 85, 91, 146, 149, 152
Fisher, E., 39, 40-1, 231
Fitzpatrick, P., 60-2, 68, 231
formal discipline, 75, 76-81, 83, 100-1, 102-4, 109-10, 132, 134-5; absence of, 181-97
formal group pressure, 188-98
formal joint disciplinary tribunal, 135-6, 145-76
formalistic sociology of law, 51-7
formality of law, 13-14, 32, 33, 38, 40, 41-2, 45, 47, 49, 51-7, 61, 71, 72-3, 77, 98, 110, 189
frameworks of law, 48, 52-4
functionalism, 1, 2-4
functions of law, 1, 2-4, 19, 20

Garfinkel, H., 10, 11, 231
Gemeinschaft, 5, 7, 11, 24-6, 67, *see* community structures
Gesellschaft, 5, 10, 11-14, 24-6, 67
Giddens, A., 62-3, 64, 65, 66, 67, 68, 99-100, 231
Gierke, O., 47-8, 49
Gouldner, A., 86, 234
government, 102-3, 104, 105, 106, 134, *see* state law

groups as a source of law, 47, see formal group pressure; informal group pressure
Gurvitch, G., 18-19, 20, 22-3, 47, 48, 49, 50, 51-7, 68, 98, 231

Hart, H., 1, 3, 231
Hauriou, M., 49, 50-1
health and safety rules, 72, 76, 86-7
Henry, S., 82, 89, 92, 100, 101, 123, 223, 224, 231, 232, 234, 235
hidden economy, 75, 79, 129, see pilfering; fiddling
hierarchy, differentiation and specialisation, 11-12, 55, 179-80, 203-16, 208-19
historical specificity, 133-4
Hoebel, E., 1, 3, 232
horizontal pluralism, 47-9, 50-7, see pluralism
human agency, 62-9, 208-9
humanism in law, 31-2, 35, 39, 45, 116-17, 181, 206
Hunt, A., 3-4, 22, 35, 66-7, 232

ideal-type theorists, 21-6, 47, 96-7
ideological processes, 2, 4, 18-31, 33, 34, 35, 36, 37, 38-9, 41-2, 43, 45, 46, 56, 61, 67, 68, 71, 83, 84, 85, 88, 89, 92, 98-100, 116-17, 145-78, 179, 180-1, 197, 216-17, 222, see legitimation
individual manager as a semi-autonomous part, 97, 99, 116-17, 121-3
individual trade union representative as a semi-autonomous part, 97, 99, 120-3, 157-8
individual worker as a semi-autonomous part, 97, 99, 126-31, 172-6
individualisation of deviance, 11-14, 72, 74, 76-7, 78, 88, 90, 158-9, see collective conflict; ideological processes
individualisation of punishment, 15-16, 77, 79, 80-1, 158-9, see medical model
individualistic structures, 11-14, 19
industrial democracy, 93, 132, see participation in justice
industrial relations legislation, 102-3, 105-6
industrial tribunal, 102-8, 136-7
industry as a semi-autonomous part, 97, 99, 104, 115
informal detection, 135, 181-2
informal discipline, 73, 74-5, 82-92, 93-6, 123-6, 168-72, 181-97, 198
informal group pressure, 181-8, see formal group pressure; shaming
informal institutions, 45
informal joint disciplinary tribunal, 135
informal law, 4, 8-9, 18, 20, 32-62, 67-8, 85-97
informal rules, 85-92, 181-4
informalities of disciplinary procedure, 121-3
informalities of law, 2, 33, 34-7
Institute of Personnel Management (IPM), 100, 101, 232
integrated theorising, 4, 32, 33-4, 47, 50-7, 58-69, 70-1, 92-3, 96-7, 98-100, 180, 216-19, 222
integration to group, 5-9, 11-13, 47, 51
interdependence of disciplinary systems, 150-7, 177, 179, 180, 181, 197, 207-8
interdependence of management and union, 119-20, 121-3, 157-66, 177
interdependence of structure and action, 59-69, 92-3, 96-7, 216-22

Index 241

interests and private justice, 116-31, 134, 140-1, 152-7, 199-203
interpenetration of semi-autonomous parts, 98-100, 130-1, 132-3, 145, 177-8, 179, *see* autonomy; penetration
intimidation, 191-4, 204, 206
investigations, 134-5, 138-9, 151, 159, 162

joint disciplinary procedure, 89, 90-1, 133-78, 224, 225, 227, *see* participation in justice
Jones, D., 72, 76, 77, 80, 81, 232
jury, 14, 138
Justices of the Peace (JP), 138

Kamenka, E., 6-7, 12-13, 14, 15, 24-6, 32-3, 66, 67, 232
kangaroo courts, 189
Kelson, H., 1, 2, 233
kinds of law, 47, 48-57
King, M., 10-11, 16, 27-9, 233
Kinsey, R., 82-3, 233
Knorr-Cetina, K., 64-6, 230, 231, 233

labour supply, 113, 114
law, autonomous generation of, 47-8, 49-50, 51-7, 104; depths of, 47, 49-57, 98; forms of, 4-31, 70-97; layers of, 47, 49-57, 98
law of advancing rationalisation, 22
law and associations, 47-8, 49-51
law and customs, 1-4, 7, 13, 32-3, 49, 57
law and economics, 70-1, 72, 73, 102, 107
law as education, 11-14, 42, 73, 76, 77, 79, 80-1, 86, 105, 116, 190-1
law and groups, 19, 47-57, 58, 179-220
law as interaction, 57-62, 70-1, 85-92

law as process, 57-62
law as separate from people, 2, 4, 13-14, 15-17, 25-6, 30, 33, 38-42, 46, 58-9
law as social engineering, 35
law and the state, 2, 14-17, 40-6, 47-8, 49-50, 52-4, 60-1, 69, 70-1, *see* state law and private justice
law-centred anthropologists, 20-1, 57, 58, 61
legal developmentalism, 17-26, 82-4, 86, *see* legal evolutionism
legal ethnocentricism, 20-1
legal evolutionism, 17-26, 48, 53-4, 73, 82-4, 86, 96-7
legal functionalists, 1-4
legal language and law words, 13, 102, 109-10, 137-8
legal pluralism, 18-19, 21-31, 33, 46-62, 85-92, 98
legal positivists, 1-2, 20, 32, 49, *see* positive law
legal purity, 2, 33, 36, 37, 38, 89, 91, 98
legal realism, 32, 33, 34-7, 41
legal rules, 3, 13-14, 51, 57, 59, 60
legal universalists, 1-4
legitimation and authority, 5, 6, 8, 43-6, 72-3, 74, 76, 77, 78, 80, 83-5, 86, 90, 93-6, 118-19, 137-9, 145-78, 179, 190-1, 203-7
legitimation through diversification, 150-7, 177, 179, 180, 181, 197, 207-8
legitimation through duality of law, 145-50, 197
legitimation through participation, 118-19, 141-78, *see* participation in justice
levels of law, 47
living law, 2, 18, 23, 49-50
Llewellyn, K., 1, 3, 34, 233
lock ins and lock outs, 82-3
Longmire, D., 39, 41, 43, 233

McConville, M., 36, 229
macro-theorising about law, 1-31, 32, 34, 62-9, 70, 71-85, 86, 88, 92, 98, 99, 210-16, 220-2, see structural theorising
Maine, H., 18, 233
Malinowski, B., 8, 20, 57, 234
management, 75, 77, 78, 79, 85-92, 97, 99, 102, 103, 105, 106, 108, 109, 110, 113, 114, 116-17, 118-19, 125-6, 133, 134, 135-6, 139-40, 157-66; as a semi-autonomous part, 116-19, 129; themselves subject to discipline, 155-6
managerial justice, 98-131, 134, 135, 150, 151, 177, 223, 225, 227, see corrective-representative model of discipline; punitive-authoritarian model of discipline
Mars, G., 89, 123, 126, 234
Martin, J., 102, 234
Marx, K., 1, 19, 234
Marxism, 62
Marxist sociology of law, 19-20, 66, 67, 70, 82-5
meaning and law, 4, 23-4, 30-1
mechanical solidarity, 5-8, 11
mediation, 39, 45, 58
medical model of justice, 15-16, 27, 28, 77, 78, 79, 80-1, 90, 91, 109, 128-9, 173
Mellish, M., 85, 86, 87, 88, 234
micro-theorising about law, 30-69, 70-1, 85-92, 98, 208-9, 220-1
Moore, S., 59-61, 62, 68, 234
multi-paradigmists, 27-30, 47, 64

National Joint Advisory Committee (NJAC), 77, 100, 102, 104, 234
natural justice, 77
natural law, 1-2, 3, 31
networks, 180, 182-3, 192-3, 194

neutrality, 13-14, 23, 30, 77, see legal purity
normative controls, 89, 90, see informal group pressure

open justice, 36-7
organic solidarity, 5, 11
organisational size as a factor in disciplinary policy, 74, 78, 90, 94, 100-1, 102, 181, 186, 204-5
ostracism, 8, 58, 95, 96, 187

Packer, H., 10, 234
Parsons, T., 1, 3, 22, 62, 234
participation in justice, 33, 37, 39, 42-6, 75, 77, 78, 79, 80, 83, 84, 85-92, 100-1, 118-23, 132-78, 224, see accommodative-participative model of discipline; community justice
Pashukanis, E., 14, 19, 84, 234
paternalism, 74, 84, 90, 93, 132, 133, 150, 224
peer group discipline, see collective justice; community justice
penetration, 60-1, 92-3, 96-7, 98-131, 177-8, see interpenetration of semi-autonomous parts
penetration of community of employees: by individual employee, 172-4; by participatory justice, 168-72, 178
penetration of community justice: by capitalist structure, 210-19; by elite groups, 198, 203-7; by individual workers, 181-2, 183-5, 190-7, 198-203, 205; by sexist attitudes, 211-13; by state law, 180, 187, 205-7
penetration of individual employees: by community justice, 174-5, 186-94, 199-203; by management, 126-8, 157-63

penetration of management by trade unions, 119-20
penetration of managerial justice: by community of employees, 123-6; by economic conditions, 112-14; by individual empolyees, 128-9, 129-30; by individual managers, 116-17; by industrial and corporate influences, 115; by state law, 100-12; by trade unions, 117, 119
penetration of participatory justice: by community of employees, 117-8; by economic conditions, 149-50; by individual managers, 163-7; by individual trade unionists, 167-8; by state law, 136-41, 146-50, 177; by trade unions, 153, 167-8
penetration of state law: by managerial justice, 100-12, 115; by participatory justice, 141-4, 146-50, 176, 177
penetration of trade unions: by individual unionists, 120, 157-66, 167-8; by management, 140, 153, 157-66; by managerial justice, 118-19, 140, 153
people's courts, 26, 42, 43
perks, 87, 163
philosophy of punishment, 75, 79, 109, 155-6, see sanctions
pilfering, 75, 87, 115, 128, 130, 141-5, 146, 152, 159, 166, 170, 171, 173, 174-5, 176, 223, see theft; fiddling; crime and deviance
plea-bargaining, 36-7, 121-3, see bureaucratic model
pluralism, see legal pluralism
plurality of private justice systems, 150-7, see legitimation through diversification
police, 102, 111, 135, 138-9, 104, 142, 146-7, 151, 152, 188, see company detectives
politics of informalism, 33, 38-46, 88-9, 92
politics of law, 18, 21-30, 33, 35, 36, 95
popular justice, 38, 39, 41, 42-6
positive law, 1-3, 17, 19, 24, 30, 32, 33, 34, 35, 36, 37, 42, 47, 49-50
positivism and crime, 15-16
Pound, R., 2, 34, 35, 234
prison tribunals, 40-1
private justice: forms of, 71-97; as multi-stage process, 134-6; as semi-autonomous part, 100-15
private policing, 134-5, 138-9, see company detectives
probation officers, 16, 28
profit and co-operatives, 209
protection: against managerial justice, 139, 153, 156, 158, 160, 161, 162, 163-6, 171-2; against state law, 141-5, 176
punishment, see sanctions, penalties and punishments
punitive-authoritarian model of discipline, 72-3, 74-5, 77, 80, 85-6, 93, 96, 98, 100, 224, see crime control model of justice

radical conflict, 44-5, 46
radical theorising, 44-5, 46, 62-3, 66, 67, 70, 71, 81-5, 86
Ramundo, B., 42, 43, 234
rationality, 11-13, 15, 22, 79
records, 16, 102, 105, 128, 143, 147, 148, 152, 164, 166, 175
recruitment, 184-5
reification of law, 38-9, 70, 85, 88
relationships and discipline, 179, 181-5, 192-207, see community justice
Renner, K., 14, 19-20, 70, 234
representation hypothesis, 65-6

repressive law, 6-8, 72-3, 74-5, 82-3, 84, *see* crime control model of justice; status passage model of justice; shaming
reprimand, 135
research methods, 223-8
responsibility and socialisation, 210-11
restitutive justice, 12-13
retribution, 6-8, 72, 73, 80, *see* philosophy of punishment
revolution, 215-16, 222
Rich, R., 27, 29, 234
ridicule, 8, 21, 58
Ritzer, G., 27, 29, 234
Roberts, S., 13, 14, 20-1, 57, 58-9, 61, 68, 230, 234
Rogovin, E., 43, 235
Ross, E., 35, 48-9, 235
rule creation, 1-3, 23, 47-8, 49-57, 60-1, 72-3, 74, 76, 78, 86-7, 90, 94, 96, 104-6, 176, 190-1
rules and interests, 70, 72-3, 74, 76-7, 78, 80, 85-92, 93-4, *see* interests and private justice
rules and meanings, 85-92

sanctions, penalties and punishments, 6, 8, 9, 10-11, 14, 16, 20-1, 39-40, 48-9, 72, 73, 75, 77, 79, 80, 82-3, 84, 87, 89, 91, 95, 96, 101, 103, 121-2, 124, 128-9, 135, 136, 142-3, 146-50, 152, 153, 154-7, 158-9, 165, 168-78, 181-98, 205-7
Santos, B., 46, 235
Schur, E., 4, 235
Scraton, P., 82, 84, 235
self-discipline, 73, 74, 77, 79, 83, 126-8, 186-8
self-help and mutual aid, 182, 183, 223
separatist anthropologists, 20
sexism and discipline, 211-12
shaming and stigma, 6, 7, 8-11, 21, 48, 58, 75, 91, 95, 96, 136, 147-50, 168-76, 186, 193-4
shared decision-making in justice, 93-6, 132-78, 179-219
social construction of law, 1-4, 17-31, 32, 36, 37, 56, 61, 67, 68, 71, 84-5, 89, 92-3, 96-7, 98-100, 104-6, 117, *see* ideological processes
social control, 4, 6, 8-9, 19, 20-1, 30, 32, 33, 34, 35, 41, 43, 44-6, 48-9, 57-62, 70, 71, 85, 88-9, 92, 97, 98, 99, 100, 101, 132, 133, 140, 145, 150, 154, 156, 177, 179, 180, 183
social status, 5, 6, 7, 10-11, 13, 45, 74, 75, 78, 79, 90, 91, 94, 95, 147-50, 168-78, *see* shaming; status passage model
social structures and law forms, 1-31, 70-97, 210-19
social workers, 16, 28
socialism, 180, 213-19
socialist legality, 14-16, 19-20, 41, 42-3, 93-6, 180, 216-17
sociality, 51-7
socio-legal change, 217-19, 222
sociological jurisprudence, 33, 34-7
sources of law, 23, 47-8, 49-57
South, N., 82, 84, 92, 235
Soviet Union, 42-3, 145
spontaneous rules and law, 18, 23, 47, 50, 51-7, 61, 72, 74, 89, 94
state law and private justice, 68-9, 70-1, 89, 92-3, 96, 98, 99, 100, 101-12, 134-41, 145-50, 177, 180, 187, 205-8
state as a semi-autonomous part, 60-1, 97, 99, 102-12
status passage model of justice, 6-7, 10-11, 27, 28
strikes, *see* collective conflict
structural conditions, 1-2, 4-17, 34, 62-9, 71-2, 73, 74, 78, 81,

82-3, 90, 92, 93, 94, 96, 97, 99, 102-8, 112-15, 133-4, 149-50, 179-80, 201-19, 220-2, 224
structural theorising, 4-31, 37, 47, 59, 62-9, 70, 71-85, 88-9, 90-2, 96-7, see macro-theorising
structuration, 62-3, 65
substantive justice, 6-7, 25-6, 39-41, 58-9, 74, 91, 181
suspension, 79, 80, 91, 101, 108, 124, 135, 143, 146, 147, 152, 159, 161-2, 172, 174, 176
systematic sociology of law, 51-7
systems theory, 65

tariff system, 14
Tay, A., 6-7, 12, 13, 14, 15, 24-6, 32-3, 66, 67, 232
theft, 74, 78, 87, 102, 108, 111-12, 115, 128, 140, 141-5, 146-7, 152, 156, 173, 188
Tönnies, F., 5, 7, 11-12, 235
Toulemont, R., 56, 235
trade unions and employee representatives, 73, 74, 75, 77, 78, 79, 80, 88, 90, 93, 97, 99, 101, 103, 107-8, 109, 110, 112, 113, 116, 117-23, 124, 135-41, 142, 152-3, 155, 156, 157-68, 177; as semi-autonomous parts, 97, 99, 119-23
transfers, 79, 80, 91, 101, 135, 166, 167

typology of disciplinary forms, 70-97, 225-8

unemployment, 83, 112-14, 149-50, 194
Unger, R., 7, 15, 23-4, 66, 67
unintended consequences, 64-5
unitary perspective, 78
United States, 9, 40
universalism, 1-4, 17, 32, 50, 56, 57, 61, 104, 180
unorganised law, 23, 47, 51-7

values and standards, 1, 2, 3, 5, 30, 34, 72-3, 74, 76-7, 78, 85, see interests and private justice
Versele, S., 38, 39, 235
vertical pluralism, 47, 49-57
victimisation and vindictiveness, 134, 164-6, 189, 192-3, 199-203
visits as sanctions, 191-3, 205-7

wage deductions, 80
warnings, 79, 80, 91, 95, 101, 103, 105, 128, 135, 142, 151, 152, 173, 196
Weber, M., 1, 8, 14, 22-3, 235
Whelan, C., 38, 39, 235
witnesses, 109
women and discipline, 211-12
workers' courts, 42-3, 89, 92

Young, J., 5-6, 14, 15-16, 29, 235